1975

DIALOGUES ON THE FUTURE OF MAN

DIALOGUES
on the
FUTURE OF MAN

FREDERICK PATKA

PHILOSOPHICAL LIBRARY
New York

TO THE MEMORY OF NIETZSCHE

"Man is a rope, tied between beast and overman
—a rope over an abyss. A dangerous across, a
dangerous on-the-way, a dangerous looking-back,
a dangerous shuddering and stopping.

"What is great in man is that he is a bridge and not
and end: what can be loved in man is that he is
an *overture* and a *going under*."

Thus Spoke Zarathustra

CONTENTS

Note to the Reader   9

Chapter I—The Encounter with the Stranger   11

Chapter II—The Proposal of the Visitor from the Outer Space   25

Chapter III—The Break   49

Chapter IV—The Affair   57

Chapter V—Toward a New Way of Life   69

Chapter VI—The Evolution of the Superior Man   85

Chapter VII—The Progressive Extinction of the Family   113

Chapter VIII—Children Are Individuals, They Belong to
             Themselves. Problems of Love and Sex   157

Chapter IX—A Different Life Style in the Age of Total
            Automation in a Unified Universe   205

Chapter X—The Future of Education as a Creative Process   239

Chapter XI—The Ultimate Meaning of Ethics and Religion   283

Chapter XII—Epilogue   325

NOTE TO THE READER

Reading through the pages of this book, the question will come to mind whether the main character, Noesis, and his friend, Gynea, are fictional types, mere imaginary beings, or, perhaps, they had actually come from another world as the representatives of a much more advanced civilization and culture? Similarly, the reader could have doubts as to the reality of the two 'contactees,' Knox and Marisa, the earthly counterparts of the superior persons from outer space.

We consider these questions irrelevant and insignificant in view of the incomparably more serious problems challenging the future of man on this planet.

The real questions to be weighed throughout the reading of the dialogues are only a few. First, is the criticism of man's cultural history on earth true or false? Second, do the new ideas proposed by the visitors from outer space make any sense at all?

Everyone is aware that modern man is standing at an important crossroad in his history today. He is faced with the very real danger of total annihilation through atomic warfare. Could it be that the only way out of this impasse will be found in the ideological regeneration of man, in his willingness to discard his outmoded ideas, his traditional principles and prejudices? Could this alone free him from the dead weight of his worn out codes and institutions that are no longer functional and meaningful to him? The very condition for the possibility of further progress lies in man's courage to bury his dead and to care for the living, to strike new paths, open new vistas and horizons, thus creating the conditions for a more enlightened and meaningful existence.

9

Ask yourself the following vital questions:

1. What will be the fate of the present religious beliefs and organized church life?
2. What changes will morality undergo in the near future as new values appear on the cultural horizon?
3. Will the slow disintegration of marriage and family life lead to its final extinction?
4. Is man heading toward collective enslavement or to the fulfillment of individual freedom, equality and brotherhood on an inter-planetary dimension?
5. Can one think of our existence without nationalities, races, politicians, wars and law enforcing agencies?
6. Is our economic life developing toward the unification of the whole process of supply and demand on a global scope by the process of full automation? In other words, what is the future of capitalism and communism?
7. Increasing leisure time, will there be more intensified search for artistic and scientific creativity or else man will vegetate in utter boredom and nausea?

The answer to these questions is much more serious and pressing than satisfying the prurient curiosity of the so-called saucer-cultists, who try to escape from the emptiness of an unwanted life into the fantastic, imaginary and unbelievable figments of their overwrought imagination.

F. P.

Chapter One

THE ENCOUNTER WITH THE STRANGER

It was late afternoon, brief fragments of time heralding the slow coming but steady approach of a beginning and an end. It was the beginning of the end of another day of light, running its eternal course of endless duration, to be embraced and enveloped once more by the rising shadows of darkness, step by step, moment following moment, till night would wipe out things, shapes, colors, sounds—life itself, drowning everything in the unfathomable depths of stillness, silence and blind nothingness.

A man was visible at some distance on the top of a hill, the silhouette of his figure sharply imprinted against the changing colors of the distant horizon. He was standing motionless, his feet planted slightly apart, as if waiting for something to happen or someone to come. His erect posture, neither tense nor loose, but firm, his arms folded on his chest and his head held with proud self-confidence, gave the impression of someone totally conscious of his power, a master dominating all reality around him by his presence, ready to face everything and fearful of nothing.

One could not tell his age simply by looking at him. The expression of his face, dominated by large eyes of an unusual clarity that heightened their irresistible power of penetration, seemed to suggest not age but rather a knowledge of many worlds seen and many things familiar only to those of his kind. There were no visible traces marked by time on his high forehead, framed by rich strands of hair. A faint smile at the corners of his mouth betrayed a consummate blend of wisdom and joy. He seemed to exist in freedom, independent of time and space,

11

innocent of fear, suffering and defeat. His whole being revealed the embodiment of a superlative affirmation and love of life.

His attention was suddenly caught by the shape of an approaching man, still an indistinct shadow at the foot of the hill, barely visible in the dimmed twilight. The newcomer walked very slowly, almost aimlessly, dragging himself as one who had no reason to be there or anywhere else and no purpose to his motion either, being indifferent to both moving ahead and standing still. He seemed not to care about anything, except the annoying burden of carrying about a much abused and exhausted body.

His slow climb was stopped, once or twice, by the attack of a persistent cough that shook his fragile frame; then he would start to move again, hands in pockets, his head bent down and his eyes fixed on the small patch of ground before him. At one of these unwanted stops he caught sight of the lonely figure on the hilltop. Without any sign of surprise or any change in his slouched posture, he resumed his unsteady steps toward the man whose presence seemed a matter only of indifference to him.

When he had come to within a few feet of the Stranger, he muttered some unintelligible words which could have been a greeting or simply one of his usual curses. Then he sank to the ground, breathing heavily, and glad to be at the end of his painful exertion. The Stranger took one step toward him, his eyes on the still body of the expected visitor. He noticed the thick beard covering the lifeless features of his face, the long and unkempt hair hanging in sticky strands. The clothes covering his emaciated figure—faded, shabby dungarees, a stained, smudged grey sweater, and torn sandals—completed the image of a man displaying all the symptoms of despair, weariness, disgust and nausea, the will to nothingness, the embodiment of living death.

After a few moments the visitor opened his eyes. There was no passion or desire left in those eyes, no hope and no life, just dark ruins left by a wild fire that had started too soon and died even faster. He must have seen too much and wished to see no more. . . .

Finally he sat up and took his first look at the man standing next to him. He found it strange that this unknown individual looked steadily, unflinchingly and straight into his eyes, for he was already too familiar with the evasive and furtive glances of the city people whose only concern had seemed to be to avoid his inquisitive looks of times past, when he still had the desire and the hope of finding in their eyes the promise and the confirmation of a future worth anticipating. But this was different. The Stranger's glance was pure, clear and clean; there was no sign of reproach, contempt or hidden hatred in those eyes, just the open expression of a total knowledge and understanding that required no explanations and asked no embarrassing questions.

"So, you made it after all. You didn't sound very convincing on the phone," said the Stranger, just to break the silence and the mounting tension of uneasiness, growing between the two unknown to each other and ignorant of what to expect.

"Yea, I made it all right," answered the newcomer gruffly, not trying to hide the resentment in his voice. "I wish I hadn't . . ." he added in a tone of accusation.

"But then, why did you go through the trouble of coming anyway?"

"Well, you wouldn't believe it . . . but it was just a stupid thing; I mean, it was your voice and your accent that made me want to find out who the hell was still after me and for what idiotic reason. . . . It's stupid, isn't it? Like everything else in this goddamn world. . . . Besides, it makes no difference at all what I do or I don't do. . . . So there. . . ."

"You mean that there's a lot of nonsense in your world, downright irrational and. . . ."

"Why not say crazy and that everything stinks, that there is no meaning to anything and even the questions about meaning turn out to be meaningless? . . ." the bearded fellow hastened to recite, almost mechanically, the slogans circulated among the rebels of subterranean caves.

"If what you've just said were true," replied the Stranger, "that would make you one of those who're crazy and stink. . . ."

"And suppose I am one? Sure, not the first and not the last either," mused the rebel, finding some comfort in his conviction

13

that he was right, that he must be right, because almost everybody who had courage, would say so.

"And the majority is always right, is that it?" asked the
Stranger in a challenging voice.

"The majority be damned, if you mean the flabby people, the
public —our lovable mankind in general. . . . I meant only those
who . . . how shall I say it? . . . Well, I meant those who're
like me and think as I do, the ones the middle-class bourgeois call
the 'drop-outs' of society and life . . . if you know what I mean."

"I think I know it, and this is one of the reasons I wanted
to meet one of you, not any one of those well-adjusted hypocrites. . . . But, would you mind telling me what you think,
how you think and what you're after?" asked the Stranger with
sincere curiosity. He noticed that his question made the rebel
more tense and nervous, almost irritated.

"What do you mean?" he retorted indignantly. "Do you expect
me to start lecturing on philosophy, on values, life, happiness and
the rest of the academic garbage? Don't you think that this place,
the time and especially my own disposition rebel against it? Besides, I think you heard me saying that I believe that everything
is absurd, didn't you?"

"Yes, I heard you saying it with no small satisfaction on your
part. Shall I take it as your fundamental premise?"

"Well then, that's it, take it or leave it. It makes no difference
at all. But I meant to ask you a few questions of my own, all
right?"

"Go ahead and ask all the questions you want to. Thus we
shall get better acquainted."

"First of all, I find it very strange that you haven't asked anything about me so far, I mean, who I am, where I live, how I
live, my name, my past and my whole beautiful life story. . . ."

The Stranger smiled with reassurance and said simply: "I don't
have to ask any of those questions about you for I know it all.
Didn't I call you on the phone?"

"Come on, that's nothing. . . . Probably you fished that number
out of the book. I get crazy calls almost every day from all sorts
of odd guys. . . ."

"All right, then. If you wish, I shall introduce you now to your own self. And you won't like all that which I'm going to say. . . . Your name is Edward Knox, you are twenty four years old, you live in a second-floor apartment on Washington Square, the rent being paid by your estranged father. Since you left college, after only five semesters of renewed probations, you became a drifter, going from one job to the next, never finding anything to please you. You filled the emptiness of your days with the so-called pleasures of the joy-makers. Occasionally you've even tried pot, I mean drugs, without getting hooked to it. You've had quite a few bad trips though. . . . So you went through the days of your life as if it were an unending picnic, picking each time what the whim of the moment dictated, trying to satisfy an unsatiable will to live. But the more you picked and ate, the hungrier you became, till your nervous system refused to react to any more excitement, from sheer exhaustion. But you've never experienced any great passion that would have dominated your whole being and given direction, content and meaning to your existence. You stumbled from one illusion to the next, all of them ending in disillusions. Finally, you even got tired of your own self, you cursed and damned everything, life itself, as an unwanted burden. Now you can hardly stand your own being, which is why you're trying so desperately to drown yourself in the semi-conscious daze induced by drinks, sex, and drugs. When you entered college, your ambition was to become a writer, but you never got beyond the clever use of your four-letter-word vocabulary. . . . Shall I say more, and talk about your family, your mother? . . ."

"Shut up, you! . . ." screamed Knox, his fists tightly clenched, ready to attack. Then he thought better of it and said with difficulty: "I've heard enough! It's pretty accurate, I guess; you must have done some digging or pot-peeking of your own. So you've got good nerves, a strong stomach, and the cheap taste of a gossip hunter. . . . But you must have your reasons for playing private detective; right? Well, what are your reasons? What are you after? What do you want? And, first of all, who are you?

15

Your whole manner, your speech, everything about you tells me that you must be a stranger, a foreigner, true?"

"A foreigner I am and I intend to remain such; but perhaps not in the very same meaning you give to the term. . . . My name —if it means anything to you—is *Noesis*. Since I've been living here, I've collected all the papers you people carry—social security, driver's licence and a collection of credit cards—by which you are trying to fake some identity in the eyes of others. My accent will remain with me because of the peculiar nature of the sounds which make up your language. And as to my specific reasons for wanting to contact you, I have a simple proposal to make, and I'll leave it up to you to accept it or reject it."

"What is it?" asked Knox, without much interest.

"Would you like, Edward, to end the meaningless flow of your wasted days and. . . ." Noesis could not finish his sentence, because Knox errupted in a strange, almost hysterical laughter, full of cynical, ironic and sarcastic derision.

"So I found you out," he managed to say between two bursts of uncontrolled emotions. "Yes, I guessed it right. . . . You must have been hired as the agent of the good samaritans, the fishermen of lost souls, the all-loving humanitarians, the salvation army of preachers and grace-peddlers, the self-righteous moralists, the fanatics of eternal truths, the hallucinated believers in immortality and the beyond, the mystics of divine revelations, the exclusive, wholesale and authorized dealers in redemption and the ushers of heaven and hell. Is that it, my dear Noesis?"

Noesis listened attentively to the torrent of words gushing forth from Knox's obsessed mind. He waited a while till Knox regained some of the self-control available to him, then he said, calmly, choosing his words carefully: "You must have suffered unjustly at the hands of those who pose as the guardians of truth, justice and love. You must have discovered the ugly hypocrisy of the false prophets, and you've paid for that discovery with the loss of your faith in the value of your own life." There was no pleading, no pity and no attempt in Noesis' words or in the tonality of his voice to console, to persuade, to win over, to

16

pressurize, to convince. His words sounded as an implacable verdict, based on undeniable facts.

Knox realized then that there was no danger to his freedom, but rather an unusual respect for him, without the compassionate sentimentality of the weak, in spite of the offensive words that he had hurled at Noesis, whose face had not changed from the tranquil serenity of undisturbed peace which seemed never to leave him, giving the impression of a person who could neither be offended nor flattered. He felt somewhat ashamed of his words and wished that he could match respect with respect and the confidence granted to him as a token of friendship. He tried to make up for his mistake by saying:

"I understand, you're not one of those head-hunters, you're not out after my scalp, you don't want my soul, you don't want to make a convert, a penitent, a holy man out of me? . . ." He said it as if he were trying to convince himself, fighting his inveterate fear and doubt whenever faced by another human being.

"Edward," said Noesis, "learn to take my words in their true and precise meaning: I do not want anything from you; not now and not in the future, should our relationship continue after this bad start. I'm not after your life, your freedom, your independence and I don't want to enlist you in the service of any 'good cause,' or anything of what you mentioned before. Therefore, fear nothing, no matter how difficult this might be for you."

"But then, I don't get you. . . . I'm getting even more confused. You said you have a proposal to make, and now you assure me that you don't want anything from me. That doesn't make any sense to me, Noesis."

"No, it doesn't, for the simple reason that when you hear the word 'proposal,' you associate it necessarily—you can't help doing so—with someone's greed to take the better of you, perhaps, in return for some money. . . . The only way you can think of one man's relation to another is in terms of onesided or mutual exploitation. You have become a use-value in the eyes of your fellow men, and you look upon them in the very same fashion. 'To use and to be used!' There's the key to your motives. . . .

17

Everything is just a commodity at the disposal of prospective consumers. To consume and to be consumed. . . . And when you run out of victims, you turn against your own self and it becomes self-consumption, self-use and abuse. Your life to you is not more and not less than petty cash to be spent at the first drugstore, bakery or tavern. . . . Finally, when you've exploited your own self and become bankrupt, you start blaming and cursing everything as stupid, crazy, absurd and meaningless. . . . It's the whining and the wailing of the impotent who does not know that he himself is the only cause of his impotence. But, perhaps, there is and there could be—because there ought to be—another way, a more noble form for man's attitude toward himself and others, don't you think so?"

"Oh, yes, and I can name a few, if you care to listen!" said Knox.

"I do care to listen, Edward, so tell me, what are they?" inquired Noesis.

"Well, I shall mention first the creed of unselfishness, the gospel of selflessness, the evangel of disinterested dedication and service for the good of others, also called the philosophy of altruism. And I suspect—after what you just said—that your unnamed 'proposals' must belong to one of these 'higher,' 'superior,' and 'noble' categories. Because if it isn't selfish, then it must be unselfish; since you have no interest in it and you're not thinking of any advantage of your own, no profit is involved, no gain is planned or anticipated, you must be the proponent of the altruistic crap. . . . Am I right or wrong, Noesis? It's your turn to speak."

"Thank you, and I'm sorry to disappoint you once more, but I mean no harm, and if I contradict you, it's not because I am a No-saying spirit, just for the sake of saying no. That would be childish. You are wrong, Edward, because your mind is caught in an alternative, the opposition and the conflict between self-interest and the interests of others, which forces you to make an either-or choice, between selfishness and so-called selflessness. If you choose the first, you're told that you're a narrow-minded egotist who lives for the sole purpose of satisfying the

18

hungry greed of his own desires and whims. You're branded as an immoral person. If you choose the second, that is, the service of the common good, the good of others, then you feel gipped and rightly so, for you don't like to think of yourself as a fool. Not being able to find your way out of this double dead end, you tell yourself that there is no solution, no answer, and no use in trying to find one. You become even more convinced that nothing makes any sense, that the world is absurd. . . ."

"But isn't it? You said it yourself, I mean you implied it, when you were lecturing on the either-or contradiction, didn't you?"

"I did not say so, and I didn't imply that sort of thing either. Because I can think and I know of another possibility, above your either-or dilemma."

"I'd like to hear it, although I'm a skeptic by nature and I don't believe in anything unless I can see it. I'm not ready to swallow any more the pill of unearthly bliss. . . ."

"First you're going to listen to the third way, if you care to call it such. Then, perhaps, you'll see it in action, in reality, how it works in life, if we shall ever come that far."

"Why do you sound so mysterious, like you're talking to me from a distance of millenia, or from the promise of some remote future to come?"

"Let's forget that for now and let me tell you about the third way you asked me to explain. Or shall I drop it?"

"No, no, go ahead, say it, it must be interesting, even if it turns out to be just a beautiful dream never to come true."

"All right, Edward, call it the way you want to, I can't change that right now. So, listen. I'll start with a few examples, well known to you, because they're taken from your life here. Then, I shall invite you to think along with me and draw your own conclusions."

"You know something, Noesis? You sound like that old tramp from Athens; Socrates was his name. I remember having read some of his stuff—dialogues they called it—as a freshman assignment. Ever heard of him? I used to like him, then. . . ."

"Then what?"

"Well, I was told later that he was just an early example of a

19

psychological case. I mean to say that Socrates was maladjusted and neurotic, and he tried to justify himself before his fellow citizens as the revengeful gadfly of irony, bullying and posturing as a cross-breed between an ignorant bastard and a would-be prophet. So I lost respect for him and his stuff. . . ."

"Who told you that, Edward?"

"I guess it was one of our philosophy instructors who liked to show that the great men of the past weren't great at all, because greatness has never existed and can never exist. Of course I was only nineteen then and I took his word for it, though I felt a little funny about this passion of his to confuse, to ridicule, to make a joke out of everything, no matter what it was. But now it doesn't matter any more. It's over. Anyhow, let's hear the examples you were going to give me, remember?"

"Yes, I do. But allow me, please, to say that we, I mean, I know of Socrates and think of him as one of the very few who could have given a better turn to the development of your culture on earth, had he not been killed—very typical of your people— and his doctrines distorted. But back to my first example. It's about a gardener."

"A gardener, you mean? It sounds trivial and a very pedestrian thing to bring up in connection with this philosophy you're going to tell me about!"

"Think that way if you wish, but I know that the highest is also the simplest and least complex. Also the most difficult to explain to those who never learned to see the obvious, because it's so obvious. You're impressed only by the confusion of the unintelligible, the worship of the unknowable, and the glorification of the controversial. And you call it sophistication, the hallmark of wisdom and scholarship."

"What about the gardener, then?"

"Well, let's assume that he is a free man—an almost extinct species among you—and that he can afford growing his flowers for the simple pleasure he derives from making life germinate, grow, reach for the sun, achieve its fullest perfection and beauty, the truth of its being, of its kind. Can you image this?"

"Oh, yeah, there's nothing to it; it's just a hobby, you know, one of the thousands you find in those 'How to do' books you get in any dimestore. I don't see anything unusual or extraordinary in your gardener's hobby. I'm sorry, but I don't. Period. Besides, it sounds like the romantic fad of nature-worship, the idiocy of that other sick fellow, Rousseau, I think. . . ."

"I didn't ask you to like my gardener or the growing of flowers, or to ready yourself for getting back to Mother Nature, did I?" replied Noesis, still patiently. "What I am asking you to do is to see the obvious and—using the jargon of psychology—to discover the motive, the why, the goal, the purpose and the meaning of his work. Can you do that?"

"I guess I can. It's simple and stupid. Probably he is an old fellow, too old to have some fun with the fair sex, and he's killing time, dodging boredom and frustration by growing flowers as a miserable substitute for the pleasure of his good old days. What do you say, Nocsis? Am I right or wrong?"

"You're wrong again, Edward, on several counts. But the worst of all is within you. I mean what you've lost and what makes you blind and deaf to everything. You take pleasure—just like your philosophy instructor—in reducing everything to the smallest, in making it look insignificant, unimportant, trivial, common and vulgar, in order to feel justified when you dismiss all things after you've destroyed them by emptying them of all meaning and value, turning them into the lifeless image of clattering bones. Then you feel prepared and free to start your gloomy and sick moaning about the absurdity of the world, not realizing that it's you who banished and forbade all values and meanings from it. Because, Edward—and I mean no offense—you can't afford to look at anything great, noble, sublime, strong and beautiful. That would prove your philosophy to be just the projection of your own chaotic condition. That's why you have to act like any barbarian of the past: destroying whatever stands on its feet, reducing it to ruins and dust, because that's the only habitat or environment congenial to him. It is the resentment, the hatred of life by those who betrayed its challenge."

"That was a nice speech, Noesis. You're a skillfull orator. How many credits in rhetorics did you pick up in college?"

21

"None!"

"But you went through college, didn't you?"

"I did."

"What was your major?"

"Knowledge."

"What do you mean? You're not making any sense!"

"Aren't I, Edward?"

"No, you're not! What do you mean by majoring in knowledge? What knowledge? Are you trying to say that you majored in all subjects, that you're a universal genius, that you know all about everything? Is that what you mean?"

"I did not claim omniscience, just knowledge and more knowledge about everything that exists as the highest and most valuable of all pursuits, the only meaning and happiness open to all those who experience delight in learning, thinking and creating."

"Where did you go to college?" asked Knox, with mounting impatience.

"In my country, Edward," Noesis answered simply.

"Which is your country, Noesis? Your name tells me that you must be from Greece. It sounds Greek to me anyway. I had three credits in Greek before I flunked out of that course."

"The name is Greek, and it means *Knowledge*, but I like to think of it as my *alter-ego*, that is, the symbolic expression of my being and my unlimited quest for more knowledge."

"That sounds good too. But then you're Greek, aren't you, Mr. Knowledge?"

"Have your fun, Edward. You can't help it and I don't want to change it. Not right now. Only when you'll be ready to change it yourself. For nobody can do that for you. And if you like to identify me as a Greek because of the name I use, go ahead. But I don't like these labels; they define, they circumscribe, they limit and—to that extent—they also separate, divide, and oppose, instead of integrating and unifying. Since labels and nationalities have no meaning for me, I invite you, Edward, to look at me as a rational being. That's all."

"What about calling you Mr. Logic, then?" continued Knox. "That's a Greek name too, and comes from Logos, which means, among other things, idea, speech, discourse, reason and so on. I remember that much."

"Look, Edward, it's getting late. Soon I shall leave you and probably you'll have to go too. I have no time for this joking. That's not the reason I wanted to make your acquaintance!"

"This is the first time that you sound a little bit irritated and annoyed, Noesis, and a little frustrated and disillusioned too. Sorry, pal, it's your own fault. You, who call yourself Noesis, Knowledge, a rational being and refuse to identify yourself any further, you should have known better when you picked me from the list of subscribers or when you saw me coming up to you on this hill. You made a mistake. Shall we call it quits and a 'see-you-never'?"

"If you wish, Edward. Remember what I said about respecting your freedom and independence? I still do."

"And what do you want, Noesis? Do you want me to go and forget about this stupid incident?"

"My wish has not changed. Neither has my purpose in being here with you. It's still the same and will remain such. We . . . I mean, I do not live by the desire or the whim of a fitful moment."

"But you did not make your proposal yet," said Knox, with some aprehension and pleading in his voice.

"When I started to, you cut me short, Edward, to empty the gall of your hatred, on the assumption of a mistaken identity," stated Noesis firmly.

"And we didn't get to the end of your parable about the gardener either. I still don't know what's going to come of it. . . ."

"In other words, Edward, you're not so dead yet as you like to think you are. You still have some curiosity left within you, some glowing coal under the ashes of your own fire. Shall I take this as your desire to keep up our acquaintance?"

"Well, you're different and interesting, Noesis, though I don't like some of the things you said, and I don't understand all of your words. That is reason enough for continuing our conversation."

"That's true, and . . ."

But Noesis could not finish his sentence. A ball of light of a blinding radiance was descending in their direction from above at a tremendous speed, as if falling freely, its size increasing every moment. Knox threw himself to the ground, covering his face with his hands. Seconds later, he heard the sound of something heavy touching the ground, just a few feet from him. The blinding light subsided then, and he could open his eyes. First he saw Noesis standing next to a huge craft of some sort, bigger than a house, shaped as two saucers turned upon each other, lip by lip. He noticed a row of blinking lights—white, blue and red—running around the rim of the craft. He could hear no sound, but felt a strange sensation of heat coming from the machine. The next moment a door opened in the side of the craft and Knox saw Noesis walk up some kind of a ramp and disappear inside the strange thing. The door closed noiselessly from within, and the next instant the craft took off straight up into the sky, its color changing to orange and then to white. Before he could do or say anything, the craft was out of sight. Then he was looking up into the darkness, his arms stretched out in the direction where it had dissapeared, and he heard himself shouting: "Noesis! Don't go away! Noesis, come back! Come back, Noesis!"

But the stillness of the night choked the sounds of his dying voice.

CHAPTER TWO

THE PROPOSAL OF THE VISITOR
FROM THE OUTER SPACE

Several weeks had elapsed since the mysterious incident on the hill. Knox could not remember how he had gotten back to his apartment in the city. The only thing he was able to recall, the morning after that frightful experience, was a maddening confusion in his mind, being unable to control the disorderly wild race of his ideas and emotions. At times, he had difficulty drawing a clear line of demarcation between his bizarre dreams, his recurrent nightmares, and the reality of his body and of the things around him. He would not leave his apartment because of a nameless fear of the unknown that seemed to have changed his whole attitude toward himself and his life. He felt that he had lost his old identity, while the new one had not yet taken shape. The thing he had seen on the hill stood out by itself as the only one experience that counted and made everything else seem small, unimportant, unattractive, without value or meaning. The narrow horizons of his previous concerns seemed to shrink to the emptiness of nothing at all, for he knew that a new dimension was open to him, unique, fantastic, unheard of, a secret that belonged to him only, a hidden treasure and hope, the promise of something surpassing all his former dreams and expectations. He would not contact anybody, would not answer the phone or open the door, for fear that, by stepping back into that world, he would spoil and lose the pleasure, the happiness of his unique adventure.

A few days later he felt strong and brave enough to make his way to the hill. As he caught sight of it from a distance, his heart began to pound wildly, his breathing became faster and almost painful, and he felt the first drops of nervous perspiration on his forehead. He was now walking faster and faster, then breaking into an uncontrolled run uphill, feeling no pain, no exhaustion. He stopped at what he took to be the landing site, and stared stupidly at the ground at his feet. But he could see nothing. Then he knelt down to examine the rusty red color of what seemed to be some circular depressions in the ground, where the grass had been scorched by the pressure and the heat of what he took for the landing gears of the craft. He moved on his knees from one spot to the next several times to prove to himself that what he was seeing was really there and true. He had to make sure for his own sanity's sake that it wasn't hallucination. Then he sat down next to one of the round holes in the ground, his head sunk to his chest, his hands touching the spot. So it was here, he told himself, reassuringly. It was real, it had really happened, it existed, it was not the making of his deluded mind. He laughed with the joy of an escapee from some torture chamber of untold horrors. He felt like kissing the ground, like jumping up, dancing, yelling, shouting with joy for having recaptured his sense of reality. He waited till the pressure of his emotions subsided, then got up, slowly, straightening his body and lifting his head toward the endless void of infinite space. The ground on which he was standing was a platform, a springboard from which to leap and to fly up into the invitating depths of unknown worlds. He heard himself repeating, over and over, Noesis' name.

He walked home in a pensive mood, seemingly unaware of things, people and the deafening noise of the rush hour. One could read in his eyes the rebirth of light, the youthful energy and expectant vitality of the resurrected. The vision of a new life was taking shape in his mind, building on his new certainty that we are not alone in the universe.

Then his old enemy of nausea and agonizing depression attacked him again. He felt his energy draining from him, his hope beginning to seep away, his enthusiasm changing into the nagging pain of futile despair, until he felt the cold hands of lifeless

26

anguish choking him once more. He threw himself on his bed, hoping to drown into the comparative bliss of unconsciousness.

The following day he decided to forget all about the whole affair, to defend himself against the anguish of a hopeless hope for the impossible. And the shortest route to this end would be to look up the other fellows, whom he had neglected entirely for the past two weeks. But he also made up his mind not to let anybody learn anything about his recent experience. He would put up some plausible excuse—sickness, maybe—to justify his absence to his fellow rebels against the bourgeois establishment. So he went, in the afternoon, to their favorite and almost exclusive side-walk café, the colorful hang-out of the hairy-type.

It was rather early in the afternoon when he got there, for the gang never got together before five or six o'clock. Since there was nothing to his taste then at the movies, he sat down at an empty table and sipped his first drink, watching the busy, well-conditioned passers-by, the regimented subjects of the Organization. It was a kind of inverted pleasure he gained from looking with contempt and disgust at the endless parade of the nice, clean, responsible, and respectable units of this great society. The pleasure came from his knowledge that he was not one of them. They could not enlist him in the stupid rat-race of Pavlovian mazes. He was free, he was different, he didn't conform, he didn't submit, he dropped out, he rebelled and kept on protesting through his appearance, every detail of which was contemplated to be a living contradiction of what middle-class people regarded as the 'right' thing. He began to enumerate and summarize in his mind the symbols of his protest. People worked—he didn't, or if forced to by the cursed necessities of his stomach, only on an *ad hoc* basis, part-time, never full-time. The 'serious' people believed in success—he laughed at the idea; the 'responsible' people planned a career—he loathed the glorification and the glamorizing of prestige, fame, glory, so-called greatness, promotions and the nerve-wrecking competition of the social and professional climbers, who were paying for the race with their ulcers and heart conditions; the 'well-rounded' people dressed carefully by putting on the 'latest' uniform dictated by the manipulators

27

of public taste—he chose casual, comfortable clothes, every piece was chosen and designed so that it neglected the public's standard of elegance and grooming; the 'mature' people were conscious of the psychology and the value of a clean haircut—possibly crew-cut—and a cleaner, closer shave—and he despised cleanliness —it stunk: his long hair and bushy beard were the symbols of saying No; he thought that they must be also deodorized—who knows, perhaps also pasteurized, homogenized and enriched with their daily communion at the breakfast table—the vitamin pill— needed for an extra dose of energy—and he rather developed hydrophobia, a fear of, or, perhaps, just an aversion to, water, soap, deodorants and toothpaste, being proud of that added defiance at cleanliness. He preferred whisky to water, cigarettes to vitamins and nothing for the skin. He took a strange pleasure, mixed with nausea, in analyzing the nervous faces of the 'respectable' tax-payers and 'charitable' contributors to every 'goodcause.' They seemed to move as if being driven, hunted, chased or persecuted; they were running under the merciless drive of obsession and compulsion. Invisible hands seemed to hold the strings attached to the feet, legs, hands, arms and the necks of these marionettes, who jerked obediently at the slightest pull of any one of the many ties that kept them tied to . . . what? To life, they said. And they made an effort of faking some nice front of agreeableness, politeness, kindness and warmth whenever they parted their tight lips for a well studied, officially prescribed and efficiently helpful, mechanical smile. Perhaps, Knox told himself, they were anxious to prove that they brushed after every meal, and got no cavities. No, they didn't have any cavities, just the big cavity on their shoulders which they could not help having and carrying, with the lightness typical of emptiness and vacuum. Self-righteousness was carved and frozen on their tense faces, the consciousness of being useful and efficient, for they lived on Geritol. Whenever they forgot the letter or a line of the well memorized roles they acted out for themselves and for the sake of others—thus lapsing into the expressionless stupidity of revolting barbarism, heightened by the nervous blinking of their evil eyes—they pulled themselves up and to-

28

gether again, with ill-concealed embarrassment, for this is what they believed to be right, and good, and clean, and effective, and . . . maddening!

As he shifted his chair with disgust toward the wall, he became almost paralyzed, unable to complete his motion, half-sitting, and half-leaning, supporting himself with his left hand pressed against the marble top of the table. He was stunned, shocked and stupefied at the same time. His eyes widened to an unusual size, his mouth hanging half-open, as though he had been hit or electrified and reduced to helpless immobility. The image of a man, sitting alone at the table close to the wall seemed both real and illusory. Knox rubbed his eyes once or twice, wanted to say something, to get up and walk toward that image, to touch it, to convince himself that he was not seeing things. But he couldn't control or overcome his inert passivity. Then he saw that figure—he did not dare to decide whether it was only an image or reality for fear of destroying it—getting up from his seat, his eyes—the same magnetic power as of those he had seen once before—resting on his face, as if inviting him to follow. So, almost mechanically, he obeyed. The man walked down the sidewalk with slow, measured steps, heading toward the entrance of a hotel. Knox followed him into the lobby, saw him ask the clerk for his key and move toward the elevator. Knox felt irresistibly drawn by that image. In a few moments, he found himself in his room, face to face and alone with Noesis!

"Hello, Edward!" Knox heard the familiar sound of his melodious voice.

"Hello, Noesis, that's you again, isn't it?" muttered Knox, his words scarcely audible even to himself.

"Sit down, Edward, make yourself comfortable. It's I, Noesis. Try to relax and regain your composure. You're not dreaming, you're not deluded. It's not hallucination, it is real, actual, existing," said Noesis, while sitting down in one of the armchairs. Knox calmed down somewhat and obediently followed Noesis' suggestion. He was searching for words, he wanted to talk, to say something, start a conversation as a relief and to be released from the tension that was still holding him in its grip.

29

"If you want to have a cigarette, go ahead, smoke. It doesn't disturb me." Noesis was giving Knox time to recover from his upset condition. "I hope you don't mind my returning and forcing you to come with me here?" he asked Knox more from politeness than prompted by actual doubt.

"You know that I don't, I think nobody would, especially after that . . . how shall I call it . . . that sighting on the hill, right?"

"Of course," answered Noesis matter of factly, with understanding. "I also know what you want to talk about, all the questions which plague your mind because of an almost public hysteria about so-called flying saucers and visitors from outer space."

"Then it's true and you must be one of them, aren't you?" explained Knox with excitement.

"If you mean all the hoaxes, fabricated by the childish or, perhaps, just fertile imagination of the so-called cultists, the fantastic stories repeated in the so many UFO books, newsletters, pamphlets, and what not—then I'll have to say no, I'm not one of those 'space brothers,' as they call them. But if you can leave out the miraculous, the unbelievable and the downright idiotic fabrications of opportunitists, the self-styled 'scientific-ufologists,' the absurd claims of the 'contactees' and their even more incredible messages, gospels and revelations about a paradise lost and found in outer space—if you can discount all that exploitation of your credulity by unscrupulous dollar grabbers—then you are right in saying that it is true and I am one of them. But tell me what did you mean when you called me 'one of them'? Who are 'they'?" asked Noesis. He was smiling and looked inquisitively into Knox's eyes. Knox tried to coordinate his thoughts, but he felt like a child holding a big box containing his Christmas present, anxious to open it, but unable to do so without the help of his elders. He felt only the undeniable presence of Noesis, and the desire to know him better.

"What I mean," answered Knox, "was the truth about life existing in the universe and that you came from there, whatever world, star, planet, galaxy you're from. That's what I meant."

"There shouldn't be anything so extraordinary about all this," said Noesis simply. "Doesn't life exist on your planet? Aren't you real? If so, then why should it be made exclusive and unique and restricted to your planet only? Just because you didn't know of it, because—so far—you haven't had any objective evidence and proof, because you haven't succeeded in breaking loose into the immensity of the cosmos? And, unfortunately, with the present methods of your outer-space program you're not going to get much farther than the moon. But that's a different matter," Noesis cut short the current of his own thought.

"I guess you're right in everything you say. I remember that some of our scientists—at least those who are not hindered by their provincial and dogmatic myopia—speculate on the possibility of life existing on other planets, but they never get beyond pure theorizing."

"Besides," interrupted Noesis, "they always fear the possibility of falling into disrepute and ridicule at the hand of their colleagues, without forgetting the moral and religious obstacles either. Your people disapprove of thinking beyond the narrow limits of your sunsets. That would upset quite a number of their 'eternal and infallible' truths."

"You have a strong point there," Knox hurried to show his agreement and his delight in discovering that Noesis did not seem to think highly or favorably of the supernaturalists. He himself had lost his faith in the 'beyond.' He had plenty of reasons to doubt the sincerity of the agents of beatific visions one was supposed to contemplate from the dark quarters of one's grave.

"Yet, I repeat," continued Noesis, "the existence of life in the universe should be more than a hypothesis; rather, it is just the logical and real consequence of the principle of the organic continuity and uniformity of the so-called matter and its forms of manifestation throughout the cosmos."

"Would you care to explain what you meant, or how I should understand the principles you've just mentioned?" demanded Knox.

"Certainly!" replied Noesis. "What I mean is the simple fact that the stuff out of which everything is made—life included—is the same, identical, uniform, and continuous, wherever you find

31

it. And there is no reason to suppose the opposite, that is, the discontinuity, heterogeneity and diversity of the one and the same energy. The structural combination of the elementary particles of energy is and can be varied, but no matter what new configurations it builds up in the process of evolution, the principles, the laws, the code of the blueprint remain the same. Your planet, as you know it, is part of a small solar system, which is part of a galaxy, which in turn is part of the orderly coexistence of countless other galaxies, and so forth without end or limit. But the important thing to grasp is that the nature of the part is no different than the nature of the whole of which it is a part. That's simple, isn't it?"

"In other words," Knox was trying to catch up, "no matter how far one penetrates into the cosmic space, one would find the same things. Am I right in concluding this?"

"Not altogether correct; but a principle already known to some of your philosophers could give you a better insight. They spoke of the eternal recurrence of the same. Now let's add to it these three words: 'under different forms,' which means: if we assume that the total amount of energy in the universe is finite and if we think of time as an endless duration, then it follows that the combinations of which matter is capable had been realized many times over, but 'under different forms.' It is the unity in variety, the sameness in diversity, the uniformity in plurality, the simplicity of its effects and combinations."

"Then it is the same and not the same. But that's a contradiction." Knox was trying to justify his lack of comprehension of what Noesis expounded.

"All right, Edward," Noesis said patiently. "I shall give you a simple example that should clear up the apparent contradiction. Suppose a child gets a limited number—which can also be a very large number—of building blocks. Suppose also that this child, being intelligent, has many ideas of his own, and that there is no limit to the time he can play with those blocks. You can anticipate that the same blocks will be arranged in an almost endless variety of different structures, combinations and forms; nevertheless, there is a limit to the number of possible combinations because of the finite number of blocks. So, one concludes, everything reoccurs again and again, eternally, while only the forms of the combinations vary with certain limits."

"I understand that much," nodded Knox. "But I don't see its relation or connection with the existence of life on other planets."

"Nevertheless, there is one, and try to follow this thought: if life evolved on your planet—and there is no doubt about that— if the laws and principles of the cosmic stuff are the same, if conditions similar to those prevailing on your earth exist elsewhere, tell me, why, for what reason, shouldn't it have occurred and exist also elsewhere? Just because the idea is so new, and it has not become, as yet, part of the common belief of your mankind? And, finally, my presence here in this room gives you the immediate proof and evidence that it did and does exist. . . ."

"But if I told my friends about you and everything I've seen, they wouldn't believe me anyway!" Knox added rather disappointed.

"People's beliefs, opinions and prejudices—even if they are shared by the large majority—do not change facts which are absolute. The only standard and measure of truth is reality, not numbers, statistics, and majority votes," Noesis tried to convince his rather slow disciple.

"But they will demand evidence, proof, demonstration, which nobody—including my own self—can provide at the moment, right?"

"As far as the demand for evidence is concerned, it's true that we have not provided signs, miracles for the population of your world at large. And we shall not do so for a long time to come," Noesis stated with firmness.

"But why?" Knox was pleading. "Why, for what reason do you keep back such a stupendous news from them? Why do you leave them in doubt and create the best opportunity for the cheap money-grabbers to exploit the excited fantasy of the masses?"

"First, because we do not owe such information, I mean, it's not our obligation to do so; secondly and most important, because the news is—as you correctly stated—so stupendous. This

33

means that it would create a global hysteria, disorder, disorientation and their worse consequences, such as armed conflicts, of which you have had, throughout your history, more than enough. Thirdly, because the knowledge about the universe being populated would bring along an immediate collapse, first, of your religious and moral beliefs, codes and values. This would be followed then by the total revaluation or devaluation of your outlook on life itself, causing the sure disintegration of your present social, political and economic system."

"Do you really think so?" Knox argued skeptically.

"Yes, we do think so! And it's not only a matter of opinion, feeling or fear on our part. We know it from similar experiences in some other parts of the universe. The reason is quite simple, and please do not take what I'm going to say as an offense. It is your very primitive level of evolution and culture which forbids us this large scale disclosure of what you already know. You have to understand that the process of evolution, its form and rate, is not uniform throughout the universe. Neither is it the same in terms of its start, duration and extinction. The so-called time is different. I think you know that there is nothing static, stationary and stagnant or, shall we say, dead in the world. Motion, change, transformation, birth and rebirth applies to everything, from the smallest particle of energy to the immensity of unknown galaxies. We are in an ever-changing, dynamic, living universe. Your own life, Edward, is constant activity and change; while you live, you're constantly changing biologically, mentally and culturally. Therefore, it makes only good sense to assume that the many worlds in the universe are not at the same stage, point or level of development: some civilizations are incredibly more advanced than yours, while still others are millions of years behind yours."

"If this is so—and I don't see the reason why it shouldn't be—then I regret and resent that I was born to live on this earth which—as you said—is on a very primitive level. . . . I wish I could blame somebody for it or at least change it. . . . I would also be ready and glad to say a final good-bye to our beautiful world, only if I could go to some better place. . . ." Knox was musing ruefully, letting his imagination get the better of him.

34

"I'm sorry to disappoint you, Edward, but that is not possible. I do not promise you rides in our space crafts or visits to your nearby planets, and enjoyable company with space girls as it was already claimed by unscrupulous frauds and crackpots. Besides, it would do you no good. You have to take my word for it. But let's get back to the question of evidence and the reasons for not breaking the news on a global scale."

"I'll listen to the rest of your reasons," Knox said with decreasing enthusiasm.

"Rest assured, Edward, that the persons responsible for the international peace of your world—not only your politicians—but your scientists, have been informed and instructed by us regarding the policy to follow in order to slowly educate the population of the globe, preparing them step by step for the mature and responsible acceptance of the news. I don't think that you're so conceited as to imagine that you are the only person who'd been chosen to receive the revelation about the secrets of the universe. You're not the first, not the only, and not the last one either."

"I didn't imagine that I would be . . ." Knox said apologetically. "And I agree with you on the need to educate our people. But, so far, there has been no official recognition about the truth of flying saucers. On the contrary, people still complain about the secrecy, the censorship of the Government, and especially of the Air Force, their policy of explaining away most of the sightings, even those of reputable, reliable and educated people. What do you say to that?"

"They have no other choice left, if you understand and agree on the disastrous consequences an official recognition would entail," answered Noesis.

"Let's just say that I agree. . . . You don't give me much choice, do you? But tell me this, if you can, why are you so interested all of a sudden? Why the close observation of our world now? Why not before?"

"If you were familiar with the historical records, which are being dug up by some writers and published with tolerable accuracy, you would know that the observation of the world by extraterrestrial visitors has been going on, almost without inter-

35

ruption, for a long time. The reason for its increase in the past quarter of a century is due to two important technological advances of your science: the knowledge and the power you acquired in the field of nuclear physics and your first attempts to communicate with and travel in space."

"Why should you care about that?"

"Because of the kind of people you are, Edward. Do I have to remind you again that your whole history so far has been the bloody record of revolutions and wars which means of murder and mass extermination? And unfortunately, whatever advance you've made in science, its knowledge was immediately put to the service of improving your skill in destroying and killing each other. Take the existing atomic weapons, the arsenal of your A and H bombs, and the real danger it represents, first of all for your own civilization. Instead of putting your knowledge to the technological and cultural betterment of your lives, you take pride in being capable of wiping out life from the surface of your planet. Should that happen, that fact in itself would not represent any threat to out own peace and security, especially if you knew about the superiority of our own power, which we don't use for belligerent purposes. As you saw for yourself, the very existence of our space ships renders all your hardware obsolete."

"That's true," agreed Knox at once.

"But can you imagine what would happen if this same blood-thirsty race finally succeeded in their space projects, being able to approach and attack our world, armed with their devastating weapons? They already know how to deliver a playload on the moon, in which there might also be included an atomic warhead. And what guarantee do we have that it will not happen? I told you that your historical record proves the opposite."

"On the other hand, you're superior enough to prevent it, aren't you?"

"Yes, we are and we intend to do just that. This is one reason for our stepped-up surveillance of your world."

"I did read in a saucer-book written by some scientist that— according to what he says—you have already mapped our entire globe, surveyed all our military installations, the testing grounds of our defense projects. Is that a fact?"

"That's only a small part of what we've done so far. We do not like to take chances, especially not with a race of people whom we justly call mechanized and motorized barbarians, if you'll excuse the expressions, which are nevertheless correct. We can switch off, all at once, whatever source of energy you have and need for the functioning of your peaceful or belligerent machinery, without the loss of a single life."

"Then the accusation that you're hostile and ready to invade the earth by force, to take over, is false?"

"That is false and, at the same time, a typical example of extrapolation or unwillful projection of the accusers' own dispositions: barbarians can think of, or rather imagine, everybody only in terms of their own identity and intentions."

"Why do you insist on calling us barbarians?" Knox seemed to jump to the defense of his own people.

"I called you mechanized or motorized barbarians, and that term contains the paradox, the contradiction of your present condition," explained Noesis, without getting emotionally upset.

"Would you care to justify your position?" asked Knox.

"Certainly. First of all, you've made some progress in the field of science and its practical application, technology and industrialization. To this extent you're a small step ahead and above the primitive savages living in the jungles. In fact, you could be even farther advanced scientifically today, if you hadn't waited almost two thousand years, due to your ethical, superstitious and religious views, which have been the constant enemy of your cultural emancipation and enlightenment. And this brings me to the second part of the term, barbarians, that is. For in the field you call humanities—including your social, political and moral ideas —you are not better off than your barbaric ancestors. The bloody record of your past and recent history is the indisputable evidence of its truth. Your true nature becomes manifest through your actions. Only you don't like to name what everybody knows, instead you invent all sorts of rationalizations, giving so-called good reasons, or at least good intentions, for your evil causes and deeds. And this is the paradoxical and contradictory predicament

37

of your condition. It is also the source of all your sufferings and miseries. I remember the first time when I came to this world of yours. The thing which impressed me most was the almost total absence of joy and happiness in your lives. It's very rare to see one of you as the embodiment of a meaningful existence. I'm still waiting to see the first happy human being. But I don't have to tell more about that to you, because you're one of the many who's totally disillusioned and disgusted with your present way of life."

"That's true again, but what can we do about it? There seems to be no solution, no way out, no hope for anything better, just the certainty of everything getting worse and worse, running its necessary course of decline, till the whole nonsense collapses. . . . Or, you tell me, Noesis, is there a way out?" Knox challenged his host.

"Yes, there is, but no magic formulae are available," Noesis volunteered cautiously. "What I mean is that no one can bypass the natural and necessary steps in the process of evolution. A child cannot turn into an adult overnight; neither can a savage become a civilized and cultured person by moving into a big metropolis and imitating their way of life. There's no short cut to learning, developing, maturing and acquiring wisdom. One can do no more than assist to this process, giving the right directions and goals, removing the obstacles and preventing the possibility of getting lost while under way toward that goal. In one word, one who knows can teach those who don't but these must be willing to learn and to improve themselves."

"I'm not so sure about the efficiency of teaching and learning, and I've got reasons to feel that way. Probably you know that we've had several—how shall I call them?—great teachers, philosophers, wise-men, enlightened spirits, whose goal was to decrease ignorance by shedding the light of their knowledge. And look what has come of them? They were stoned, crucified, poisoned, murdered, exiled, or silenced. I really don't believe that you can teach anything to anybody. Everyone learns only through his own experiences, and the stupid ones keep on making the same mistakes over and over."

"In other words, you're denying the very possibility of evolution as such?" Noesis tried to make Knox see the hidden contradiction in his sham wisdom. "That would deny the evidence of the progress you've made so far, in spite of the persecution of your best. . . ."

"I'm not trying to quarrel with facts, I'm not that stupid," Knox retorted almost offended. "What I meant is that only a few, very few individuals are capable of reaching for higher values, whereas the rabble, the mob keep on vegetating and multiplying their own kind."

"But there is a promise and hope at least for the superior types of men, those of ability, who can be educated and educate themselves?"

"Oh, sure, no doubt about that. On the other hand, what is the weight and power of these few exceptions when one thinks of the large masses of half-domesticated herd-animals, for which there is no promise and no hope to ever become true human beings? And if you add to that the fact that the principle of natural selection can't work nowadays as it did in the past because it seems to be the desire of all democrats and humanitarians to perpetuate the mediocre, the average, the inferior, even the sick and degenerate—then I don't see how the higher man should prevail. I can see the opposite though: the existence of the superior man will be made impossible through the cultivation of the type opposite to his own. Now, can you see why I'm so skeptical about the future of man? There's one more point: there are limits to educability, which should be taken for what they are. You cannot educate everybody, and those few whom you can, will go only to the limit of their individual capabilities. The large mass of mankind shall always be what it has been: a multiplication of zeroes by zeroes."

"Well said, Edward! But don't you see that you were saying, in different words what I had in mind and what I had said before? When I referred to those who are willing to learn and improve themselves, I wasn't thinking of the lowest type of human beings. My view is selective and to that extent also aristocratic. It's the opposition between quantity and quality which are inversely proportional: the higher the quality, the lower the quantity, and vice-versa."

"But you realize it, don't you, Noesis, that you are denying the democratic and collectivist utopia of education for all? That's a very unpopular and also very dangerous point of view to defend nowadays."

"It may be so for you, but not for us; we have no such problems and conflicts any longer. But we shall discuss that later on, if everything goes well. Right now, Edward, I'd like to come back to my proposal, that I could not present to you when I first mentioned it on the hill. Remember?"

"Well, what is it that you have on your mind?" asked Knox without much curiosity and enthusiasm in his voice and manner. "Is it in the line of some extraterrestrial, celestial crusade or revivalist campaign? If it's anything like the charitable, humanitarian and welfare programs for 'the greatest good of the greatest number,' you might as well save it for yourself or somebody else. I'm sick of all those projects designed for the improvement of our beloved brothers. I haven't got the spirit or the blood of the good samaritan, the social and socialist workers, the devotion of the civil-rights heroes, the unselfishness of the promoters of happiness, of universal progress and the future paradise or whatever you want to call it. . . ."

"I see you're quite fed up with the creed of altruism. . . . Well, I don't blame you. And you would make your greatest mistake by assuming that I am some kind of a redeemer, a savior sent from heaven, the angel of light, the magician of miracles and the rest of it. But our values are not based on or derived from public benefit. So do not fear that I'm going to burden you with any unselfish dedication to the good of mankind. . . ."

"You've said that already. I remember it and it's fine with me, so far, but it's time now for you to come out with it and state your proposal. I forgot to tell you that if it's money or espionage or anything along that line, you've got the wrong guy."

"So far you've told me all the things you hate, loathe, and don't care for. Is there anything, Edward, one thing, only one, which you would like to accomplish just because *you* want it?"

40

"That's a hard question to answer and kind of personal too. . . . But I don't mind telling you how I feel, rather, how I used to feel some time ago, during my college years. You know I wanted to be a writer and I knew that I have what it takes to be a good one, I mean, ideas and the ability to express them, to communicate them, to dramatize them. . . . First I started writing some short stories about what I considered essential, important, significant, and noble in man's life. My stories were sent back by the publishers with the same objection from all of them: while they allowed some good praise for my imagination and style, they criticized the idealized and stylized image of my characters. . . . 'Life is not like that,' they told me. 'Write about people as they are; modern man doesn't want dreams, fantasy-thinking, romantic vulgarities. . . . You have to be more realistic, down to earth, and honest about it.' Then I started to imitate what they call the naturalistic method in presenting real man and real life. . . . Oh, I learned what they actually meant by realistic. I read the trash of those who 'arrived' and were held up as the greatest riddlers of man's soul. All that glorification of the nil, the glamorizing of the senseless, the mournful bewailing of our own tragic lot, the graphic description of what people actually do in their bedrooms. I've tried that and I succeeded. My stories were accepted. They were published. I was praised as a new promising talent of the future. They paid me well too. . . . Only that kind of success didn't please me. I couldn't keep it up because I felt I had betrayed something within my own self. I had betrayed the promise of life, I was enshrining garbage and wrapping it in sly sophistication. And when I finally got sick of it, I dumped it. . . . And I've never written one single line since then. . . . So there you have it, Noesis, and I don't know why I said all this to you. I couldn't repeat it to anybody else."

Noesis kept watching Knox while he was telling him the short-lived story of his defunct ideals, observing the presence of unconcealed suffering, the helplessness of one who had lost all ability to hope, to believe, and to feel, because of the tragic absence of the will to live, to value and to create. He understood that the true reason behind Knox's strange rebellion was his last,

41

ill-conceived and desperate protest against a society that had banished values, greatness and meaning from life, while senselessly fomenting the cult of the irrational, the small, the low and the depraved. He also knew that he had a difficult case at his hands, almost as difficult as to resurrect, to bring back to life those who cynically celebrate their being sick unto death. An idea occurred to him that could perhaps reverse this dangerous process of rushing headlong into final tragedy, and said:

"Edward, do you remember my example about that gardener? . . ."

"Yes, I do, but I haven't given much thought to it. If you care to finish your parable, I'll listen now, if it's any good. . . ."

"I want you to grasp the idea behind it, the motivating power, the purpose and the justification, the meaning and the sanction in the gardener's passion and pleasure in growing his flowers."

"I think I told what I find in it. Is there anything else to it?"

"There are several things to it, but the most important and the most significant for you is only one point, that the gardener's activity was the expression of his own will through an action whose only reason was the fact that it was self-chosen, self-imposed, self-determined, self-directed, that is, self-willed, autonomous, and free. He wasn't growing those flowers for sale, to impress or to please his neighbors or to make them envious. He wasn't thinking of how they felt about it, whether they approved of it or not, whether it represented any value and meaning for them. The only motive was that it was the thing he wanted to do and nothing more. Therein was also his pleasure and his happiness. That one reason was sufficient upon itself—requiring no outside sanction and motive whatsoever. It was the manifestation of his own desire and his ability, the meaning found in the active exercise of his powers, willed only for its own sake. It was the living manifestation of personal freedom in the absolute sense of the word. Freedom from others and freedom to live and to act the way one chooses to be. The contents and the meaning of his life and activity were not made dependent upon anything outside his own being. It was self-contained and owned only by himself. It had a meaning and a value only for himself and that was sufficient."

"Why should that be so important for me. . . . I don't see the connection," Knox remarked impersonally.

"You'll see it in a minute. . . . Ask yourself the question why you became so deeply disgusted with writing. What was the mistake you've made? What was the wrong premise you started out with in your career?"

"What was it?" repeated Knox with some animation.

"You've committed the fateful error of making your life, your ideas, your goals and values dependent upon the approval or disapproval of the others. You acted as a child, the typical extrovert by nature, whose every action is other-directed and subordinated to the sanction of those around him."

"But I didn't!" Knox protested. "When I started I wrote the way I thought I should write. I didn't ask anybody to vote on it!"

"At the start you didn't do it, and it was good. But when you were faced with the collection of your rejection slips, your faith in your own self quivered and broke down. You yielded, you submitted, you conformed, you accepted their will, you allowed them to fix the terms by which you would be allowed to exist as a writer. You betrayed your own will, your own principles, your own standards. You sold out your mind, you set a price on your soul. You capitulated, you gave in, you put up, you resigned, then you obeyed. You ceased to function as a free self sufficient person. And do you know why you did all that?"

"Why?"

"Because you wanted to write at any cost, to become a writer not for the sake of the writing itself, not for creativity's sake as such, not even for the pleasure you ought to have experienced in being creative, but for the desire to impress, to show, to display, to function in public, begging for their approval and being mortally afraid of their rejecting you. Which means also that you evaluate your personal worth by the public's reaction to your own mode of functioning, whereas it should have been the other way around: your own worth and value should be known to your

43

own self first and its recognition by the others should be a matter of no concern to you."

"Do you have anything else to say?" Knox inquired uneasily, as if offended by Noesis' words.

"Just one more thing. It's about your present condition. Your rebellion, your being a 'drop out,' a wayward or marginal existent. The true meaning of your passionate and fierce protests. Your defiance, your almost aggressive ostentation of the fact that you believe you've walked out on society."

"But I have! Haven't I? . . . I think I have, I know I don't belong to them and I don't want to. To hell with it! To hell with all of them! I hate their guts, their sights makes me throw up, I hate them, I despise them! They nauseate me, they fill me with contempt and disgust!" Knox had begun shouting, with increasing vehemence, his indictment of the others.

"All that may be true, but your immense hatred gives you away. . . ."

"What?" Knox almost screamed.

"Your hatred shows that you still belong to them in a way, you've never broken with them altogether, because you haven't become free within your own self. Your endless protest is just the reverse side of the same coin called love. You're bound by hatred, you're not free. This is why you make such a point of showing yourself to them by sitting at your sidewalk café, in the greatest traffic, in the midst of those whom you have supposedly damned. You cannot forgive them the fact that you were hurt by them when they disapproved of your ideas. Now it's your turn to pay them back through your apparent walk-out, actually a form of hidden desire for your revenge, unconfessed even to your own self. And, listen, Edward, since I know that what I'm saying is true, and that I do not make the judgment of my mind depend on anything else but my own ability to know and to reason, I'm not going to ask for your agreement or approval. Remember, though, that you can't lie to your own self. That is one thing which is impossible. Your reason won't let you get away with it!"

Knox felt uncomfortable and uneasy in his armchair. He tried to evade Noesis' inexorable eyes. He felt like jumping up from his place, run out of that room and keep on running. He closed his eyes, but still could not avert Noesis' steady gaze. He wished he could wipe him out of reality, but he also knew that those eyes would never cease to look at him. He felt helpless and beaten. It was the truth in Noesis' words that had knocked him out. He felt a sudden desire for a drink or something stronger to banish out of sight those burning lights on Noesis' face. He wanted to say something to keep up his protest, to disagree, to prove him wrong, to laugh at him, to be cynical or sarcastic, to escape the irreversible verdict he had just heard Noesis pronounce. He felt naked, the mask of pretense had fallen off his face, there was no place to run, to hide or to escape. He knew that he couldn't kept up the show any longer. It had lost its meaning, even the pleasure he used to have from his acting out that odd role in a nonsensical show was gone. He felt finished.

Noesis sat motionless in his place. The calm composure of his body, the unflinching steady glare of his eyes, the relaxed position of his whole self, without any sign of lazy informality, translated the image of a man totally at peace with his own self, taken as the only form of life possible to him.

After a protracted silence, Knox whispered almost inaudibly: "What's your proposal?"

"I'm one of the persons who came to this world with a definite purpose that I chose for my own self: while others are completing the work of surveying your planet, I decided to take part in the ideological aspects of our mission."

"The work of a missionary, then, but this time on an interplanetary scale," Knox said incisively. He couldn't help introjecting his biting criticism.

Noesis did not show any sign of being disturbed by Knox's impertinent remark. His patience revealed the quality of a wisdom needed when one has to deal with small children who cannot help being stupid and uncooperative, while, at the same time, depend on the help of those whom they oppose. So he continued explaining his intentions:

"It will be my pleasure and its justification too if I'll discuss

45

with you the causes of your social, political and moral problems and also to disclose some of the ideas, principles and values by which we live on our own planet. I believe that you need a new philosophy of life, a new frame of reference, in order to remedy your present condition of confusion and decadence. A new intellectual climate must be created—without which your future evolution will be doomed to failure. Of course, I shall not be able to give you the full account of our own way of life, because the conditions needed for applying it to your situation are not present in your world. Besides, if I mentioned them to you, you would not understand them, nor would anybody else. Our civilization and culture are at least fifty thousand years older and ahead of yours, though we measure time by standards different from yours."

"I still don't see my part in it. Or do you expect me to become a self-styled prophet and to preach your new gospel from the housetops? I hate the very idea of thinking of it. I haven't got the preacher's blood in my system."

"Neither do I, Edward, and your part shall be—if you accept it—another one. I had in mind a simple suggestion: If our discussions should continue—and you'll have to decide that too—why not write down their contents in a book and have it published?"

"So you want me to go back to writing, to write down your ideas but not my own, is that how you figured it out?"

"Not quite, Edward. Only if you should happen to agree with those ideas, because they make sense, would I ask you to do it."

"Why don't you do it yourself? You're smarter than I am and you don't need me as a docile ignorant. Write it down yourself, have it published on your planet, print millions of copies, billions of them, and shower them down from your spaceship. That way you take care of its distribution, you need no advertising, because the spaceship will be its best promoter. I guarantee that it will stay on the best-seller list for years, as the first book from outer space, only its popularity will not be measured by the clicking of the cash-register. . . . And I might read it myself, if I found it any good and to my taste. I shall propose to have you nominated as the man of timeless centuries—not only the man of the year—and be given all the trimmings and decorations in medals and awards we hand out to our best. Well, this is my counter-proposal! What do you think of it?"

At this point the telephone in Noesis' room started ringing. He got up from his seat, walked over to the phone and lifted the receiver. He kept listening attentively to the unknown party at the other end of the line, whose voice couldn't be heard. Then Noesis began to talk in a strange language that did not resemble any of the sounds which make up our speech. The total effect of the sounds was pleasant, a combination of melody, rhythm, cadence and harmony. The words did not seem to have more than three syllables each. Its modulation and tonality reminded Knox of a system of symbols that must be very simple, precise and efficient. He wished he could understand what Noesis was saying. After two minutes, Noesis put the receiver down, walked up to Knox and said:

"You'll have some time to think over my proposal. Right now I'll have to invite you to leave."

Noesis words sounded firm and final, allowing for no 'ifs' and 'buts' and 'howevers.' Knox got up and walked straight through the door that Noesis had opened for him.

CHAPTER THREE

THE BREAK

Knox found himself in the street, walking in the direction of the sidewalk café. Nothing was clear and settled in his mind. Nothing could fill the blank sheet of his consciousness. He wasn't thinking at all, and couldn't even if he had wanted to. He felt being possessed by his emotions, freely playing their wild games, one chasing the other, then returning again to the center of his awareness. He was being torn apart inside by the conflicting nature of his feelings that made him so helpless, unable to coordinate his thought and come to the root of his conflict. There was, first of all, his intense anger, but he couldn't discern whether he was angry with Noesis or with himself, or both. Perhaps his hatred involved everything and everybody, the whole of life. He couldn't explain to himself either why had he behaved so stupidly in the presence of Noesis? Did he hate him or like him? If he did hate him, he wished to know the reason, why? But he couldn't be sure that what he felt for Noesis was hatred, because up till now his hatred had been the combination of contempt, nausea and disgust. And he couldn't apply any of these feelings to Noesis. It would make no sense. It wasn't hatred, he was quite sure. Then it had to be something else, but what? He kept asking himself. He thought of resentment as a possible answer. If it was true, what did he resent about Noesis? Was it his superior state of being that gave him an acute attack of inferiority feeling? He wasn't sure of that either. No, it couldn't be, because he knew that he admired Noesis as well as envying him. On the other hand, he was certain of resenting that Noesis had unmasked him before himself, and shown him the inside

49

story of his strange condition. He never liked the idea that others might discover his true being. He liked to see that all well hidden, even before his own self. He didn't welcome the knowledge of standing naked before somebody's eyes. He took it as an intrusion of his privacy. Even more annoying was his awareness that the unmasking of his twisted self made any future attempts at playing the same game of self deceit impossible. He saw clearly that his insight meant also a loss, imposing the necessity to invent some new role to learn and act out. However, he didn't feel like putting up that new effort. He saw no reason why he should, and had no desire to it. This must be, he told himself, what people mean when speaking of somebody being concerned, bankrupt and at the end of his resources. The mounting frustration within himself told him irrevocably that his self-analysis was correct. He wished he could reverse the march of the time, turn the calendar back before the day he first met Noesis on the hill. After all, it was rather pleasant to live the way he did— without responsibilities, plans, goals, without serious commitment to anything, just as a self-exiled outsider, enjoying whatever pleasures he could collect. No thought about the future. He used to enjoy his role of being the bad conscience of his time. But now that bad conscience became rather his own than anybody else's. He cursed himself, everybody and everything. Life would never be the same again, it couldn't be. At the same time, he was ignorant of what it would be or ought to be in the days and months to come. In a way he was glad that he did not commit himself by either accepting or refusing Noesis' proposal. He enjoyed the benefit of remaining undecided. It allowed him the freedom from the responsibility to choose and act. He preferred floating in nothingness than living in reality.

Suddenly he found himself in familiar surroundings. It was his favorite hang-out of not so long ago. The group was there, just as usual. His first impulse was to pass by. Strange! He wanted to plunge back, head on, into the atmosphere of an illusory form of non-existence, but not this way. His friends had caught sight of him and he didn't have the courage for an open defiance, to walk out on them. So he joined them at the table, ordering a drink from the waiter. He wanted to say something, but couldn't find the right words. He just sat there in silence, staring blankly into space. One of his friends finally broke the silence provoked by his strange attitude:

"You look hung up, man! What's got you shook? Your old man stopped feeding you the monthly pittance?"

"No, no, I'm not broke yet, not quite. That's a miss. . . ."

"Where've you been? asked another subterranean creature. "S'been more than a month, I guess. . . . You used to be one of our regular irregulars."

"Got in trouble with the cops, heh?" questioned the third modern barbarian. "That's it, and this time you ran out of connections to get lose right away."

"No, no. I've got it. . . . He's gone over to some group of some kind, something new and different, promising a new pleasure pit unknown and unexplored yet, right?" Another devotee of hedonism threw in his guess.

"I don't buy that! No. That's not it. We've invented and explored everything, every imaginable kind, form and source of kicks . . . down the line of what the fat-heads label as 'abnormal,' and Ed was always the first to take his lion share from both inventing and enjoying it. So it can't be that. There's nothing new. It must be something else." That was the opinion of the pragmatist of despair, which means the senseless, avid and hungry chase of any kind of fun, not because there was any meaning to it, but just because of its opposite: because there was no sense to it, as there was no meaning to anything. It was the irrational pursuit of the irrational, because it was irrational and fun.

There was no reaction from Knox, neither agreement nor denial. The group became more and more puzzled by his mysterious silence and his stubborn refusal to give them any hint, any lead, to help them find the answer to their mounting curiosity. As a last attempt, another bushman, known as the Bull, was ready to shoot at Knox what all of them thought to be the greatest possible sin and treason, his voice heavy with ridicule, sarcasm and hidden reproach:

51

"Knox, listen. I think I know the truth about you. Even the unbelievable change in your behavior makes it right. You've committed the unpardonable sin, you betrayed your and our cause, you broke the oath you took when you dropped out of the Establishment. You're a turn-coat, you've been one all the time, but this time the chips are down, the colors are out in the clear. You went back to the so-called good, decent, virtuous, responsible and hard-working flock of bourgeois life and happiness."

Everybody expected Knox to jump at the throat of his accuser, but to the astonishment of all, he only lifted his glass to his lips and slowly reached the bottom of it. His eyes were fixed on his accuser, steady, unmoved, transfixing him with its glare. He put down his glass with measured precision, sat back on his chair, his legs crossed, and moved his eyes around the circle of the group. He paused a few seconds catching the eyes of each of the fellows, as if wanting to make sure that he got the best, the most detailed and precise image to be remembered in the future. When he had examined the last face, he stood up, straightened as if in defiance, and turned away, without letting one word fall from his tight lips. He walked away with slow but steady steps, without looking back. The group was struck dumb with astonishment at this unexpected behavior. There was a general confusion and embarrassment, each one trying unsuccessfully to bring the situation back to what they called normal. Fortunately the waiter came to their rescue, asking his customers if they wished anything, and each one hurried to ask for another drink, king-size this time. Apparently something was clogged up in their throat that needed a good flushing and lubrication. . . .

Knox kept going his way with only one desire and destination in his mind: "Let me get away, let me go as far as I can," he kept telling himself. "Let me unfasten the ties and the lies that kept me prisoner to others. Let me separate myself from the closeness of everything and every single body, let me divorce myself from the bondage of togetherness, no matter what its name, form or purpose. Let me wash myself clean from the dirt that accumulated on me through human contacts. Let me free myself from any 'common' cause, goal or problem. Whatever is common to many is also vulgar, ordinary and cheap, if for no other reason that its being shared by everybody. Let me seek deliverance in loneliness, in my solitude, in being alone, that is, all-one by myself. Rather alone than in the sickening company of people who invent common issues or ideas of protest and rebellion, as an excuse to come together and to stay that way. It's all the same anyway, whether it's the gospel of middle-class non-entities, or the bad tidings of those who take delight in stinking. It's nothing, nothing, of no consequence, a zero. Let me empty my brains of the slimy mud deposited by ignorance that parades as wisdom. Let me clean my heart from the drippy, schmaltzy sentiments of the clean and also from the wild torrents of frenzied insanity!"

It was getting late. Knox thought of walking home. He didn't want to take the subway or the bus, he loathed the idea of being crammed in tight with others in the compact closeness of the cars. He noticed that a fear was growing within him of late, an irrational aversion mixed with nausea, worse than any of the attacks he had in the past. It was a deep repulsion of all other human beings, whenever forced to touch them or to be touched. He invented for himself the term 'anthropophobia' to define his state of mind. He was hungry, but the same disgust kept him from walking into a diner. The sight of public vegetation, the spectacle of many hungry stomachs being filled without any concern with taste or manners, the sounds of slurping, chomping, munching, crunching and inevitably burping in between and after, with the cutting odor of burnt grease as an added delight and fringe benefit! . . . "No," he thought, "I'd rather stay hungry and walk back to my apartment." He avoided the busiest and noisiest streets, choosing the side-streets, not minding the extra time and fatigue it would mean to him.

He had not realized that it was already late in the evening when he finally shut the door of his apartment. It was his last gesture to lock out, to seal off reality and people out there, that wonderful something named life. He felt relieved and safe in the security of his loneliness, in the privacy of his apartment. He grabbed the first thing he found in his refrigerator and sat down at his desk, a thing he hadn't done for a long time.

He opened one of the drawers, taking a glimpse at the title of the last story he got published in some male magazine. He had called it "The Dawn Starts at Twilight," a story about a man in his late fifties or early sixties, who was trying to make sure that he was not going to miss any of the last kicks with the young chicks to be had for some dough. The story ended with the non-hero despairing of life, after discovering that the hormone shots had not fulfilled the promised flare up of passions of some forty years past, and he shot himself for that reason only. He knew then and now that the whole thing was just cheap crap for the cheap kind.

Then he looked at the last drawer on the left side of his desk, without touching it. It was in that drawer that he kept the manuscripts of his first trials and errors, when he still looked upon the profession of writing as a noble vocation, pregnant with hope, promise and meaning. He was afraid to reach down and to open that drawer. He realized—now—what such an apparently simple move would mean to him by its consequences. But the words of Noesis' proposal kept ringing in his mind, like the nagging insistence of an unwanted phone call, without being able to lift the receiver and slam it down again, in order to silence it. Certain doubts fed the undecided ambivalence of his consciousness: "What if it's too late?" the question sounded heavy with its fatal finality. . . . "Is there such a thing as the resurrection of one's spirit, the possibility of making a new star? Even if it were possible, was it worth all the disciplined concentration of the mind, required for creating something of value and meaning? And for what purpose, anyway? Perhaps to throw the best of his mind into the vulgarity of the market place? Pearls should not be thrown to the swine," he remembered vaguely, "for they would trample them and attack their owner. How true!" He sighed in exasperation. But next he remembered Noesis' words explaining the gardener's only reason and satisfaction for growing his flowers. . . . "Did that mean," he reflected, "that every creative act contains in itself its own reason, justification and sanction, without becoming dependent upon the arbitrary or artificial recognition, reward or rejection?" It was now clear to him and beyond any shade of possible doubt, that that was the only answer.

Chapter Four

THE AFFAIR

Knox slept through the whole night and far into the late hours of the next morning. It was a deep, profound and undisturbed sleep, a total submergence into the unknown regions of the unconcious, a complete abandonment of one's entire being to total non-being. There were no dreams he could remember when he opened his eyes, slowly recovering the awareness of himself, watching the gradual emergence and awakening of his existence, taking shape in reality once more. He felt the pleasure, the gratifying sensation that accompanies the state of total relaxation of mind and body. He floated in a half-world without any strain, tension or effort.

He found it both new and strange that his chronic feeling of fatigue left him, or at least it was nowhere that morning. The experience of over-all tiredness so well known to him was gone. No matter how much he used to sleep or relax, he always felt sleepy, exhausted, worn out, ready to collapse. He suspected that his condition had not been due to work or diet. He hadn't put in a full day's work for months, while not refusing the promptings of his appetites either. He tried to remember the technical term used to know from the jargon of psychology. . . . It began with something like neur . . . neurosis . . . no, it wasn't that . . . though the first syllable was the same. . . . He gave up the effort of remembering, and fell asleep again.

The hated sound of the doorbell forced him back into reality, announcing some unwelcome intruder. He never could stand the obtrusiveness of people, not even on the part of his friends. It must be the mailman, he thought, or perhaps some door-to-door salesman, a new one for sure. Those who had tried him out once before, never did so again and for good reasons. He hoped this time that by not answering the door, the biped would give up and take off.

But it did not work. The unknown visitor wouldn't retreat from his door. Now he not only rang the bell, but started knocking on the door as well. He was forced to get out of bed, put on his robe, readying himself for the use of his most effective vocabulary, both to repay the nag and to scare him away for good. He opened the door violently, planting himself in an aggressive position and shouted:

"What the hell . . ." he stopped the torrent of his abusive language, the words stuck in his throat. It wasn't the mailman or a salesman, or the police, nor was it some good soul soliciting dimes for some disease of unheard name which was killing thousands of innocent children every hour, every minute and every split second, proved by the authoritarian rigor of infallible statistics. . . . It was the person whom he had least expected to come up again to his doorstep. It was Marisa. This name alone was enough to resuscitate countless memories, how much more so, immensely more so, the actual presence of the person standing not two feet away from him, as if just risen from the dead. . . .

Marisa did not wait for an invitation to come in. She walked straight into the room, passing by the flabergasted Knox, who clung to the doorknob for support. Her next move was to free an armchair from the load of clothing, shoes, magazine, empty paperbags, remnants of food, and every imaginable and unimaginable articles, piled on top of pile. . . . Then, without pronouncing one single word, she sat down on the armchair, crossed her legs, produced a cigarette from one of her pockets and lit it, throwing the book of matches on the table in front of her. She leaned back on the chair and took her first good look at Knox, who was standing in front of her, in the middle of the room, dumbfounded, unable to recover from the shock of her unexpected presence.

"Make yourself at home," quipped Marisa ironically between two puffs of smoke.

Obediently, Knox sat down, unable to remove his eyes from her face, almost stumbling over the pile of junk which Marisa had thrown off the armchair, as he motioned toward the other chair. He reached for a cigarette in his pocket, fumbled around for matches, and, finding none, let out a muffled curse. Spotting Marisa's matches on the table, he reached for them and finally lit his cigarette, which had been hanging from his mouth. He wrecked his mind desperately in search of something to say, but even the conventional "hello" died on his lips, as he realized the utter stupidity of it. Marisa watched his every move through her narrowed eye-lids, an ironical half-smile on her lips, as if thoroughly enjoying Knox's embarrassment. Finally, she broke the silence, saying:

"So there you are! I knew it! I knew I would be right from the beginning. I told them so! Knowing you? No reason for alarm here!"

"What do you mean? What are you talking about? Told what to whom? Alarmed about what?" Knox was totally stupefied.

"Your friends, dear, that's who." Her voice became even more derisive and contemptuous. "Those nit-wits, worrying themselves to death about you, for lack of any better kicks."

"Worrying about me? What for?" Knox asked rapidly.

Marisa let out a hiss through her lips, and shook her hand in the air in a gesture of dismissal: "About a big fat nothing," she finally uttered.

"What do you mean? Would you finally explain yourself for mercy's sake?"

"Those nincompoops got the crazy notion that you had killed yourself or something. Ha! Ha! You of all people! Kill yourself! Now that's a good one, eh?"

Knox almost gagged on his cigarette smoke. "What?!" he gasped in bewilderment.

"My dear Edward," said Marisa, uttering each syllable with the greatest care. "Your sweet bunch of bosom-pals are jittering with fright that you committed suicide. That's all. Do you get it now? Suicide!"

"But . . . but . . . why? Who gave them that crazy idea?"

inquired Knox still dumbfounded. He had never felt so alive in his life.

"They, I mean, the Bull and another pet came to my apartment last night, and told me about your behavior yesterday at the café as absolutely unheard of. They said that you just sat there, without uttering a word, taking all kinds of provocations, not even cursing or anything, as if you where not quite there . . . you kept on drinking whatever you had in your glass, and mind you, only one glass, while looking at them with the empty eyes of a moron. Then suddenly you got up, and walked straight out on them. And all this after weeks of absence. Now this *is* strange coming from you, isn't it?"

"So you came over here expecting to find my dead body . . ." added Knox rather disappointed.

"They begged me on their hands and knees to come and see."

"And why didn't they come themselves, if they were so concerned?" Knox was regaining his composure.

"Because, my dear Edward, they are a very brave bunch. Suppose you were dead and they would have to call the police, eh? That would have been a pretty messy job on their hands, now wouldn't it? They like to become involved with the police, you know, they just love it," added Marisa, exhausting the scale of contempt expressible in human voice.

There was a momentary pause. Marisa uncrossed her legs, stamped out her cigarette in an ash-tray overloaded with buts, knocking a few on the table, sat back on her chair, and crossed her legs again.

"And suppose I hadn't answered the doorbell," inquired Knox with curiosity. "Or suppose I had been out this morning. What would you have done then?"

"Nothing to it," shrugged Marisa, "I would have called the janitor and had the door forced open."

"And what if you had found me dead?" by now Knox was amused.

"So what?" answered Marisa indifferently. "I would have called the funeral director and arranged for your funeral. The world wouldn't have lost too much with you. Or what did you expect from me? Bitter tears?"

"No, Marisa, I didn't expect any such thing. . . . Not from you . . ." Knox had regained his self-control completely. He grabbed the ashtray, dumped it into a plate full of scraps of food sitting on the table, and placed it back where it had been. He said, putting out his cigarette: "So now, your mission is complete, Marisa. Go and tell the boys that I'm alive, fit as a fiddle, and that I send them by best regards."

"Alive? You?" Marisa emitted something like a sarcastic little grunt. "You hang on to your so-called non-death for the simple reason that you haven't got the guts to put an end to the meaningless flow of your empty, wasted hours. You're a coward, Edward, that's what made me so sure that your body and errr . . . soul, if that's what you have, would be still clinging together when I got here." She seemed to derive a special pleasure in heaping insult upon insult.

Knox didn't reply to her last biting remarks. Instead, he appeared to be thinking hard. Finally he said:

"You know something, you're not making a bit of sense, my dear Marisa."

"And why not, pray tell?" she answered defiantly.

"For several reasons, my dear . . . whatever noun I should attach to this adjective." Knox was master of the situation oncemore. "First, if you were so damned sure of finding me still on this side, then why did you take the trouble to come? Just to do a favor to the gang? No, that's not it. You're not such a good samaritan as to run errands for others. You look out for yourself first, last and always."

"What are you trying to get to?" Marisa asked with marked irritation. The poise of her initial self-assurance seemed to have slackened a little.

"You'll see it, Marisa, in a little minute or less. I'm sure that you know it yourself, but it sounds better if I said it. It'll give you another chance to deny it and I want to hear you denying it. But as to the other point I want to make. . . . Reversing the case and assuming that I had really done away with myself as

61

the fellows thought I had—then there was no reason for you to hurry over here. Death is an absolute, the only absolute in the mind of those who sell life-insurance, which they should rather call by what it really is, namely, the policy signed by you as the declaration of your own death sentence. . . ."

"Stop it, Edward," interrupted Marisa. "I don't like your crude attempts at philosophising. . . . You're not as good at it as you would like to think."

"Let's leave this part out. We won't discuss this for reasons of my own, all right?" Knox observed calmly. "However, as you can see for yourself, not even my death-as-a-fact hypothesis can provide you with an acceptable excuse for coming here."

"I told you already," replied Marisa with mounting irritation and uneasiness, "that the only reason I came to this hole of yours was because the boys had begged me to do so. Can you imagine them involved with the police? Even if they got away with the question of homicide, a search of their dump wouldn't be the best thing that could happen to them, now would it? You know very well what they would find there. They would have ended up in jail."

"This hole of mine, you say," said Knox referring to Marisa's definition of his apartment. "It wasn't always a hole, now was it, Marisa?"

"Whatever it was in the past, it isn't now," said Marisa almost in a whisper. "But getting back to your buddies. . . ."

"I understand their fear, sure I do. But I still can't see how your news to them, whatever it might be, I mean, my being dead or alive, could have changed anything. Least of all your act of unselfish self sacrifice, being so eager to inquire after me." Knox's voice had a quality of irony in it, and he was enjoying the situation more and more. "Well, Marisa, what do you say to this?"

"Perhaps your logic is worth a C in a mid-term exam, Edward. . . . But your arguments are not altogether convincing. You give me the impression that you are trying to convince your own self rather, to produce the first sparks of your hope. . . . Maybe you'd like to believe that I took this opportunity as a chance to come and look at your charming face. . . ."

"Charming is not the word you used in the past, Marisa. It was another one: 'interesting' you used to say, remember?"

Marisa reacted as though she had been unexpectedly stung by something. Knox had touched an exposed live wire that had given her a shock. The sudden expression of suffering that clouded her face for a moment reminded one, however, of the acute pain one feels when a bandage is torn, with one violent jerk, off a half-closed wound. She recaptured her composure, though, but her still, straight and rigid posture on the edge of the chair betrayed the amount of effort she needed to control her welled emotions. She reached for another cigarette, held it between her tightly pressed lips, her hands obeying with difficulty her will to hold the burning match without trembling. Then she leaned back on her chair and closed her eyes.

There are some rare instances in human existence, called the limit situations or marginal experiences, such as an immediate threat to man's life or other psychological traumatic experiences, involving a heightened intensity of stress, anxiety and dread. Psychologists tell us that the person, while experiencing this limit situation, is capable of reinstating vividly, in a flash of insight, all the contents of his subconscious and unconscious mind. This person relives in a state of concentration and rapid succession of images all his past experiences.

It was this marginal experience of emotional stress which brought about in Marisa the detailed memory of her first love affair with Knox. It started with her initial infatuation with him during her first year in college on the occasion of the traditional Harvest Dance. Knox appealed to her as a potential genius in the field of creative writing. And Knox naturally cultivated that idea very dearly. This emotional involment flourished into a fully grown love affair, leading, as it is most of the time, to its consummation in sexual love. Neither Marisa nor Knox realized the possibility of Marisa getting pregnant which is what actually happened. Instead of legalizing this affair in the form of marriage, Knox insisted that Marisa abort the child. With mixed feelings of guilt and fear, Marisa went throught this experience, hoping that the incident of pregnancy and its removal will not deterioate their loving relationship. Knox, however, took the absence of Marisa as an opportunity to cool and end the whole affair. To establish a lasting relationship with any girl was the farthest thing in his mind. On the other hand, he had to confess to himself at least his emotional attachment to Marisa whose love toward him was beyond any doubt. In spite of everything, Knox was not ready to commit himself any further. His love of freedom and independence seemed to him to be his first priority.

It was during this situation of psychic ambivalence that Knox had made his strange acquaintance with Noesis on the hilltop, with all its consequences and changes in his entire person and outlook on life. He thought he understood Marisa's behavior toward him, as well as her reason for coming to his apartment on that morning. He had tried to reason his way into Marisa's motives: as long as she knew, he thought, that he was still engrossed in the activities of the pleasure seekers and joymakers, she had kept away from him. But the news about his long absence from the joint of the rebels and especially his silent walkout on them seemed to have aroused her curiosity. And now she had come to find out whether that change had been for the better or worse. He was glad to learn now that Marisa had not forgotten him altogether. In spite of her contemptuous hostility toward him, there still was some remnant of a tie between them. He was intelligent enough to understand the dialectics of human emotions, hatred being just the reverse side of one's unconfessed concern and perhaps even love. He was also aware of the fact that now it was his turn to help Marisa and also himself, by changing the tone of their conversation for the better. He hesitated to put in words what both of them knew about the true reason for her visit. That would be in bad taste and defeating their attempt at a reconciliation. Consequently, Knox volunteered the first step and said:

"Marisa, I think I owe you an explanation, if you care to listen." His attitude was serious, his voice sounded sincere and Marisa seemed to be pleasantly surprised.

"I'll listen."

"Perhaps I should start by apologizing for my attitude toward you," Knox continued. "I will not try to embellish or whitewash what happened. No amount of rationalization or blaming can replace the facts of reality or the truth about ourselves."

Knox noticed a faint smile on Marisa's lips, with some contempt in its expression. He hastened therefore to add:

"If you now think that I'm only acting again, which means lying, I can't help that. I know that I mean every word I say. Neither am I trying to appeal to your sympathy. I'm not asking for your pity, nor begging for your forgiveness. Don't look at me as though I were a sorrowful penitent, a convert crawling on his belly, ready to kiss your feet. It's first of all for my own sake that I'm speaking. Besides I'm accepting only my part of the whole affair, I'm not ready to carry your guilt too."

Marisa listened attentively, still hesitating whether to give Knox the benefit of a doubt. She expressed her state of mind by saying:

"Your words, your present manner do not remind me of your former overpowering arrogance and impatience of before. This much seems to be true. . . . But, tell me, how shall I know that they represent your true self? It's so much unlike your whole being and appearance. What guarantee can you offer me to prove the sincerity of your words?"

"Right now I can offer you only my words. I realize that only my future actions will lend to them full weight and validity."

"You mean to say that you broke for good with your gang?"

"That's what I implied when referring to my future actions. . . ."

"But why didn't you tell them so?"

"Because I don't owe them such information," Knox replied firmly.

"And you owe it to me?"

"I owed to you only my apologies, Marisa. If I mentioned something beyond that it wasn't because I was prompted by any feelings of obligation. Whatever I'll do from now on will concern first of all my own self and no one else."

"But why did you mention it to me, then?"

"Because you were asking for some guarantee."

"And there was no other intention or motive to it?"

"None! And try to see the point I want to make: perhaps you thought that my hidden purpose in presenting you my apologies was to win you over again. Work up a nice reconciliation. Make up for the past and to ask for a new beginning. But I didn't hint this at all and I'm not going to. I'm not asking you to stay with me, to come again."

"In other words, you couldn't care less!" Marisa sounded almost offended.

"I didn't say or imply that either."

"Then let me ask you this," said Marisa impatiently, "do you care or don't you?"

"I do only under certain conditions."

"What conditions?"

"On the condition that you also care and not less than I do."

"And suppose I don't?"

"Then you don't, and neither do I."

"You expect *me* to make the first move in order to count on my responsibility, right?"

"No, that's wrong again. What I mean is that I respect your freedom, and that I count on your free choice as the only possible way of establishing a dignified and meaningful relationship between us. Which also implies that you owe me just as much respect for my freedom as I owe it to you."

"Which means," Marisa continued, "that there would be no more tricks and plays and false pretense to cover up some hidden plan of yours?"

"You're perfectly correct in assuming that."

Marisa seemed pensive for a moment. "This sounds too good to be true," she finally said. "It's almost unbelievable. People don't change so suddenly and fundamentally. Morally they don't change at all."

"That's true again," Knox confirmed.

"But it doesn't apply to you, right? You're the exception that confirms the rule."

"I might be one, yes."

"This whole thing seems so mysterious to me. . . ." Marisa

seemed genuinely puzzled. She had been hoping for some change in Knox, but this certainly surppased her wildest hopes. "Tell me, Ed, what happened? I must confess that I'm almost confused. You don't want to be looked upon as a convert and a penitent, but, pardon me in saying so, you certainly sound like one. . . . What's the new idea, the new cause that won you over? Are you going to became a member of the lay apostolate crusade?"

"Nothing could be farther from me than that!" Knox couldn't help laughing. "You should know better than that!"

"But . . . then I can't make heads and tails of it."

"I understand that feeling, Marisa, and I wish I could help you out, but I can't."

"Why? Why can't you? Did you pledge some secret oath of silence?"

"No," said Knox quite amused at seeing Marisa so befuddled.

"Then speak up and drop your airs of mystery, will you?"

"I can't. Not for the time being."

"Then you force me to keep on guessing. Let's see. . . . Ah! You're going to get your book published?"

"That book hasn't been written yet!"

"I'm not going to ask you whether you're going to write it and what it'll be about. . . . I had heard many of your plans and ideas before." Marisa became annoyed at this point.

"That's true," admitted Knox.

"What's on your mind, Ed? What kind of a game are you playing this time? Tell me before I slam your door from the outside for good."

"You're free to close my door from the outside any time you wish, Marisa. As for my plans, perhaps I'll be able to tell you more about them the next time, if there will be such a time."

"Are you planning a trip?"

"No, I'm not planning anything of that kind."

The telephone shrieked, interrupting Marisa's impatient inquisition. Knox answered. Marisa could faintly distinguish the voice of a man. He was asking brief questions, and Knox's answers were limited to a simple Yes to each one of them. He then put down the receiver, and turned toward Marisa. She noticed the

67

satisfaction in Knox's eyes immediately. She wanted to know who that man had been.

"Sorry, Marisa, I can't tell you that now. Perhaps if we meet again in the near future." Knox did not sit down again, but remained standing in front of her as a silent indication that he didn't want to continue their conversation any longer. Marisa understood the hint, got up, ready to go.

"I'm going out myself," Knox said. "If you care to wait, I'll be ready in a minute and we can leave together."

Marisa agreed. They walked silently together to the first corner, then Knox excused himself and walked away in the opposite direction of Marisa's apartment.

CHAPTER FIVE

TOWARD A NEW WAY OF LIFE

Knox rapped on the door of the hotel room where Noesis was staying. He immediately recognized the familiar sound of his pleasant voice in the short "Come in." It was not actually a room, but an apartment, containing two adjacent units with a private bathroom. It offered every facility needed for comfort, without the disturbing ostentation of superfluous luxury. The hotel had been built recently, in a quiet suburb, away from the hustle-bustle of the crowded downtown quarters. Knox found Noesis sitting in an arm-chair, reading a book. As he entered, Noesis placed the book on a small table, next to his seat, stood up and greeted his guest. Knox noticed the spontaneous and effortless ease of his precise and elegant motions. Here was an example of perfection without a trace of studied artificiality, characteristic of traits acquired through long and painful training. Underneath the casual slacks and white shirt his live and powerful body represented the translation of his whole being into visible form—the energy of his superlative consciousness and will. Noesis extended his arm, offering Knox his hand, a symbol of greeting and a seal of agreement. Knox understood the full meaning of that gesture: in returning Noesis' handshake, he had taken an unworded oath. The expression of their steady gaze was a more powerful seal and confirmation than any superfluous words.

Then Knox's glance rested on the book which Noesis had deposited on the table. He was overcome by an irresistible curiosity:

"I see you had been reading before I came in," he said cautiously. "Would you mind if I looked at your book?"

"Not at all," answered Noesis. With this, he handed the book over to Knox, inviting him to sit down and make himself comfortable. Knox proceeded to examine it carefully. It resembled any other hard-cover book. He noticed, however, the expensive quality of the binding, the fine paper. Though the book was rather voluminous, its weight was not in proportion to its size: it was astoundingly light. He could not proceed any further with his inspection, because the contents were totally alien to him. The characters were unlike anything he had ever seen before, including Greek, Gothic, Cyrillic or any of the symbols of Oriental writing. He had to give up, and handed the book over to its owner. His only comment was in the form of a question:

"What is it about? Is it fiction or non-fiction? Philosophy, science or art?"

"Your questions imply a certain division and departmentalization of knowledge, which is your way of classifying the domains of reality. The result of this method is the growing plurality of endless specializations in a particular field. Usually it becomes narrower by every step, knowing more and more about less and less. Thus one necessarily loses sight of the whole perspective of reality, making the imperative of integration a practical impossibility. Its further harmful result is the problem it creates in the field of communication between people belonging to isolated branches of knowledge. It becomes almost impossible to utilize that which has been observed in any one of the isolated fields of knowledge by all the others."

"But there is no other way of doing it!" Knox was searching for a justification. "Where could we find at least one single mind capable of assimilating all the available knowledge and powerful enough to take it one step further even? It would be impossible, even for those universal geniuses. Then you have to consider also the time element! The productive or creative years of any man—optimistically speaking—number only fifty, but usually much less. A man would have to live for centuries in order to make a systematic attack on all the areas of knowledge! But that's a utopian dream, fit for fiction writers only."

"Have you ever asked yourself what would have happened to

man if he had never dreamed or had stopped dreaming? Perhaps it would not be altogether incorrect to regard what you call reality —especially the visible facts of civilization and culture—as the incarnation, the translation of man's dreams. What is an automobile, if not the physical form and shape of an idea running on wheels, the latter being also the translation of another dream, and so on and so forth, down to the last detail?"

"Are you equating dreams with ideas?" Knox interposed.

"I had in mind only the dreams of the creative imagination. But you prefer to call them fiction. Even the short breath of your own history teaches you that which is taken for granted today, as matters of fact—air travel, radio, television, atomic power, the exploration of outer space—would have been rejected as the phantasmagoria of demented people just a few generations ago. And here you have one of the causes for the slow progress of your civilization on earth. There have always been the bigoted dogmatists, the provincial conservatives, the prejudiced realists and the narrowminded rationalists, who have rejected many new ideas because of their own lack of vision and courage."

"Coming back to what you where reading, how should it be called if our criteria are not valid?" Knox pursued his quest to learn. He took out a pack of cigarettes and offered it to Nocsis, who declined his invitation to smoke.

"I'll try to make myself understood. Our knowledge is based upon and starts with one fundamental premise derived from reality. It is the principle of the organic continuity and unity of all being, which means that all the laws governing reality, scientifically expressed in the various fields, are reducible to one code, one formula, one blueprint only. Reality is one and not broken up into disjointed fragments that can't be made to fit together again."

"What are you trying to say, Noesis?" Knox exclaimed with surprise. "Do you mean, for example, that art is the same thing as mathematics, and mathematics is identical with religion, which, in its turn is not different from physics, and that's no different from psychology, which again is equal to astronomy, or anything else?"

71

Noesis was pleased to learn that Knox was such an intelligent conversationalist, having the ability to think. Then he replied:

"If I said right now that you are correct, you would not believe me, for obvious reasons. Your intellectual habits, the result of the way you were taught, prevent you from adopting a more comprehensive view. But I shall add this to clarify my point: you have to learn to assume the evolutionary point of view. You must look upon reality in an historical perspective, as a constantly unfolding process of becoming, an uninterrupted flux, change and motion, a dynamic and dialectical strife to reach ever higher forms and states of being, while all the time obeying the law of the one and all pervading source of energy."

"If you continue the metaphysical flights of your imagination, Noesis," Knox interposed, "you'll end up with the idea of God, as most of our philosophers in the past did."

Noesis smiled with understanding and continued his explanation:

"You don't have to fear that I'm here to announce an interplanetary gospel, as the founder of the first cosmic church and religion. I'll come to the phenomenon of religion in general later on and in more detail. But right now I want to say in this respect only this: What you associate with the idea of a god or gods is no more than the projections of primitive anthropomorphisms and wishful thinking. But let's leave this for now and get back to what I was going to say. I was going to explain the idea of the mind interpreting perspectively the progressive manifestations of the one cosmic energy, out of which everything is made—no matter how diverse and sometimes even opposite and conflicting these forms may appear to an observer caught in the web of one particular method or frame of reference. Have patience and bear with me awhile and then you'll see what I'm driving at," he added, perceiving Knox's confused expression.

While lighting another cigarette, Knox realized that Noesis was enjoying this discussion immensely, as if he were at that moment in his most natural element. Occasionally he raised his voice, got up from his seat, walked toward him, trying everything within his means to bring him to better understanding. There

72

was, however, no trace of impatience or nervousness in his whole attitude, his gestures being rather a consequence of his passionate love not only for knowledge, but also for communicating it.

"Go ahead, Noesis," he said, "I'm neither impatient nor tired of listening yet. But this whole idea you're talking about is very unfamiliar and new to me. So, it's possible that I'll reach a point of saturation, when my mind can't take any more. When that'll happen, I'll let you know. Right now I have a great desire to hear you say more."

"Very well, then. Suppose I give another turn to our problem and say that the present situation of fragmented specialization of your knowledge is a necessary stage in the process of evolution? Does that mean anything to you?"

"So far, so good," Knox said encouragingly.

"Then you must also realize that—and I mean no offense by saying this—that you're just at the beginning of your quest for knowledge."

"You must have some valid reasons to be able to afford such a serious remark."

"Yes, I have, and I wish I could give you evidence for my claim."

"But why can't you? Is it taboo or is there somebody up there, I mean out there, who forbids you to reveal it?"

"Nothing of that sort. To forbid to learn, to think, to reach for truth and to punish him if he did so, is one of the most sinister chapters of your history. And the contradictory aspect of it was that they forbade truth while claiming knowledge of so-called higher truths."

"What prevents you then from telling me?" Knox insisted.

"It's you, Edward, and nothing else."

"What do you mean by that?"

"What I'm going to say now, Edward, will not please you; but since I have to say it, I must ask you not to take it either as an offense or as the vain ostentation of unjustifiable pride. Try to be as objective and rational as possible, not letting your feelings determine your reactions."

"I think I'm neither a child nor a sensitive neurotic corroded

73

by his feelings of insecurity and inferiority," Knox replied with remarkable dignity.

"Well, then, listen to my question: have you ever had the frustrating experience of trying to explain an important principle or idea to a small child without succeeding?"

"Yes, I have . . ." Knox agreed.

"Then ask yourself this further question: was it your fault, your lack of knowledge, your inability to communicate it, or was it rather the immature condition of the child's mind—natural at that early stage of development—that was responsible for your failure?"

"It was the child's invincible ignorance and nothing else. But are you trying to hint, Noesis, that I'm in the same primitive condition compared to you and your alleged superior knowledge as the child was in relation to me?"

"I'm sorry, but I'll have to say that your condition is even worse than that of the child's. Of course I don't mean only you, but the whole of mankind, its best scholars included."

Knox found it rather difficult to swallow this verdict without any objection, therefore he said:

"Since I don't think you make irresponsible statements, I'm going to ask you to defend your position."

"If I tell you that I can't, you'll think that I'm a fake or a posturing impostor. Probably something similar must have been also the child's reaction to his frustration when you couldn't lead him to the insights you wanted to communicate. But you know all the time that your inability was caused by the child's condition and not due to your ignorance. Perhaps I should add this one more remark: The degree or the level of one's development sets the limits to one's understanding and educability. In your educational psychology courses you call this the principle of 'being ready,' and readiness presupposes the process of differentiation, maturation, leading to development. This principle, however, applies not only to the rate of individual growth but also to the whole cultural history of the earth's population. The higher includes and presupposes the lower degrees of perfection in an eminent and superior form. But the same does not apply to the lower. Do you follow me?"

"I think I do . . ." Knox was hesitant to agree fully. "But in this case your coming here and your proposal become meaningless, a futile attempt at the impossible, in virtue of what you've stated. I'll never be able to understand what you'll tell me, assuming that my immaturity and primitivity are at fault, correct?"

"In principle you're right," Noesis consented. "Nevertheless, the situation is not that hopeless. Following the above example about the child, there are at least two things one can do: first, one can ask the child to accept the truth he doesn't understand, through the faith he has in the authority of his elders. Second, and this is the better way of doing it, one can present the ideas in as simple words as possible, thus setting the directives for the child's future development and also helping him, gradually, slowly, to overcome the temporary obstacles or limits to his educability. And this is what I intend to accomplish."

"It would be rather difficult for me to regress to the level of the innocent credulity of a child . . ." Knox confessed his lack of enthusiasm. "I used to consider myself, regardless of the stupid things I've done so far, as a young adult, not a child."

"I'm not asking you to regress, Edward, but to progress. I realize that it's hard for you, or for anyone else on your level, to see the gap and the distance that separate us. You don't have and cannot have the higher horizons and perspectives we have already achieved."

"Do you really think that man on earth is as primitive as that?" Knox remarked skeptically. "You can't deny all the progress we've made so far!"

"Nobody wants to erase the obvious. But I shall try to express myself better. First a small example. There is a difference in perspective for a man standing at the foot of a mountain and for another standing on its very summit. The same change in perspective occurs when you travel in an airplane and much more so when you're orbiting the earth in a space capsule. You must have seen some of the photographs your astronauts brought back. . . . But these examples illustrate only one change in the horizon of one's perspective, you can call it spacial. Then there is also the time element and its relatively new dimension. . . ."

"Are you going to give me now a briefing on Einstein's theory on special and universal relativity?" Knox interrupted Noesis' presentation for the sake of a needed break.

"Not quite," Noesis smiled in understanding response. "Only insofar as it tells you something with regard to the idea of evolution. We are not going to discuss right now whether time is real or unreal, whether it is something in itself or only the accidental consequence of motion and change. Let's assume, therefore, that what you call time, duration, succession, continuity and lasting, including its psychological counterparts—past, present and future—are something useful as a frame of reference for the coordination of events." Noesis paused for a moment, then said: "I hope that the terms I'm using are not too abstract. . . . If they are, please interrupt me at any time you wish and feel free to ask any question that might come up in your mind."

"Don't worry, Noesis, so far I can follow you. And I have also made up my mind to give you as hard a time as I can, as a means to prevent boredom!"

"There's nothing better, Edward, than a good intellectual contest, the thing in which our friend Socrates was a master."

"And what about Aristotle? Why don't you call him your friend? Anything wrong with him?"

"Aristotle will be also very useful for us, Edward, if we leave out the Platonic element in his thought."

"And also its baptized version by Aquinas, I guess?"

"Agreed. But let me get back to the question of time and evolution. I'd like to finish today at least one thing and it's getting late. According to your units of measuring time—very arbitrary, artificial, conventional and limited to the perspective of your solar system only—you have your seconds, minutes, hours, days, weeks, months, years, centuries, all disposed according to the present, the past and the future. You write now, for instance, October 4th, 1974, 11.35 P.M. In physics and astronomy you

76

needed larger units, and you invented light years, taking the velocity of light as an absolute standard of measurement."

"But isn't it an absolute even in Einstein's theory of relativity?"

"In Einstein's theory it's so and its plausibility lies in the fact that it has worked so far within your present limited perspective. . . . But there is still what we call geological time and also cosmic time, used in reference to the birth, evolution and present age of your solar system and planet. Now you should widen the horizons of your time perception and think—you can't imagine it—in terms of thousands, hundreds of thousands, millions and billions of years past. . . . Next, project against that immensity the few years of your own history and the really insignificant number of years—one hundred and fifty or two hundred years—as the age of your scientific analysis and progress. What does that tell you? Think it through and draw your conclusions."

"You want me to say that we are absurdly primitive. . . ."

"I want you to say it only if it sounds right to you because it is true, because it expresses and identifies the facts of reality, that which is and exists. I want your rational consent and agreement only. Nothing else matters."

"Okay, Noesis. I agree because it is so . . . no matter how much I resent this one truth. . . . I wish it weren't so though. . . ."

"Wishing won't do. . . . You said absurdly primitive because you like that expression of 'absurd.' You used it at our first encounter. . . ."

"You remember everything, don't you?" Knox laughed at Noesis' precision.

"We can't afford forgetting because the loss of knowledge means the shortest and the fastest way to relapse into ignorance, decadence and primitivity. But your primitivity is not due to forgetting, but to original ignorance, for which you're only partially responsible. The successive stages in the process of evolution follow their necessary course. There are no jumps or gaps in nature, although it can be arrested for a while, either through willful abandonment of the mind and by errors or mistakes in learning."

"Could you, Noesis, give me some illustration for our primitive condition? I'd like to hear and know what you think about us on this planet."

"I'm quite willing to do just what you're asking. I was going to come to this point myself, but let's get it out of our way right now. First, I'm asking you again to use your imagination and project in into the future. Can you imagine what life on earth will be like, let's say, one hundred, then five hundred, then again when you'll be writing 4974 A.D."

"Nobody can see everything the future promises to us, but sometimes I wonder myself . . . I also resent—as I have already told you—that I was born into such a primitive age as ours. No matter how much we pride ourselves of our achievements in science, industry, technology and so forth, one can anticipate the enormous difference and superiority in the way of life simply by allowing a normal progress in the development of our science, for instance. Those who'll be living in 4974 A.D.—unless everything will be blown up by our madmen who posture as the redeeming apostles of mankind's fate—shall look upon us perhaps with the same contempt or compassion as we look upon the primitive savages still living on the stone age level."

"I see that you understood what I meant by the gap and the distance that separate us . . ." Noesis was glad to acknowledge.

"But please continue and give me other reasons and more evidence for our primitivity," Knox insisted.

"I hope your desire is not an exercise in masochism," Noesis remarked with a faint smile. "If we look upon you in the perspective of evolutionary time, then I'll have to say that you got off the tree just the day before yesterday and crawled out of your caves only last night, still possessing and preserving your bad animal instincts. . . ."

"Are you going to refer again to our bloody history? You've mentioned that already. Say something else. Don't repeat yourself," Knox was teasing his friend.

"Certain truths are worth being repeated for their serious consequences. . . . But I'm going to say something else, not to bore you with bloody truths. . . . Suppose you go down to Brazil and pick yourself an Indian from the jungle who lives on the banks

78

of the Amazon River. You take him with you, you fly him out of the wilderness and in less than twenty four hours you've installed him in an air-conditioned luxury apartment in New York City. You will also see to it that in no time he comes to look in every respect as any other 'modern' man. You might also give him a Cadillac with a chauffeur in uniform. In less than a week he can be conditioned to push the correct buttons of his many gadgets in every room of his apartment, the all-important bathroom included. He will also learn how to chew gum, to puff from an expensive cigar and to mix his own coctails. At the end of his process you ask yourself the question: what have you accomplished? What do you have now?"

"A 'modern barbarian, motorized, mechanized and well conditioned.' Isn't this the answer you expected me to give you?"

"One hundred percent right. And let me add this: you don't have a better human being, only a living paradox, the personification of the principle of contradiction, a shameful caricature."

"And I'm to use this example as the illustration of what you think of us and the way you look upon us 'modern barbarians.' . . ."

"Right again, with this note to add: you are civilized to a certain extent, but utterly uncultured."

"I thought that civilization and culture were synonymous terms!"

"Not in my vocabulary, not in the way I interpret them and the meaning I attach to those concepts."

"Explain yourself. Let me hear what you have to say about this."

"With pleasure. This is one of my favorite points I like to make clear. So listen. Your Indian became suddenly civilized as far as all external things and appearances are concerned. But you have to make sure that he makes no mistakes in running his mazes and, above all, that he doesn't open his mouth."

"You mean to eat and drink? It's relatively easy to teach him some table manners. . . ."

"No! Not that, oh, no! I meant his speech!"

79

"Apparently you are biased against his native tongue, Tupí-Guaraní?"

"You know I don't mean that! And if I had meant it, you would immediately say that you would teach him the language of Shakespeare! But what I meant is *what* he has to say, if anything at all. The level, the meaning—if any—of his pre-logical, pre-conceptual and mythical consciousness, rich in black magic and supertitions. In this sense I mean that he is a civilized barbarian only."

"And that is the picture of the population of the earth?"

"That is correct, allowing for a very small minority as an exception."

"And where would you place me?"

"My dear Edward, you're the most promising potential exception!"

Knox had enough sense of humor not to get offended and joined Noesis in his laughter.

"Do you know, Noesis, that the majority of our people would reject your distinction between being civilized and cultured?"

"There we go, back again to numbers and statistics as the measure of truth!"

"Regardless of that. Maybe even in spite of it, you couldn't convince them anyway!"

"I know that and it doesn't disturb me in the least. I like to say sometimes that truth is not for everybody to see."

"This sounds arrogant, discriminatory and anti-democratic."

"And it is nevertheless true for this simple reason, not everybody, as a matter of fact very few, is intelligent enough and qualified to discover, to know and to value the superior and exceptional perfections. And you can't have it any other way!"

"They'll brand you as a snob and a high-brow!"

"I think that you're just as far removed from people's opinions as I am. . . ."

"Thanks for giving me some credit for that!" Knox hurried to emphasize the point.

"But of course!"

"If people asked you to define your terms and clarify you

80

distinctions—without dragging in again your blessed Indian and his ignorance—what would you say? You see, in college we were always asking for definitions."

"Well, I would make a distinction between material goods and cultural values. Or, even better, between values wanted for their own sake such as philosophy, science and art, and use-values, which are only means to guarantee man's mastery over energy, space and matter, setting him free for the pursuit of the first category of values, which represent culture, while the others stand for the state of civilization only. I could also draw a line of demarcation between being and having, if you can see the point I'm driving at. . . ."

"I've lost you here. . . ."

"But it's simple. Your people try to work out some kind of self-esteem by identifying themselves with their 'having,' I mean their possessions. And they also believe that the more they possess in things, the better they are. However, no money in your pocket or in the bank or its equivalent in objects can make you a better human being. This is very simple, I'd say. . . ."

"That's true. But money helps, you know. . . . It soothes your nerves."

"No doubt about that, but its value is contained, limited to and circumscribed by its usefulness only. There is no carry-over from it to the meaning of your life."

"Then I must conclude that in your eyes only the philosopher, the scientist and the artist are actually human beings. . . ."

"Or the combination of all three in one person, whom we call the superior type of man. . . ."

"You mean Nietzsche's superman?"

"I don't object to that name as long as you know what you're talking about."

"But that leaves out almost everybody!"

"Indeed, it does."

"And you mean to tell me that on your planet you have only superior men?"

". . . and women!"

81

"But . . . what happened to the average, mediocre and the inferior men?" Knox was perplexed.

"That I'll explain to you next time. Do you know that it's almost 2.30 A.M.?"

"You mean you want to call it a day, right?"

"Right. Later on we'll have to go into all the aspects of your culture and civilization and analyze the truth about their moral, social, political and economic principles. . . ."

"I see, Noesis, you've made up your mind to undertake another 'revaluation of all values' as Nietzsche looked upon his philosophy. That should take quite a long time and effort. . . ."

"I have all the time I need. What about you?"

"Perhaps my trouble is that I have too much time, if you know what I mean."

"I know. I told you already that I know you were dropped from college, you hold no permanent job, you're short of money and your father is not willing to keep you alive at his expense."

"Don't get the wrong impression, for I didn't ask for money or help! I've always managed things one way or another. I only wanted to reassure you that I have more time than I need or can use."

"That's not so. You'll need all the time you have if you want to go ahead with our plan to write down our dialogues. It'll hardly give you time for anything else if you want to finish it in six months or so. Therefore, I was thinking of considering this work as your job, a full-time engagement, and of myself as your employer. . . ."

"That's no good. . . . You want to help me out and you dress up your charity in commercial terms. I won't take it!"

"As you wish. But let me remind you, you'll have no time for anything else if you start writing, and second, my reasons are selfish, insofar as that book will give me as much pleasure as it will to you. I'd like to think of myself a co-author, so that it shall be also my book. It's only fair and just if I pay you and make sure that money will not be an obstacle in our way."

"How do you make money? Where do you get it from? What money is it?" Knox was overcome by curiosity.

82

Noesis took out his wallet and showed its contents to Knox: they were regular U.S. dollar bills. Then he added with a smile: "This money is neither counterfeit nor stolen nor looted. It's earned. Some of us are employed as research scientists in your institutions, even in the top secret government projects, and they are very highly paid for their superior contributions. . . ."

"Have you ever been in such a position before?"

"Yes, I have, but not in this country. I worked as a microbiologist under an assumed name."

"What's your pseudonym in this hotel?"

"Anything you wish . . . Jack Smith will do, for instance. . . ."

Noesis laughed as a mischievous child. Then he invited Knox to eat something, for they were both hungry. Knox expected to get some outer-space wonder-food, but he had to put up with ordinary ham and cheese sandwiches only, which Noesis took out of a small refrigerator. While they were eating, Knox remembered that he'd have to start writing his book. He told Noesis about it, expressing his doubts whether he would remember all the details of their first meeting and the present one. As an answer, Noesis reached into his pocked and handed a small rectangular box to him. It was not larger than a pack of cigarettes.

"What's this?" inquired Knox, surprised.

"It's your secretary," Noesis answered. "It's something like a taperecorder, but instead of a tape we have in it a small unit called a 'memory cell' which registers and recalls everything we've talked about so far. By pressing this button, it'll play it back to you. You can take it with you, but I wouldn't advise you to show it to anybody. In the event that you should change your mind and decide to try and put it on the market, it wouldn't work. We have means to destroy it and to render it useless. Don't try to open it either, because by that you'll destroy its contents."

"But I wasn't going to do anything of that kind!" protested Knox.

"I didn't mean to imply such a thing. I merely wanted to warn you. Incidentally, I almost forgot to set the date for our next meeting. Suppose we make it after you finish typing the material

83

we have so far. I'll call you in about two weeks or so from today. At that time you'll also receive the first installment of your payment."

Knox felt pleased with this perspective and also the friendly attitude of Noesis. There was no strain, no tension, suspicion or fear in their relationship. There was rather mutual confidence and respect.

Then Noesis pressed down the small button of the 'memory cell,' and Knox heard his friend saying:

"So, you made it after all and you came. . . ." But when it came to hearing his own voice giving Noesis his first answer, he asked Noesis to turn it off. . . .

CHAPTER SIX

THE EVOLUTION OF THE SUPERIOR MAN

The phenomenon of life has been described by philosophers and scientists as a spontaneous activity from within, a self-initiated process of actions and reactions, an organically structured complexity of chemical elements in which every part performs a necessary function aimed at the goals of self-preservation, growth and reproduction for the exclusive benefit of the individual agent, resulting in its well-being. Thus the only value and meaning one can attach to life is and cannot be different from the goals life sets for itself: to come into being, to preserve itself, to develop and to enrich itself, in one word, to live. Life's purpose is self-contained, it is a reason unto itself, needing no outside sanction or justification. Its value is immanent and not transcendent. It cannot be subordinated to anything else. It should not be sacrificed for any goal alien to itself. The meaning of life is to live it.

The opposite of life is death, and its first symptom is the absence of activity, passive and purposeless inertia, mere being with no reason to it. There are different forms and degrees of dying. Any activity that defeats the purpose of life, proves itself to be suicidal. In man's case, for instance, the condition of aimless and meaningless drifting and floating will sooner or later bring about the early symptoms of a slow death through boredom, weariness, despair, nausea, will to nothingness. This is death when held in contrast to the joyous affirmation of life through a sustained intelligent pursuit of well-reasoned ends toward man's highest purpose, the attainment of his happiness, as the result of a meaningful and creative activity.

85

All this had been running through Knox's mind since his last conversation with Noesis. He was engaged in an activity very few people perform, all appearances to the contrary notwithstanding: he was thinking. He was analyzing the precise contents and meanings of the ideas he had taken over from others. This was new to him, never before had he made any attempt to assume a critical and logical attitude of mind, required for the dissection of its contents. He was using, for the first time in his life, his power to formulate judgments by carefully examining the relationships in meaning existing between his ideas. Then he moved on to reason out the conclusions implicit in his accepted premises, examining the validity of both. He was taking careful inventory of his mind. To his surprise, he discovered that there is pleasure and joy even in the tension and the effort required to perform the acts of conscious examination and self-scrutiny. He saw himself as fighting his way through a dark fog, slowly emerging from its oppressing presence, experiencing a relief that he had never felt before.

Knox did not believe in miraculous cures and rebirths. Nevertheless, he had to accept the definite changes which were taking form within himself. He felt renewed even physically. The chronic disposition of his general tiredness, sleepiness, along with his almost permanent nervous tension, his frequent headaches were decreasing day after day. His appetite, too, improved, he felt the power of his youth returning into his muscles and limbs: his stooped posture was gone, his steps became firm and resilient once more. Standing before the mirror in his bathroom he took a long, penetrating look at the image of his own reflection, imitating his own acts. The change in the expression of his eyes impressed him most: they were looking back at the corner of his month, his lips were held together, revealing the same quality of firmness and resolution of his eyes.

Suddenly he felt the desire to see the features of his own face, hidden under his bushy beard. Obeying his first impulse, he searched for a pair of scissors and his shaver. In less than an hour he had freed his face from its rebellious decorum: he was now looking with satisfaction at himself, smiling as a sign of welcome and self-acceptance. To complete his desire at self-liberation, he hurried to the first barber to have his feminine looks removed.

Back in his efficiency apartment, Knox set out to change its appearance in such a way as to harmonize with his new self. While cleaning it up, he was thinking about the truth contained in the idea of an immediate and necessary relationship of causality between the within and the without, the invisible and the tangible. He remembered the principle of man's psycho-somatic oneness or unity and its practical consequence—one's physical appearance is only the necessary effect, reflecting the kind and quality—good or bad—or one's inner psychic structure and organization. First one becomes a degenerate decadent in one's mind. Then one's external appearance, manner, behavior—whatever one says or does—necessarily conform to that psychic category and mercilessly manifest, reveal and betray their cause, the person himself. That holds true also for the good, most valuable and noble characters.

He was ready now to begin his new life, to sit down at his desk and write the first words of his book. Before making that all important move, he had the desire to call up Marisa, to invite her over to his place and celebrate together the beginning of his —perhaps also her—new life. He hesitated awhile, standing by the silent telephone, repeating mentally her number. It would be so easy! It was within his reach, it would take only a few seconds, and. . . . He thought better of it. He realized that he would have committed a mistake by calling her up and over, for he knew that neither of them were ready for the kind of relationship he had in mind. They needed time. He, in particular, needed time to prove to himself that his life and his work ought to be the first and the most significant source of his happiness, that whatever relationship he might have in the future with any person, man or woman, it should never take the place of his own self. He recalled Noesis' example about the gardener's motivation, and he felt joy at his first success at self-overcoming. He placed the 'memory cell' on his desk, took out paper and pen, ready to formulate the title of his book, to name the future child of his mind.

First he thought of a high-sounding title: "A Message to Man on Earth from Outer Space." And as a sub-title he wrote: "Interplanetary Dialogue on the Future of Man." He read it back to himself, kept pondering, then discarded it. It sounded too moralistic, didactic and preaching. It reminded him of the eye-catching titles of popular saucer-books. It was cheap and gaudy. He crossed it out, crumpled up the sheet of paper into a ball and threw it into the waste basket. His next idea was to call his book: "Death and Resurrection." That wasn't good either. It gave the impression of a religious theme. Another trial and error, landing in the wastebasket. Then he thought of one-word titles: "The Rebel" . . . still no good, he thought, and too personal, almost an autobiography. Finally, he remained undecided between two provisional solutions. He liked both: "The Message," and the simple name "Noesis." He wrote them down both, deciding that the baptism should come only after a successful delivery, which is preceded by many long months of pregnancy. He still had time to come to a final decision. Perhaps he should also hear what Noesis had to say. . . .

The first week of his new style of life did not turn out to his full satisfaction. His progress in writing was very slow. When he tried to accomplish more in one evening, the next day, while attentively editing the pages of his first draft, that extra work did not meet the standards he had set up for himself. He destroyed it and started anew. Only then did he fully realize how much damage he had done to his mental powers during the period of his revolutionary decadence. If you don't move forward, ahead and uphill, he thought, you're going to fall back, sinking downward of necessity. For there is no standstill in existence; it would contradict the very essence of life. Evolve or degenerate into non-being! Sometimes he needed all his self-control to hold out during the painful hours of not being able to fulfill what he had demanded of himself. Especially frustrating were the attacks of doubt on his ability to create a work of lasting value.

It was during one of these dark moments that he was aroused from his state of dejection by someone knocking on the door. The sounds were not insistent, rather subdued. Knox immediately thought of Marisa, but just as fast discarded that wild guess, for it was almost midnight. Marisa would not come to him so late. Why should she come at all? He hadn't called her since their last meeting, neither had she given him any signs of life. It had to be someone else. His curiosity was immediately satisfied as he opened the door and saw Noesis standing in the hall, waiting to be admitted. He couldn't repress a smile at the sight of Knox's visible embarrassment and surprise. He had never imagined that Noesis would walk up to his door just like that, without announcing himself first.

"May I come in?" asked Noesis still smiling.

Knox made a gesture of invitation and welcome, so solemn and ceremonious that it was almost comical. Noesis walked in and sat down in one of the armchairs.

"What a surprise and what a change!" Noesis exclaimed while examining his friend's new appearance. "I didn't expect it for so soon," he added.

"But you were thinking of it, expecting it anyway . . . " Knox stated his conviction, letting Noesis know that he understood things even if they were not explicitly mentioned.

"Of course! I did anticipate it and I don't have to give you the reason or the law behind it. It's so simple! And you grasped it and acted upon it."

"How would you call that law" Knox inquired.

"Let me use the name given to it first by your best philosopher, Aristotle. He called it the law of non-contradictory identity and that of causality."

"Applied to shaving and other things like that?"

"Perfectly correct. But let's not waste any more time on it. I see you've been doing some writing. . . . How is it coming along?"

"So, so. Not the best. I could be better. Want to see it?" Knox handed over the first typewritten pages which dealt with their first encounter on the hill. Noesis went through the first two or three pages and then remarked:

89

"On the whole I like it. . . . But when you describe my appearance and your first impressions, you're perhaps exaggerating or idealizing somewhat . . . I'd like to suggest—if I may—not to fall in the error of the saucer cultists who create the false image in the minds of their readers that we people from out there must be in every respect the incarnation of absolute perfection. When I walk on your streets, eat in your restaurants, work with your professionals, the people I meet don't look at me with amazement or turn around to see something very unusual never seen before. Do you see what I mean?"

"Yes, yes, I agree. . . . However, it was you who stated on several occasions that you are in every respect, that is, physically, mentally, culturally, socially, politically, economically, perhaps even religiously, far superior to us. That makes us in all those respects your inferiors. You also emphasized this point by calling us 'modern, mechanized barbarians' and what not. . . . Perhaps you've thought this over and want to make ammends?"

"No alterations or corrections are needed. On the other hand, I invite you to examine the precise meaning of what one calls superior. By what standard, measure or criterion do you assess it?"

"I mean that you're better and more perfect."

"Better and more perfect in what way?"

"Well, first of all, you know more. . . ."

"But more knowledge does not necessarily involve higher perfection in one's physical appearance. Besides, the 'more' you just used should be interpreted also qualitatively, not only quantitatively. More of the same is still the same, because the more increase in number does not yield better quality."

"In other words, a bunch of morons is still what it is: morons only."

"Well stated. But let me add one more note to this point. Quantity and quality are inversely proportional. It's the opposition between the one and the many, or the few *versus* the many. You can't have both!"

"Why not?" Knox argued.

"Because it is against the law of the universe which in its

90

evolutionary progression from the lower to the higher, from the simple to the more complex, proceeds selectively. Do you know what selection really implies?"

"I think you are trying to remind me of Darwin's natural selection?"

"So-called natural selection and the struggle for survival are not the whole story. It covers only the first stage in the evolutionary process. Besides, there is a great deal of waste in it, being left to blind chance. The next stage is the higher and more efficient form of an intelligently directed selection, based on the principle of the qualitatively superior, a stage which you have not reached as yet."

"I have the impression that we are getting back to our unfinished business from the last discussion. Remember you promised you would answer one pointed question I asked you? Do you recall it?"

"Your question was: 'What happened to the average, mediocre and inferior ones?' And now I'll try my best to expound this difficult question."

"Why do you introduce it as being difficult? Difficult for whom and why?"

"The nature of the difficulty is both scientific and moral, and it's rooted in the conditions of your existence. Where is, for instance, the science of eugenics? You may know that it started less than a hundred years ago, to be exact, in 1885 with Sir Francis Galton, and got practically nowhere since then. The reason for this stalemate is rather moral than scientific, although your knowledge of genetics and microbiology is of a very recent start."

"I think I know what you're driving at. . . . It's the moral-religious taboo raised against any attempt at trying to improve man's genetical outfit. The very name 'breeding' is immediately branded as immoral, sinful, criminal, because it allegedly attempts to treat human beings as if they were animals only."

"Why don't you state the rest of the usual objections?" Noesis encouraged.

"Because I don't know enough about it. . . . Well, let me add this: whenever the topic of 'breeding' is brought up, people immediately start talking either about man's inalienable rights of a free, independent person, or else they piously remind us of man's higher, supernatural origin, as God's creature, created after His likeness and image, possessing an immortal soul that is to live for ever in heaven or in hell. . . ."

"I'm glad you see the problem in its full context and also the difficulties it involves. But let's consider each of its aspects one after the other. Certainly when you're going to write down the novel ideas I'm proposing, and especially when the public will read it, you're going to be subject to all kinds of abuse."

"I'm quite aware of the fact that we're now considering one of those 'forbidden' questions. Knowing my brothers, I can anticipate all the 'nice' things they are going to heap upon me . . . I'm glad that at least we don't live in the Dark Ages any more, so that they won't be able to burn me at stake for the greater glory of the Almighty God."

"You forget that there's another burning awaiting you. . . . In the eternal fires of hell," Noesis reminded his friend ironically.

"Oh, yes, the divine barbacue complex, the sadism of an eternal roasting process to delight 'the good and the just' and to prevent heavenly boredom," Knox rounded off this portion of thought.

"I guess we have to ignore this unwelcome situation and face the facts as they are. The first idea refers to the well known principle of man's unity, oneness, wholeness and integrity, in opposition to the old Platonic and Christian dualism which created the unfortunate conflict in man—the soul-body dichotomy —we look upon life, man's included, as a natural bio-chemical process only. What they call organic and physical, different and opposed to the mental, psychic and spiritual, should be taken for what they are, namely, two different aspects and manifestations of the one and the same reality, of the same cosmic stuff or energy, which through the ascending process of complexifications reaches ever higher forms of perfection, becoming conscious of itself in man."

"But this first idea," commented Knox, "does away with the dogmas of creation, of the separate existence of the soul after death—immortality—the doctrine about man's original sin, the fall. Perhaps many other revered truths of the old tradition. This alone would be enough to offend most people's cherished feelings and beliefs, calling for their passionate reaction."

"I hope you're not afraid of all that, or are you? You have to get used to the idea that you'll be an outcast, living perhaps in self-imposed exile. Your name will be that of the worst evildoer, the sacrilegious slanderer and destroyer of man's highest hopes, in a word, the incarnation and personification of all sins and evils, the devil himself."

"So much the better. I've always liked Mephistopheles and I still prefer his spirit to the pious humility of those who delight themselves in their being despicable in their own eyes, calling this a virtue," Knox added with sincere contempt.

"That's how it'll be," Noesis said with conviction. "But let me elaborate further on the phenomenon of life as a natural event in the course of evolution. The first and most important conse quence of it is the understanding that there is no separation and much less opposition between so-called matter and spirit. The latter—I emphasize this point once more—is only the new quality emerging from the fortunate combination of the diverse quanta of energy, building up the amazingly complex structures of living organisms, each one displaying the perfections proper to their stage and level of development. This means that what is usually called as man's 'higher' powers, such as his mind, the degree and depth of his intelligence, his self-awareness, his freedom, his creativity, in a word, his 'soul,' is the direct and immediate product of the laws governing the process of heredity, the intricate mechanism of genetic composition (genotype) and its outward effect or appearance (phenotype).

"But this is the doctrine of crude materialism . . ." Knox remarked on the side.

"Look, Edward, I find it very amusing and at times even irritating when I hear your people using such terms as 'matter and spirit,' as if they knew what they are, not realizing that they're talking about something totally unknown to them. If I asked you,

93

for example, what you mean by the word 'matter,' what would you say?"

"Well, I'm sure that the outdated Newtonian frame of reference would not do. . . . The laws of his universal mechanics do not apply below and beyond man's perceptual level of consciousness. They're good only in the perspective of reality commensurate with man's sensory equipment. . . . Then, if we move to the region of atomic and subatomic particles or quanta of energy, the ultimate essence or identity of matter still remains obscure and mysterious. It seems to disappear into what the physicists call either wave frequency or certain foci in the general field of energy. I wish we had the answer!"

"You'll have it as soon as your scientists are ready to discard many of their inherited preconceptions and devise assumptions, methods, tools and to begin experiments aimed at penetrating into the core of the cosmic stuff. But you can't pick up a needle with a snow shovel. For the same reason, your knowledge about the laws and nature of gravity, magnetic fields, cosmic rays, the secrets of motion, space and time are totally insufficient. Our travel in space was born on the day when we learned the true nature of these things and made use of that knowledge for our purposes. And don't ask me again why don't we help you out, because I already answered that question."

"So there's nothing else for us to do but to sit back and wait for the chance discovery of something spectacular?" Knox said, frustration in his voice.

"That's not what I meant. For there is already a great deal of knowledge available to you, for instance in the field of genetics, that you could apply for the betterment of man's condition, by improving the quality of his bio-chemical outfit."

"But that can't be even started, because of the moral prejudices we mentioned before. . . . So I see no hope!"

"Don't be a pessimist, Edward. Certainly it'll take some time until the first condition for the success of eugenics will be achieved."

"What is this condition you call first?"

"The removal of man's mental and moral blocks or inhibitions!"

94

"How can that be accomplished?"

"Don't you see that this is what we're doing now and what you'll achieve through your book? Or don't you believe that ideas are more dangerous explosives than dynamite?"

"Suppose we reach that goal. . . . What's the next step? I guess it would be a program in eugenics."

"That program will consist in the application of your knowledge to direct the genetic mutations in a way such as to guarantee a higher survival value of the offspring than that of those achieved by chance only, that is, by random mating. The process of natural selection would be replaced by artificial selection, finding the best ways to vary the similarities and dissimilarities of the phenotype, either by inbreeding or outbreeding. The effects will depend also on your ability to control the genetic code of the offspring. But that involves more than the establishment of directed and selective mating."

"I'm afraid that our people would object to any such ideas, by holding up their inalienable right and their freedom to procreate as they choose. . . . Besides, they would be against any small or large scale experimentation with human beings. That would offend their belief in the absolute sanctity of human life."

"I realize that, but then the validity of these rights and beliefs should be examined and stated for what they really are or ought to be."

"Are you implying that these rights aren't absolute or holy?"

"That's correct, no matter how hard it'll be to convince especially the less intelligent, the uneducated and the primitive, without forgetting the zealots of divine origins and rights. . . . But still there's something to hope for. . . ."

"What makes you say that? What are the signs for such hope?"

"Well, take for example the changing mood in the opinions and attitudes of people toward the issues of contraceptives and abortions. . . . You couldn't have imagined such a change taking place just a few generations ago, especially among those who live in the state of submissive obedience, being ruled and dominated by the preachers of afterworlds."

95

"What do you suggest as a means to hasten this process of enlightenment and emancipation?"

"Appeal to man's faculty to understand, to judge, to conclude and to put his conclusions into effect."

"How would you go about it?"

"Well, let me take you as an example, although I realize that it would be more difficult to convince those of less education and intelligence. Suppose I asked you this question: if you were given objective evidence by experts whose honesty and integrity would leave nothing to desire, that upon analysis of your genetic endowment you're not fit and qualified to procreate, because the offspring would be just inferior being—retarded morons, for instance—would you still insist and hold on to your so-called inalienable and absolute right to procreate in spite of everything?"

"I certainly wouldn't claim such things. I fully realize that there's no right to justify the doing of the wrong, to harm others, especially those who have no means to defend themselves, for the simple reason that they do not even exist yet."

"Then you also realize that existence is not an unconditional and unqualified blessing. It can be also a burden or a curse—depending on the element of tragedy present in each case?"

"I've felt like that many times, though I don't look upon myself as an example of misgenation."

"You should also remember the truth in the wisdom of your Greek philosophers—Socrates and Aristotle—when they taught that an unexamined life is not worth living, or else, that life is worth living only under certain conditions and no others. What they wanted to say was that the mere fact of life as such is not a value, far from being an absolute one."

"That's true, but they were referring, I think, more to the social, political, economic and cultural conditions of life, not to its biological conditions and premises."

"Nevertheless, I have no doubts that they would have extended the same principle also to the domain of eugenics, if they only had been aware of its tremendous significance and consequences. They would have looked upon that science as the very first, realizing that the genetic outfit and its quality is the direct cause—good or bad—of the quality (high or low) of people's cultural life and values. In one sentence: *Bios* comes before *Logos* as the cause must precede the effect."

"*Bios* comes before *Logos*. . . ." Knox was pondering this sentence. "Well, the more I think of it, the more I like it. As a matter of fact, this principle was recognized even here among our people, but only as far as the extreme cases of degeneration were concerned. Criminal behavior, many cases of insanity have been ascribed to heredity first and to environment second."

"They should have also mentioned that the so-called environment is no better and no worse than the biological package of the individuals who make it up."

"That's true again, but you know what happened. As matter was separated from spirit, similarly culture was set apart and above man's material concerns. It's only another aspect of the same old dichotomy."

"But let's now go one step further. I'm going to ask you this question: have you ever experienced the dark feeling of resentment?"

"Yes, I have, as matter of fact quite often. . . ."

"For what reason? Have you analyzed the conditions which make its presence possible in your mind?"

"Well, let me see . . . I think I have it. Whenever I had to realize the humiliating limitations of my own abilities, and had to admit the superiority of others better equipped than myself, I felt that some injustice must have been committed by someone, somewhere . . . I felt shortchanged, frustrated, angry, ready to protest, to rebel, even to destroy. Then I had to sink into the abominable feeling of personal impotence, blaming Life, Destiny, Fate, God for my condition. Even today, when I read the works of the very few geniuses we have had so far, my respect and admiration is always marred by the shadows of envy, jealousy and disappointment with my own being . . . I keep asking myself: 'why don't I have the mind of a Goethe?' But what's the use!"

"One step further, Edward. I'm sure that if it had been within your own power to do so, you'd have changed it for the better, right?"

"I would do it even now . . . but I can't. . . ."

"And if you knew that others could have done it for you, before you were born, would you say that they should have done it as a matter of obligation?"

"Yes, I have to agree. But such is not the case; it may be like that somewhere in the distant future. . . ."

"One more point: Would you say that non-existence at all is to be preferred to a miserable existence?"

"All those who commit suicide give you the best answer, but those are the extreme cases."

"Well then, I can give you milder cases to prove the same point. It's a very obvious phenomenon. Isn't it rather a rare exception to see a happy human being, joyous, proud and powerful? The overwhelming majority of people drag themselves throughout a meaningless life, stopped under the burden of an unwanted existence, without having the proud courage to terminate the endless process of their unasked for sufferings."

"How true! It's almost a universal phenomenon. . . . Our present day existentialism is the best expression of this: the human condition and situation is described and dramatized in the darkest possible colors. And not all of it can be dismissed as the moaning and wailing of those who got lost. . . . As a matter of fact, the tragic element in life, sometimes called also the problem of evil in the world, has been with us from the very beginning of our culture. Think of the Greek tragedies, the speculations of the stoics, the trouble of the theologians to explain evil out of existence, the return of pessimism with Schopenhauer and his ubiquitous disciples. . . . The very insistence on optimism and cheerfulness, on the healthy effects of laughter, betray only man's desperate efforts to whitewash the cruel truths of his life."

"You're getting too gloomy again, Edward. . . ." Noesis tried to pull him out from the morass of his tragic mood. "Complaining is of no use, because it effects nothing. What I wanted to accomplish was only to create the insight that the human being of today is a rather unhappy and pathetic phenomenon, which

98

gives us added reasons to work in the direction of change and improvement."

"Oh, well, we've always had some enthusiasts who discovered a new formula for instant happiness. One tells you to keep smiling because God loves you. . . . But you don't feel it and you end up cursing that very idea. Another misfit writes about the power of positive thinking, which peels off like a suntan, and one ends up with positively sinking . . . and sinking deeper into cynical despair. . . . It's all trite and trifle. The solution must be in what you mentioned about man learning to control and improve the genetic code of future existents."

"I regard it not only as a noble undertaking for the future of man, but also the most important duty of those now living."

"But I can't help thinking of the enormous amount of time it'll take. Especially when I think of the ignorant, uneducated, vulgar and ordinary man, of the condition in which man still lives today in the underdeveloped countries, the millions of primitives, savages, barbarians, the neo-savages. . . . What are you going to do with them? I don't think you believe that you can appeal to their minds, which they don't have or never use. Try to tell and convince any savage that he should not sleep with his female partner! It would be the same as trying to teach self-control, self-denial and abstinence to a dog in the presence of a bitch in heat. As a matter of fact, they're even unwilling to learn something about contraceptives. Rather they keep on multiplying, without ever thinking of the means how to keep themselves from actual starvation. Apparently, man never gets tired of the persistent practice of his libidinous outlets. . . . So, I'm asking you again, what are you going to do with the large masses of uncivilized or half-civilized people, the rabble, the populace, the mob, the scum of society? Are you going to kill them off as Hitler tried to exterminate the Jews? Are you going to sterilize them against their own will? . . ." Knox became really heated up by envisioning the appalling difficulties of the problem. At the same time, he was growing more and more skeptical.

"We didn't use any of the methods you've mentioned, still we achieved our goal. But it took many long years to accomplish it.

99

One trouble with you modern men is that you developed a psychic or mental myopia, not being able to think beyond the now and the tomorrow. You live very fast, for the moment only, because you have lost your faith in yourselves and what life promises. Therefore, most of your behavior is geared at easy consumption and exploitation, a parasitic mode of existence, and very few believe that creative productivity, thinking in terms of long-range goals and ideals should come first."

"Well, Noesis, in spite of everything, I'm still far from being an idealist. What good is it to me that the superior man will live five hundred or five thousand years from now, when I know that I'll have no part in it and I'll have to keep on living under the present conditions of unhappiness, misery and suffering!"

"Come, now, Edward, you did much better before than this performance of yours. . . . You know from your own experience that the cultivation of despair leads you nowhere. Besides, without wanting to flatter you, you're not one of those who are disinherited by life. You're above the average condition of the many, whom you described with so much contempt. And, finally, remember our gardener again. . . . I'm afraid you'll end up hating that fellow!"

"All right, all right, skip it, forget it! It was one of those stupid fits I still get once in a while. . . . Go on and finish your answer to my question about the too many."

"I think I mentioned already the importance of the time element. Try to follow what I'm going to project into the future, but don't take it as a prophecy. We don't like to guess future from the flight of the birds."

"I'm ready to listen. By the way, sorry to interrupt you again, but we forgot about the 'memory cell'. . . . How am I going to remember all this new material?"

"If I'm not mistaken, it has been lying on your desk all this time and I'm sure its power of intake has not been exhausted as yet. . . . So back to my answer: can you anticipate the time when there'll be no more underprivileged countries on your planet? No more savages in your jungles? No more underdeveloped nations? No more uneducated, ignorant and superstitious hordes

100

of human beings? How long did it take your country, for example, to accomplish the highest standard of life on earth? Don't you think that with the new methods of production and communication, the progress of automation, the process of industrializing those uncivilized areas of the globe will take much less time and effort than what you needed to accomplish yours?"

"Noesis, aren't you contradicting yourself? Are you forgetting that you called us motorized and mechanized barbarians in spite of our high standard of living—or because of it! Even supposing that all what you said will occur all around the globe in, say, two hundred years, that would yield only the spread of modern barbarism, according to your premises!"

"I'm sorry I cannot give you the satisfaction of agreeing with you, Edward. Try better next time! But this time it's a miss again, for the simple reason that I don't regard your present condition here as the final stage of development. Nevertheless, it's a necessary stage, the first step out of the cave and the jungle."

"What's the next one?" Knox inquired impatiently.

"It's the progression from the state of mere civilization to the condition of becoming cultured too. . . . You seem to forget that important distinction I made. Remember our Indian whom we made into an 'instant' modern man?"

"Fine, I give in. . . . But what'll happen as to man's biological endowment in the condition of higher culture which rests on that of civilization?"

"Can't you read the signs of the time? Can't you see what changes occur in man's way of life in consequence of his intellectual enlightenment and emancipation?"

"Give me a few indications."

"Well, you'll be surprised to learn that you already know most of them. First, isn't it true that scientific, philosophic and cultural progress brings with it a necessary decline of the mythical and religious outlook on life? The more man thinks, learns and knows about himself and his world, the less he believes in supernatural beings, causes and effects? Can't you see the frantic and desperate attempts of all religious organizations to find ways to stay in business? Don't you see that so-called 'updating' is their last

101

attempt to resuscitate that God who died even in the hearts of many theologians, not mentioning the minds of the modern intellectuals? Do you know what God's death means? It means man's resurrection from the death of ignorance and superstition. Now, I ask you to draw your conclusions and make the necessary connections."

"Let me try this line. The death of God means also the removal of all the objections against the science of eugenics. It'll have . . . no, it does have a future. What's the next sign?"

"The more illumined man becomes, the easier to reason with him, right? When I was discussing with you the so-called absolute and inviolable rights of man to procreate, you understood my point right away, you agreed, and I'm sure it was not a piece of hypocrisy on your part."

"I can assure you that it wasn't."

"Fine. That means that also the others who reach the same level of understanding will have no difficulty in agreeing, especially because they will already be free from their religious inhibitions and the qualms of a morbid conscience. As a consequence, they'll submit themselves, of their own free choice and in the spirit of obligation toward their offsprings, to the necessary genetic analysis, in order to learn from this, for their own benefit and that of their future children, whether they are or are not qualified to procreate."

"I see what you mean. But I have another difficulty. The so-called proles will keep on procreating wildly with the same prolific efficiency and in no time they'll outnumber the educated ones, leading to the degeneration of, the human race by the brutal force of sheer numbers."

"Your prediction or assumption would come true only if in the race between procreation and acculturation, the former, that is procreation, came out as the winner. But I'm not sure that it will."

"I'm still inclined to disagree, just thinking of the population explosion here in my own country. Besides, the rate of child mortality decreases in direct proportion to the advancement of medical science. Am I wrong in saying this?"

"Well, your point is well taken. No doubt about that. Still it's not the whole picture. First, even in your own country the population explosion is already less and less explosive. This can be attributed, I think, to the decline of the traditional worship of large families and the rise of a more individualistic outlook on life. This trend is bound to continue. You already find many books on the market dealing with the emancipation of the woman from her glamorized housewifery. Second, take a look at the statistics in the more cultured countries on the Continent. There is no population explosion there, and, as we mentioned before, they're asking for more intelligent legislation on the question of contraceptives, abortions and divorce. I think that this is the pattern of the social-moral change to come in less than two generations in your country too and, much later on, in the other less developed countries of the world."

"I hope you're right, Noesis. But I get the impression, all the time, that you're against marriage and family. Am I right in making this assumption?" Knox bent forward in his seat, impatiently awaiting his friend's answer.

"One cannot be against something that doesn't exist," Noesis remarked enigmatically.

"I'm sure you must refer to your own social organization on your own world, not ours."

"You guessed it right, Edward." Knox seemed to be really impressed with this unexpected news. It sounded almost unbelievable. Noesis immediately perceived his friend's amazement, therefore he added: "I realize the confusion that must be present in your mind now due to this new piece of information. I know how difficult it must be for any of you to imagine a society of people without being built upon the natural unit of the family. I could go into that right now. . . . However, it's much wiser to finish one problem at a time, don't you think so?"

"I know that we must follow a certain method, an order in our talks. But, if I may ask, could we start on this new one as soon as we settle the one we're considering now?" Knox pleaded with Noesis almost as a child would with his mother. Noesis was pleasantly amused with his friend's sincere enthusiasm, and said:

103

"I'm looking forward to it myself. I know it's very important. So, let's hurry back to our present problems. Where did we break off?"

"Let me see now. . . . Ah, yes! It was the question of the race between the proliferation of the primitive versus the progression of culture which—according to you—should halt the population explosion."

"You don't seem to be convinced yet. . . . I can see it on your face. Therefore I must pose this new question: Why do people, especially the lower type, keep on procreating? Ponder this question and don't say the first thing that happens to come to your mind."

"I was going to say that it's because of the fun and pleasure they derive from sex. But that's not the whole story, I guess. There must be something else to it."

"Of course there is! Without discarding the significance of the quest for pleasure, there's also man's quest for meaning, some meaning, even if it's not any ultimate or absolute value. So far, man believed to have found in his children the continuation of his own life, a feeble form of immortality. You must consider also the circumstance that most people identify themselves and their happiness with that of their children, because they have scarcely anything better or more meaningful left for themselves. Thus, children and the holiness of parenthood, especially motherhood, are the substitutes or compensations for their basic frustrations in life."

"You're generalizing, Noesis . . ." Knox broke in. "I wouldn't make it that simple and easy, unless you want to say that having children has no meaning whatsoever, besides being the last refuge of the frustrated . . ." Knox objected in earnest.

"I didn't say that there is 'no meaning whatsoever' in having children. As a matter of fact, I do recognize that on the present level of your socio-economic development, the family institution is the best solution so far. But it's an intermediary stage only. You can see for yourself that the very tight family cohesion of before is loosening up more and more in your own society, due

104

to greater socio-economic mobility and freedom. Can't you imagine what will happen if this trend continues?"

"It'll lead to the disintegration of society with a parallel increase in social problems. That's no evolution for the better, it's rather decline and decadence!"

"I'm afraid we shall have to leave this question for later on, as we agreed upon already. Actually, what I wanted to point out was merely the fact that the more educated and advanced persons in your society—especially those engaged in a life of creative or professional efficiency—are not so family-centered and child minded. I can give you several examples if you want me to. . . ."

"Let's hear them. . . ."

"Assuming that you remember something of your course in the history of civilization and culture, you'll recall that in all ages most of the great creators, the men of genius, the superior type of human beings—the philosophers, scientists, artists, even great political leaders—did not marry and procreate at all. And those who did—such as Socrates—left much to be desired in their roles of husbands and fathers. Is this true or false?"

"So far, it's true. But are you trying to build up your case on the exceptions rather than on the rule, on the very few whom some people even label as abnormal, and not the many?" Knox objected again. Noesis persisted:

"You're fully justified in defending your point, because you think, of necessity, within the framework of your own past and present society, while I have in mind, all this time, that which holds true in our society, which happens to be its exact opposite."

"This means, then, that every single individual living on any planet whatever, ought to be a genius. They should all be the superior man and woman, the concretization of Nietzsche's dream . . ." Knox's remark was rather ironical and resentful, almost caustic.

"I'm aware of the difficulty you have to accept as real that which surpasses your highest hopes and the wildest dreams of your fiction writers. You dare not overcome the narrow horizons of your limited perspectives and I cannot help that."

"Suppose I go along with your claim. Then another important

105

problem comes up in my mind. For it follows from your promises that in your world nobody lowers himself or herself to the animalic functions of sex and reproduction. Everyone of your kind is constantly engaged in the relentless pursuit of the loftiest ideals and values. If this is so, may I ask, how does your race survive? What do you have in place of our primitive sex and all that which it entails? Were you born in a rosebush or perhaps everyone is an immaculate conception, while all of us here, on this speck of dust in the vast universe, were born by maculate conception, that is, a man copulating with a woman."

Noesis couldn't control his laughter, prompted by Knox's amusing remarks and the sudden flight of his imagination.

"You should have added a few more possibilities," he said cheerfully. "I was expecting you to drag in also the incubators, test-tubes and what not, as you find them described in some of your utopias. While reading those, we had one fit of laughter after the other! It was very entertaining indeed! However, it betrays the underlying bias of the respective authors. They could envision man's future only in terms of decadence and decline, that is, as the final triumph of technology, science and collectivism, as the absolute regimentation of life, devoid of everything one would still call human and humane. It reveals also the prejudice shared by most of your writers concerning the brutalizing and dehumanizing effect of science, while implicitly or even explicitly pleading for the happy return to the state of original naturalness in the virginal bosom of Mother Nature. The mother complex again of those who got lost on their way."

"In other words, you're denying the depersonalizing effects of modern technology, the inhuman conditions prevailing in the megapolis and technopolis, contradicting yourself once more!"

"As a future writer and a former student of the humanities, you couldn't help accepting the same prejudice against 'the hardware of science' as the chief culprit responsible for all the evils of your society. We could spend hours discussing this topic, but, right now, I have only this to say. Knowledge in itself and regardless of its nature—whether it be philosophic, scientific, artistic, social, and so on—is neither good nor bad in a moral sense.

You're confusing the scientific and philosophic quest for knowledge with morality. You're moralizing even in the fields which in themselves are morally neutral, that is, immune, independent and autonomous, free from the concepts of good and evil. They are 'beyond good and evil,' to use the expression of the advocate of the overman, Nietzsche."

"But then, and once more, why do you call us barbarians? What made us into barbarians if not industrial technology? Or perhaps we never altogether outgrew our original condition?"

"I don't want to repeat what we've covered so far. When you'll listen to the 'memory cell' you'll hear it stated at least two or three times. I meant to say only one thing. Knowledge as such —insofar as it only expresses the facts of reality—is non-moral or amoral. But it may become or be made into either good or evil, depending on whether man, the moral subject, puts that knowledge to the service of constructive or destructive purposes. In this sense, the atomic bombs are evil and the discoveries of medical science are good. Do you follow me?"

"I wish I could prove you wrong some day . . ." Knox remarked rather jokingly when left without anything to stand on. Then, he remembered that Noesis had not yet answered the question about how his people had solved the problem of procreation. He only knew that he had rejected parenthood, immaculate conception and incubators. He tried his last guess.

"I think I found the answer as to how you came into being: artificial insemination, correct?"

Noesis laughed again wholeheartedly, with a healthy ring to it.

"I'm sorry, but I can't help it," he apologized. "It strikes me so funny that you're imagining that we're professed haters of women, that we despise the pleasure of sex, just because we don't have your old patriarchal system of social life. But this is not the case, on the contrary!" Then Noesis paused as if halted by a new idea. He kept thinking silently for a while. Then he continued: "I was thinking of our next meeting. . . . We agreed to talk in more detail on the topic of family, parenthood and related questions. I realize that it's rather hard on you to be forced to take the testimony of one person only as the final verdict on the important matters we have been discussing."

"What's on your mind? What are your plans for the future?" asked Knox eagerly, not hiding from Noesis his growing excitement.

"I want to introduce you next time to one of my . . . how shall I call her? My friend," Noesis said simply, watching the changing expressions of surprise on Knox's face.

"Then it's a she, a woman, a girl-friend?"

"Again, the labels are not important. . . . But I warn you not to build up any wild and fantastic expectations. I say this because of what has been written by some crack-pots about their encounters with space-girls and so forth."

"Yes, I know. A certain fellow from South America even claimed to have been forced by some humanoids to make love to an attractive redhead from outer space!"

Both of them laughed at the vulgar stupidity of such coarse imagination. Then Knox started his questions again:

"Why do you want her to be present at our next meeting? Is it because you feel that the topic warrants and requires that we listen to the opinion of the fair and weaker sex?"

"This last remark of yours reveals your mode of thinking about women in general. I can tell you right now that we don't think in these terms about them. The war between sexes is typical of you again. You haven't learned yet what to do with the women in your lives. Basically speaking, you either enslaved them and abused them for considering them your inferiors, or you went to the other extreme of romantic idealizations. Both attitudes are wrong."

Noesis noticed that Knox's attitude had changed. He became pensive, showing signs of some conflict and indecision. He behaved as though he wanted to come forth with a problem of his own, without being able to decide whether he should or not. Noesis came to his rescue:

"What are you thinking about, Edward? Something seems to disquiet you. What is it? Don't hesitate to say it, if concerns us."

"Well, I don't know what your reaction would be. . . . It's

108

rather personal, I mean it concerns first of all only me and my private life. . . . I don't know whether I should bring it up or not. . . . I'm afraid you'll say no."

"Look, Edward, don't act like a timid child. That's not like you. It's better to make a decision. You can't make a second step if you don't take the first one," Noesis said encouragingly.

"If I remember correctly, Noesis, you've never asked me to keep quiet about our relationship, even from the beginning. Nevertheless, I haven't said a word about it to anyone so far."

"But now you'd like to?"

"I don't want to make it public or to display it in the newspapers. That would be stupid! It would destroy everything!"

"I'm glad you understand that."

"On the other hand, you see, I'd like to reveal it to one person only. I'm sure I could trust her."

"Oh! I see! It's your girl-friend this time, correct?"

"Yes. Since you mentioned that you'd like to introduce me to your friend, I thought it would do no harm if I could have her to participate at least once in our discussion. . . . Then we'd have the perfect setup: two couples facing each other. I'm sure that Marisa, that's her name, being an intelligent college student, could represent the role of the woman in the dialogue from our point of view. She could see problems I can't see. She could ask questions I wouldn't think of. . . . And, well, it wouldn't do any harm."

"What are your plans concerning her person?"

"I thought that, if this meets with your agreement, she could help me out with my writing too. She volunteered more than once, in the past, her services as a typist and editor. As to my future plans with her, I'm not fully decided yet. But that's my personal problem. . . ." Knox kept observing Noesis' face, trying to divine from its expression the nature of his decision. After a few moments of reflection, Noesis answered:

"If I agree to your request, I have one condition to insist upon. And I also know that even if you, for your part, agree with this condition now, I'm taking a great deal of risk, for one can never anticipate in what way, when or for what reason people change their minds and attitudes. . . . But then, this also applies to you and me. . . ."

"What is your condition?" asked Knox with anxious expectation.

"Nothing much. All I ask you and through you also your friend is to keep this whole affair secret and not to enlarge further the number of people involved in it. The reason for this should be obvious, besides also being in our mutual interest."

Knox felt relieved from the tension of anxiety, drew a deep breath, and hurried to assure his friend of his total agreement and loyalty. He had the impression that Noesis considered their meeting ended. Therefore, he didn't want to go back to the questions he still wanted to debate. Instead, he invited Noesis for a coffee break. But to his surprise, he preferred a glass of milk only. He appeared to be still thinking of some questions, as if working out mentally some plan for the future. He became more and more reserved, to the point of making Knox feel apprehensive and worried.

"Is there anything wrong, Noesis?" he inquired with concern.

"Why do you ask that?" Noesis replied as if coming back from the distance where his thoughts had carried him.

"Nothing, really. It's just that you became suddenly so recollected, silent and withdrawn that I thought perhaps something's the matter. . . ."

"I know what you mean and how you feel. It's one of your habits to expect persons to keep on conversing all the time when they're together, even if you talk about nonsense only, like the weather, the insignificant daily event, TV shows, foot-ball games and what not. And if somebody keeps silent for a while, this is immediately taken as a sign that there must be something wrong."

"Then there's nothing the matter?" Knox felt relieved once more.

"Not a thing! We believe that one can enjoy somebody's company through the simple presence of his person, without having to prattle all the time. Words are not the only means of communication, and not the best one either. But since we're talking again, I want to give you the first payment due to you."

Noesis reached into his pocket and took out a small envelope from his wallet, handing it over to Knox.

"Did you take out all the taxes and deductions dictated by the law?" Knox remarked mockingly.

"No, I did not. That's your problem, not ours. Some of this taxation is justifiable in view of the social and political organization you have. The rest is only legalized robbery."

"I like your definition. It's good . . . because that's what most of it is."

Noesis grew silent again. He finished his milk and stood up ready to go. There was something in his whole attitude that forbade any further inquiry. He walked to the door and left without uttering a word. Knox found this very strange. Strange indeed, very unlike the formal or informal leave-taking of most people. But then Noesis was different. . . . Was he human at all? If not, what was he? And, after all, what do we mean by being human?

CHAPTER SEVEN

THE PROGRESSIVE EXTINCTION OF THE FAMILY

Knox spent the following days trying to catch up with the material accumulated during the previous dialogues. The pace of his work alternated between the slow but steady progress from sentence to sentence and the pleasant experience of so-called inspiration, when the whole outline of a section suddenly emerged, almost ready-made, in his vision. Then ideas flowed freely one after the other, hardly giving him enough time to keep up with their spontaneous flux and speed. On these rare occasions he felt himself totally absorbed, possessed, led, becoming forgetful of time, space and even oblivious to the immediate needs of his body. But this almost abnormal intensity, the exceptional heightening of his mental acuity, were usually followed by periods of an almost total exhaustion and depression. Then he would be forced to allow himself a break. He would have to tear himself away from the obsessive power of his ideas.

The thought of Marisa kept coming back to him. Now he saw a way where he could work her into his relationship with Noesis. Had he followed his first impulses, he would have called her up right away to break the good news to her. Strangely though, he kept on delaying it day after day. It had been ten days now. Sometimes he wondered why he had asked Noesis to share his secret with her? What did that mean? Why had he got her involved? He remembered how easily he forgot girls whom he had dated before, and also those who came during their break. Why was it different now? Why couldn't he forget her with the same lightheartedness? Was it perhaps because . . . he wanted to say "because he loved her," but he didn't like that ambiguous term. His previous love affairs taught him to associate that word with his adventurous caprices only, in which there was nothing that he could justly identify as love. As a matter of fact, he told himself, what he had loved was just the sexual aspect in their relationship, not the girls themselves. They had been very welcome opportunities and means to indulge in his passions, but that was all. He couldn't remember one single case, out of the many, in which there had been—on his part at least—any serious attachment to the person of his partner. It was plain to Knox now that he had never been in love with anybody, therefore he couldn't tell what that felt like. Perhaps what he felt toward Marisa was something in that direction. . . .

He couldn't decide yet, he only knew of his longing for her, a desire not dictated by his sexual needs. Then it dawned upon him that Noesis could show up any time now and he had to make a decision. If he didn't contact her after all, he could always find some excuse to justify her absence in Noesis' eyes. Being on the verge to make a final decision, he felt a sudden desire for her person welling up in him again, stronger than ever. Another thought kept perturbing him and aggravating his condition of ambivalence: "Suppose," he asked himself, "suppose that Marisa declines my invitation? Suppose that she has left me for good and is going with someone else?" This last assumption revealed to him a new feeling, unknown to him so far: he felt jealous. Someone else! The very idea filled him with anger, hatred, despair. He couldn't bear that thought. He had to make sure. Ignorance in this matter was unbearable.

He grabbed the phone and dialed her number with trembling fingers, expecting immediate answer. Instead, there came through the receiver the sound of an uninterrupted sequence of useless ringing. . . . The more he heard that unbearable sound, the more anxious he became. He kept on listening to it much longer than necessary, just to ascertain himself that there was going to be no answer, being unable to tear himself away from the odious sound as a symbol of repeated pleading. With the last of his effort, he summoned up enough strength to slam down the receiver, lit a cigarette and walked mechanically to his bar.

114

He was amazed at himself realizing how much power his old habits still had over him. Fortunately there was nothing to drink. He kept pacing up and down the floor of his apartment, like a caged wild animal. Occasionally he would stop in front of that hated black gadget, the numbers on the dial growing out of proportion. He felt like smashing it. . . .

Then he found himself dashing out of his apartment into the street, walking fast, almost running, without knowing where he was, in what direction he was going. He was very angry at himself for being unable to control his emotions. No matter how hard he tried to cancel out the thought of having lost Marisa, he had to accept the inevitable evidence. He cared much more for her than he had ever allowed himself to admit. . . .

It was late in the evening when he got back to the apartment. He had no means to remember all the streets he had walked through in his aimless wandering. The first thing his eyes fell upon was the phone. He hated it more than ever, but he had to give in to the overwhelming power of his violent urge. He dialed Marisa's number again, perhaps out of a sheer masochistic impulse. He decided to hang on to the phone as long as he could take it. He could scarcely trust his ears when Marisa's familiar voice came through the wires:

"Hello . . . who's calling?"

Knox's heart was pounding violently, as if trying to free itself from the narrow prison of his chest. His throat was dry and he managed with an enormous effort to utter two short syllables in a dying voice:

"It's me. . . ."

Marisa apparently couldn't recognize his voice right away and repeated impatiently in a louder voice:

"Me . . . who? I can't hear you!"

Knox cleared his throat and succeeded in raising the volume of his voice to the level of normal speech:

"It's me, Edward. . . ."

This time Marisa was able to identify her party and let a short gasp of surprise escape from her lips. Then she collected herself, forced an impersonal tone into her words asking,

"Well, what is it that you want?"

"I've got to talk to you, Marisa. . . ."

"Go ahead, I'm listening. . . . Say it. . . ."

"Not on the phone. I can't!" His voice sounded almost pleading.

"What's this big, unspeakable secret you've got?"

"Could I see you someplace?"

"You mean now? Tonight? You know what time it is? Besides I have a few things of my own to look after. . . ."

By this time the shocking effect of surprise had left Knox and he was able to talk more sensibly and coherently:

"I would prefer it to be tonight, by all means. . . ."

"But why this sudden urgency? This unexpected hurry again? I'm afraid it's just another of your whimsical fits. . . . Remember? If it's something so very important you had to tell me, you had plenty of time before tonight to do so, but you didn't. What new trouble befell you this time to make you remember my phone number suddenly again?"

"I'm in no trouble at all. At least not in the usual sense of the word. I'm not sick, I don't need money, you don't have to pull me out of any mess. . . ."

"Well, if it's nothing of that sort, then I can't imagine what else there could be that you've got to tell me right away. . . . It doesn't make sense. . . ."

"I realize that . . . but . . . I'm still asking you once more if you could spare me a couple of hours tonight. I have something real important to tell you. It concerns you too, not only me."

Marisa didn't answer immediately. Apparently her curiosity was aroused by Knox's insistence and she was trying to decide.

"You can't come here for many reasons. . . . And I hate the idea of meeting you in your place. . . . I'm afraid. . . ."

"You'll be as safe as if protected by fifty body guards of the best kind, if this is what prevents you from coming. . . ."

"Don't talk nonsense! I can take care of myself in an emergency, you should know that. Look, I'll take this one more chance. I'll give you the benefit of a doubt. But I promise you, if you don't come out with your important thing in ten minutes or less, you'll never see the like of me ever again."

116

"That's a deal. I promise. Take a taxi and hurry over."

Marisa hung up with a half-hearted yes. Knox knew that it would take her less than a quarter of an hour to get there. He hurried to straighten out his room. He remembered that Marisa had not yet seen all the changes in the apartment or in his person. He waited impatiently for the sound of the doorbell. His excitement told him more about his feelings toward Marisa than he had been able to find out so far, during his lonely walks. He was very well disposed, almost happy, for two reasons; he had found Marisa and, in spite of her initial hesitation, she was coming to see him. It was in this mood that he hurried to open the door upon her arrival.

Marisa stopped short in the doorway, hardly believing what she was seeing. There, standing before her, was a young man, looking straight into her eyes, with an almost mocking smile on his face, leading her into the apartment that had no trace left of its former condition. She allowed Knox to take her coat, then sat down on a chair, still unable to utter a word. Knox kept watching her face with unconcealed pleasure, in which there was nothing of the gloating of the former beast of prey. Then he walked over to his desk, picked up the 'memory cell,' turned on the white button and waited, while keeping his glittering eyes on Marisa's face. In no time there was the clear and sonorous voice of Noesis, filling the room:

"But let me elaborate further on the phenomenon of life as a natural event in the course of evolution. The first and most important consequence of it is the understanding that there is no separation and much less an opposition between so-called matter and spirit. The latter—I emphasize this point once more—is the new quality emerging from the fortunate combination of the diverse quanta of energy, building up the amazingly complex structures of living organism, each one displaying the perfections proper to their stage and level of development."

Knox turned off the 'memory cell," placing it carefully on his desk, next to the manuscript, piled up to an impressive size. Then he sat down opposite to Marisa, waiting for her first question. He didn't have long to wait:

"Who's he? I've never heard such a wonderful voice, so rich in color and melodious tonality. Who is he? What was he talking about? What's that small gadget you had in your hands?"

Knox chuckled, really enjoying Marisa's sincere excitement.

"It's my friend, Marisa. The only friend I've got." He declared solemnly.

"But he must be a foreigner, judging from his slight accent." Knox nodded in approval. "When and where did you meet him?" Without waiting for an answer, she continued: "Let me see that small gadget. . . . I've never seen anything like that."

Knox handed her the 'memory cell,' giving her instructions on how to operate it. She kept on listening to Noesis's voice and her surprise became even more obvious when she heard Knox's voice, coming in, asking questions and giving answers. After a while, she returned the 'memory cell' to Knox, her whole being revealing the tension of impatient curiosity. Knox got up from his seat, took the first chapter of his manuscript and handed it over to Marisa, inviting her to read it. While Marisa became more and more engrossed in her reading, hurrying through the pages, Knox had a good opportunity to take a long, undisturbed look at her, letting her presence saturate his eyes and his whole being. He had no more doubts concerning his feelings toward her. The only thing he wasn't quite certain of was Marisa's disposition toward him.

In less than fifteen minutes Marisa had raced through the manuscript. She kept on looking at Knox, searching for words to express her amazement. It was only natural that she should start with a skeptical attitude:

"No! I can't believe it. . . . It's too fantastic! It's a hoax and it reveals only your over-fertile imagination, Edward. You made it all up. A pretty good piece of fiction, but not too original. . . . There are many of its kind to be found in the dime stores. . . . It's not true. It can't be! It's . . . it's too out of this world!"

"Yes, Marisa, I understand how you feel. I went through the same agony of doubt. It's unbelievable for the simple reason, that it's really and literally out of this world!"

"I . . . I wish you could give me some objective evidence, some undeniable, irrefutable, indisputable facts."

118

"You have a few already, Marisa. The change in my life. You must have noticed it since our last meeting. It was starting even then. And then there is my manuscript and, most important of all, this small instrument on my desk. . . ."

"Yes, yes. . . . But all of this is not enough, for they could be explained in a hundred different ways. And this recorder could be just a new invention of your own. The man talking with you is real, but not necessarily a citizen of extraterrestrial worlds. . . ."

"I have to agree with you again. However, that's not the end of the story. . . ."

"What do you mean? Do you have something else to show me?"

"Not right away, but in the very near future, in a few days, I'd say, if you agree. . . ."

"What are you planning?" asked Marisa with unmasked suspicion.

"Nothing you should worry about. Suppose I were to invite you to meet him and also his friend on the next time we come together. . . . Would you be willing to come?"

Marisa didn't answer right away, but seemed to be pondering over an answer. Then she said:

"What guarantee do I have that it's safe? Imagine me meeting two complete strangers, two men, allegedly from another world, without any protection, security and measures of precaution? I don't want any more unpleasant adventures. I think I had more than my share, if you know what I mean. . . ."

"You needn't worry, Marisa. From the two strangers only one is a man, the other is a woman. . . ."

"Have you seen her already?" Marisa snapped her question rather too sharply. Knox smiled with both satisfaction and understanding and replied:

"I haven't so far, but I will in a few days and you're invited to join our next discussion group."

"What are you talking about?"

"Since you haven't read all that I wrote down so far and neither have you listened to all that small thing contains, I'll have

119

to tell you briefly about what we're doing. Noesis—that's my friend's name—chose me to be the author of our interplanetary dialogues. It's my job to write down all the new ideas disclosed to me about their way of life and the probable future of our own civilization. Next time we're going to discuss the problems of family life."

"That's an old one," interposed Marisa contemptuously. "I've heard so many lectures on the wisdom of happy home makers that I'm sick of it!"

"I would be too, if we were going to repeat the same outworn questions on how to make your marriage work, how to keep your husband, how to raise your children without turning them into neurotics, and all the rest of the 'how to's.'"

"But then there's nothing left to discuss. . . ."

"Oh, isn't there! Suppose I tell you that—according to what Noesis already told me—family and all that which it involves—parenthood and children is unknown to them. They've outgrown all that. . . ."

"Then that woman or 'space-girl' is not your friend's wife. . . . What is she to him? His mistress or something?"

Knox had to laugh at Marisa's ingenuity and added: "I think he called her simply his friend. The name 'mistress' is unknown to them."

"Oh, I see! It sounds interesting . . ." Marisa remarked pensively.

"Then you accept my invitation and you'll come to our meeting. I would like it very much if you would. . . ."

"What good would my being there be to you or to them? You must have some other plans and unconfessed, hidden intentions. . . . Let's play it safe and clean this time. What are you after?"

"Of course," remarked Knox bitterly. "I should have known better. . . . I assumed too much, perhaps too soon. . . . My imagination ran away with me. . . ."

"What are you thinking about?"

"You. . . ."

"Me? Why me? And what about me?"

"Just one small insight, that's all. . . . I mean, I cannot expect you to have the confidence in me that I haven't earned yet. . . . It's natural. You had to develop the traits of mistrust, doubt and suspicion after all I made you live through. . . . And I don't want to force you into anything. But I wish I could prove to you that your fears are unfounded, at least now."

"Listen, Ed, let's have it straight, blunt and short. We're not sixteen year old children making the first acquaintance with love. We went through a lot of things together, good and bad. Many things belong to the past and there's no room and reason to get romantically infatuated. I, for one thing, am beyond all that nonsense."

"You sound very bitter, Marisa . . . I wish you weren't. But let me say this. I think I discovered the mistake we made in the past, a mistake done by very many who venture on the shaky and treacherous ground of love. Most of them move in two extremes, or somewhere in between, due to their immaturity. Either they believe in the romantic gospel of infinite blessedness coming to them through the idealized fantasies of their exalted imaginations, or they profess themselves to be so-called realists, by which they mean cool sex only, devoid of all meaning and lasting value. But both of them end up utterly frustrated and disillusioned. The first ones lose their faith in the meaning of true love, when they have to sober up under the pressures of the hard facts of reality. The latter ones get fed up with sex and the more they force it, the less satisfaction they get from it. They become practical and despaired hedonists."

"But there's no other way left . . ." Marisa confessed her agreement.

"I think there is a third way which is neither the romantic flights of the imagination nor the brutal naturalism of pleasure seeking."

"How would you call it?" asked Marisa with increased interest.

"It's an old name, very much abused today. . . . Only the name survived in our vocabulary, but its meaning and contents have been lost a long time ago. It's called friendship, Marisa. A better word than the misleading ambiguity of love and sex

121

taken together. I think even Noesis would agree with me. . . ."

"You seem to be all taken up with that fellow. You consider him as the ultimate authority on everything. You found your hero and you worship him blindly. . . ."

"I may give you that impression, that's true. But I don't think that I became blind and irrational. It's not hero-worship. It's something else. . . ."

"What is it?"

"It's respect and admiration, the essence of friendship, free from all desires to possess, dominate, own, use and exploit. And that is what the true relationship between men ought to be. . . . It's possible, it exists, it's real. I know it!"

"I wish it were the way you put it, Edward, but it isn't. You seem to have become an idealist under the influence of your friend."

"I'm not an idealist, but I think I've outgrown my previous condition of nihilism and pessimism. I know that there are values in life worth living for, and friendship is one of them."

"Why are you telling me all this?" Marisa asked not without some provocative quality in the tone of her voice.

"Because you asked me about my hidden intentions, remember?"

"Well, what are they?"

"There's only one, and a very simple one at that. I think we could renew our relationship on a new basis, that of friendship, as I understand this word."

"But these conditions are not present, Ed. You spoke of mutual respect and admiration. I think we've destroyed that a long time ago. And I don't believe in the dogma of the resurrection. Death is an absolute, not only in the physical sense, but also psychologically."

"In other words, you consider yourself dead."

"And you too. . . . Don't try to fool yourself."

"What makes you so sure about the way I am, I think and I feel now?"

"Well, you're very enthusiastic right now with your outer-space experience, but it'll cool off. It'll wear off. You'll sober up again and return to your own old self. You can't fight the inevitable. . . ."

"I'd like to believe that you don't mean all that you just said, Marisa. I'm aware of the difficulties of regaining one's stand in life. . . . As for my present condition, you've got it all wrong. This time I really mean it. I wish you could believe me!"

"Well then, let me ask you point blank: What reasons do you have to admire and respect me, not speaking about your own person?"

"I won't use the usual commonplace words, as for instance, 'because you're you' and all the rest. It doesn't sound right, it says nothing. It's too vague. I'd rather say that I see in you the possibilities of becoming a person rich in values. These possibilities are what I respect and admire. As for my own self, I think in the same terms. Besides, no matter how much you insist on your gloomy pessimism, you'd get hurt and with good reason, if I called you a person totally devoid of values, a non-entity, a zero, less than a thing. Because, Marisa, you know that you have values."

"Tell me one more thing. Why did it take you so long to call me?"

"I told you the last time we met that I needed time to see clearly."

"And now you've reached that point of clarity?"

"Yes, I have. But now it's my turn to ask you a blunt question. And my question demands a sincere answer."

"Go ahead. I'm ready."

"Well, tell me, Marisa, after all that I've told you tonight, have you decided to reject my proposal and walk out of this place for good? I'm prepared for whatever answer I get. . . ."

"Are you giving me an ultimatum in the name of the freedom you extoll so highly?"

"No, I'm not trying to coerce you. The freedom is yours to choose. . . ."

Marisa paused a while and then said: "I hope you don't expect me to make a confession of my love, to jump into your arms and the rest of the usual things people do in the name of their dramatic reconciliation."

A smile flashed through Knox's face as he said: "Thank you, Marisa. That's all I wanted to know. I hate those cheap scenes that are drowned in tears and sobs. . . . May I then assume that you'll be coming to our next meeting? You won't regret it, I can assure you of that much."

"I hope you'll let me know and. . . ."

"I'll pick you up in person."

Marisa got up from her seat, walked over to Knox's desk and picked up the bundle of manuscript pages. Then she turned toward Knox who was standing next to her and, raising the pile of paper, asked:

"Is this still my job?"

"If you want to look at it that way."

"I'd love to do the editing and the typing, if you thing I'm qualified?"

"Well, if you aren't, I'll have to fire you!"

Knox looked forward to their next meeting with Noesis and his friend with the same impatience as that of children counting the days for the arrival of Santa Claus loaded with the presents of their dreams. Even while busily writing at his desk, his attention fully dedicated to his work, this desire was ever present in his subconscious, and its full realization came to his mind with unfailing regularity. Whenever his phone would ring, he'd run to answer it, hoping to finally hear the much expected voice of Noesis. Every day that passed added to his restlessness and nervous tension, becoming almost unbearable in intensity. He could do nothing about it. He thought with regret that he should have secured his friend's telephone number. At times he was tempted—especially during his long afternoon walks—to go directly to Noesis's apartment in the hotel. But he knew how unwise such a move would be. So far the initiative had always been left to Noesis, and he had not in any way hinted that he would want it to be any different. It was this impotent passivity that put such a strain on his nerves.

His frustration reached such a degree that when Noesis finally

124

called to fix the date and time for their meeting to take place in his apartment, he almost committed the irreparable blunder of reproaching him for his delay, asking for an explanation. But the quality of Noesis' voice, the total naturalness of his words, were enough to put him back on his feet again. He only allowed himself to ask whether his friend would be present, to which Noesis answered with a good natured reassuring laughter. Knox had every reason to feel stupid for his childish behavior. . . . Nevertheless, he broke the news to Marisa immediately, who still seemed to be much less enthusiastic about the whole thing than he was.

They met in the evening of the following day. Knox was unduly anxious to learn what impression the presence of Noesis and his friend would make on Marisa. Besides, she was eager to make that new acquaintance too. Later on he remembered, half ashamed of himself, that his conduct at that meeting, at least in its beginning, had left a great deal to be desired. . . .

It is rather difficult to put into words and describe certain experiences, especially those events for which there are no parallels in one's everyday life. Noesis introduced his friend by the name of Gynea, explaining that it meant "woman" in Greek. At first, Knox had felt somewhat disappointed, perhaps because he had expected something spectacular. Marisa appeared to be feeling just the same, but she kept observing both Noesis and Gynea with the sharp perceptiveness of a woman's eyes, which would not miss the smallest details. She spent more time examining Gynea, without becoming obvious or offensively inquisitive.

She couldn't discover anything extraordinary about Gynea as long as she concentrated on details. . . . She was about five feet six inches tall, rather slim than full, her complexion tending toward the brunette type, denoting nothing of the blond fairies of fantastic tales. She was dressed with refined taste, the elegance coming from the simplicity of her attire, without any disturbing emphasis on particular details. She wore no makeup or jewelry. Her dark hair was swept back, creating a contrast to the pale white of her skin, of very fine texture. The dominant feature in her oval face were her eyes, of a dark blue color, wide and slightly slanted, calm and quiet, but revealing depth, insight and the eagerness to absorb everything they came across. The total impact of that face could perhaps best be described as being the complete opposition or negation of that prototype of feminine beauty erected by popular magazines of Hollywood, with that exaggerated emphasis on their loud and artificial sex-appeal. Nevertheless, Marisa and also Knox—as they later commented on Gynea's appearance—had to agree that there was nothing masculine about her. The sum total of her appearance was that of a woman whose beauty was the embodiment of all her inherent values. There was another trait that set Gynea apart from the great majority of women, and that was her total unconcern with her appearance, as if she took her own beauty as something natural, not to be constantly improved with artificial means. This trait only emphasized the engaging power of her whole being, existing in freedom for its own sake. She sat on the sofa next to Noesis, her posture revealing no traces of tension or uncontrolled eagerness, without, however, showing arrogance or indifference. From her person emanated the unmistakable presence of a superior state of being, matching the same quality present in Noesis. Both Marisa and Knox had to recognize the reality of an intimate relationship existing between those two persons that needed no external signs, words or gestures, to make it more evident.

Marisa was also surprised at the absence of the usual formalities and artificialities that characterize people's behavior when first introduced to each other. There were no such trite questions as 'how do you do,' or 'how did you spend your days,' about current events, silly compliments about the other's appearance, or—worst of all—the weather. Those remarks as 'how pleased I am to meet you,' or 'I heard so much about you' would have been simply ridiculous and completely out of place. Marisa felt tempted to ask a few questions about their place of origin to convince herself that the couple was actually from a different world. Fortunately she changed her mind in time. As usual, it was Noesis who began the conversation, addressing Knox:

"Do you have your secretary with you?" Since he happened

126

to look also at Marisa, Knox thought that he was referring to her, and answered:

"I think that she accepted that role. . . ."

Noesis and Gynea immediately perceived Knox's mistake. Both of them smiled understandingly. Noesis made then clear that he had meant the memory cell. But Knox, in his eagerness and hurry had left it on his desk in the apartment. . . . He felt guilty and clumsy. Noesis took another recorder from a small bag that lay on the table. Marisa kept her eyes on it trying to discover some new thing there that would perhaps betray the origin of that very unusual couple, but to her disappointment saw only a few books and notebooks. Noesis resumed the conversation:

"I was thinking of proposing the following course in discussing our topic for today. I think that we should first spend some time in analyzing and criticizing the institution of family in your own society. That would be, so to say, part one of this session. Then we could move on to talk about our own social system based on entirely different premises. That would be part two. Perhaps there will also be a third part to deal with, the topic of the relationship between man and woman—I mean the problems of love and sex—in our society. I'm sure that this question is bound to come up too. What do you say, Edward?"

"Your plan suits me fine . . . and I think Marisa agrees too!"

"Being a newcomer in this . . . circle, my opinion should not weigh too much. But before we start, I'd like to ask a few questions, if I may? Perhaps they'll sound rather stupid, nevertheless I'll take a chance, if you don't mind."

"Don't worry about that," Gynea spoke for the first time. Her voice was even more melodious than that of Noesis. "I remember when we first visited your planet, we asked quite a few silly questions till we became better acquainted with your customs and habits."

"So you've been here before. This is not your first visit here?" Marisa asked eagerly. Gynea nodded in agreement, unwilling to go into details. So Marisa prepared her questions:

"Think what you may, but it simply surpasses the limits of my imagination to think that you people do not belong to any family at all. I was told so by Ed, you see. This would mean that you neither know nor care to find out who your father was, what kind of a person your mother was. You don't have, strictly speaking, any brothers or sisters, in-laws, relatives, genealogies. You just are, practically descending from nobody and nowhere. Doesn't that bother you?"

"Let me add a little bit more to that," Noesis said in reply. "We don't have so-called races or nationalities either."

"Oh, well, I could manage myself without those two things, but as to the family, I simply can't understand. . . ."

"It's only natural that you should think the way you do," Gynea spoke again. "As I told you already, when we first came here we didn't understand what you meant by such words as family, father, mother, brothers, sisters, and the rest of the related terms. It was very strange for us indeed. . . ."

"Excuse me if I interrupt you," interposed Noesis, "but it's my proposal that we follow up our plan as I outlined it before. I'm sure that Marisa will get her answers when we come to it, and will have enough time to ask also all the other questions she must have stocked up in her mind. I hope you understand," he added turning to Marisa. She acquiesced and sat back in her chair, waiting for Noesis to formulate his first question:

"To what causes and circumstances does the institution of family owe its origin and survival so far?" He was staring at Knox, expecting an answer from him.

"All I can think of right now is the most obvious one," Knox volunteered his remark. "It's the division of sexes, male and female, their instinctive attraction toward each other, the pleasure involved in the act of procreation. In other words, exactly the same biological pattern followed by all other higher animals. . . ."

"That's what I had expected you to say," Noesis remarked. "However, is this the whole answer or should we rather look for other reasons as well?"

"Perhaps Ed should have also mentioned the direct dependence of the female, I should rather say, of the woman. The mother and her children depend on the father, whose protection and provisions, due to his freedom from the actual burdens of procreation and his greater physical strength, offer the only security and stability for them. This creates the necessary conditions of the family unit, as the only guarantee for the survival and the care of the children. And this is the setup we still have today. Frankly, I don't see any other way of solving this problem." These were Marisa's remarks, spoken with full conviction and emphasis. Noesis followed attentively every word she said, then added:

"Perhaps you would maintain the same position also regarding the development of the patriarchal system, the emergence of the larger families, ruled by the elders, developing later into clans, then tribes and other larger social units, based on common descent?"

"That's right. Actually, this is what followed as the new stage of development, when primitive man discovered the art of agriculture and stopped being a nomadic creature, living exclusively on what nature had to offer. It was through this step that more social stability and security were achieved." Marisa apparently was taking great pleasure in exposing her knowledge in the science of anthropology.

"I do agree with you once more," Noesis said. "I'd only like to call your attention to a new circumstance or factor you introduced in your last remark, in addition to the biological facts brought up by Edward before. It's the economic element, the all powerful phenomenon in the struggle for survival, the all important need to secure the satisfaction of man's immediate and most pressing needs—food, shelter and security."

"But I did mention them, only in different words," protested Marisa.

"I know you did, but I'd like you both to go a little deeper into that and consider it in an evolutionary perspective."

"I'm certain," Gynea sided with Noesis, "that you wanted to make clear that you consider the economic factors just as significant as the biological ones. Perhaps even more significant, in terms of the evolutionary process of mankind so far."

"It's my turn to say something." Knox rose to his feet. "I think I know what Noesis is driving at. The unity and cohesion of the family ties—small or large—were directly dependent on man's pressing need and want for material values. And as long as agriculture, I mean the land or nature, was the chief source and means to procure these necessities, the family was the best institution."

"What makes you say that?" Marisa expressed her doubt again.

"Why, it's simple. Think of the ownership of the land, its all important value, the strict laws governing inheritance, and, alas, also the bloody fights needed either to defend it against aggressors or to conquer more of it when the increase in the number of the members so demanded."

"There's still another point I have to bring up, lest we forget it," Gynea remarked. "It's the role of the children. On a rather primitive stage of agricultural society, the child represented 'God's blessing' in the sense that he was looked upon not only as a new consumer to be fed, but rather as an asset, as new labor, and a cheap one too, for that matter. At a very early age—as you can see it today in the countries living on a pre-industrial level—children were used and many times abused or exploited as actual producers of more wealth. Besides, to prevent the loss of land by dividing it up among them, intermarriage or inbreeding were the order of the day. There you have also the origin for the preference given to male children and the price set on the bride. Her value was measured by so many heads of cattle. It's also a well known fact that in many countries female infants were left abandoned to starve, especially when their increase in number threatened a devaluation of their price on the market, being looked upon as simple commodities. All these examples show, I believe, that in primitive societies children were wanted chiefly for their usefulness and were considered and treated as belonging to their owners, the parents, expecially the father."

Marisa didn't like this matter of fact approach. She felt that it was too narrow, onesided and crude, leaving out the psychic, moral and spiritual aspects of family life, especially the love which should characterize the parent-child relationship. She was somewhat disappointed and wanted to raise her objections. But she decided to wait and see how things would develop. . . .

130

She would still have time to protest. Noesis pushed the conversation ahead with his next question:

"What else do we know about the next stage in the development of family life?"

"Are you referring to the onset of the scientific revolution, preparing the way for the advent of industrialization and the birth of technology?" Knox inquired.

"You guessed right. Well, what changes do you see there?"

"According to Karl Marx and his associates, industrialization brought about the large scale uprooting of the peasant folk and their necessary alienation or estrangement in the new conditions of city life. Man became a proletarian, that is, one who doesn't own anything besides the great number of his children (proles) whose lot did not improve either: both parents and children were inhumanly enslaved and exploited by the limitless greed of the capitalists. . . ." There was a tone of indignation in Knox's voice.

"Perhaps one should also add the positive values of industrialization," Noesis suggested, "insofar as it undeniably raised the standard of living not only of the exploiters, but also of the exploited. . . . Look at the socio-economic condition of a worker in a modern factory in your own country, the salary he makes, the fringe benefits he enjoys and, last but not least, the house he lives in, the car he drives and the education his children are getting. All this would have been impossible even to think of in any feudalistic society, remembering also the much lower condition of the workers in the socialistic countries run by the dictatorship of the proletariat, who supposedly own everything, except their own life and freedom. . . ."

"You don't seem to think very favorably of socialism and communism," Knox observed in a rather reserved manner.

"Did you expect us to advocate totalitarian governments?" Gynea introjected her provocative remark.

"Well, I don't know . . . I'm not quite sure . . . I couldn't tell . . ." Knox hesitated. "Are you then in favor of laissez-faire capitalism?"

"If there were no other alternatives left but the choice between

131

totalitarian government and capitalism, I certainly would prefer the latter. . . ."

"But is there a third or a fourth possibility?" It was Marisa who raised this question. "Were you thinking of the modern welfare state?"

"No, I wasn't," Noesis declared.

"Then what?" insisted Marisa. "If I see what I do see and if I interpret correctly the trend toward which the Western democracies are progressing, I think we are headed toward a more and more socialized form of economic and political organization, true?"

"While the Russians, after fifty years of costly experimentations, are reviving—very cautiously—the profit motive and free enterprise?" Noesis added rather ironically.

"I know it seems rather strange, but this is what's going on, for better or for worse . . ." Knox put down his conviction.

"You're correct as far as the diagnosis of the symptoms goes. But what about the prognosis? What do you foresee as to the future form of your social, economic and political organization?" Noesis forced the issue further.

"I'm sorry to say," Knox observed, "whether you like it or not, everything seems to indicate the final triumph of socialism over capitalism, which is on the decline anyway."

"You consider it a final triumph? But then, if it's final, evolution stops, the last stage seems to have been reached and there can be no going beyond that point."

"I don't know what could come after that, if anything, but I'm quite sure that that victory will come." Knox sounded very emphatic.

"Perhaps I have to agree with you, if for no better reason than at least in terms of the necessary stages evolution has to go through. But I wouldn't call it final, not by far!"

"What does all this discussion on politics have to do with family and children?" Marisa exclaimed impatiently.

Gynea seemed to sympathize with Marisa's remark and said: "I also think we got off the main line and purpose of our discussion. If we consider first the development of the family, especially its present state and condition, we'll have a better basis to talk about what will come after socialism had its turn on a global scale."

"Thank you, Gynea," Noesis remarked. "But allow me to answer Marisa's question." Turning toward her, he said: "There is an intimate relationship of causality between economics and family. As I already told Edward, it's necessary to realize that Bios comes before Logos."

"What does that mean?" Marisa inquired.

"What he means by it," Knox volunteered to be Noesis' interpreter, " is that all the aspects of life, even the highest states of culture, depend directly on and cannot be separated from, its roots and causes: the phenomenon of life, seen in its evolutionary perspective. Am I correct, Noesis?"

"Yes, I would have said the same thing. But coming back to the question of the family itself, as Gynea suggested, I would formulate this question: would you say that there has been a slow but steady process consisting in the loosening up of the old traditional family ties, due to the increase in the amount of freedom and independence available to the modern individual as a consequence of industrialization?"

"Suppose it is the way you put it," Marisa intervened, "but do you consider it a sign of progress? I've heard the opposite, that is, interpreted as a symptom of decadence and dissolution, a real danger, threatening the unity of the family and with that the stability of the whole social system of cultured existence."

Gynea felt that she had to make certain corrections. So she said: "Marisa, I'm afraid that you don't keep the judgments of facts separate from your judgments of value. You seem to be ready to assume a moralizing attitude, perhaps too soon, I mean, before considering the facts as they are and what they tell about themselves. If I'm not mistaken, you're implying that the closer the family ties are, the better for all concerned and vice-versa?"

"But excuse me," Marisa justified herself, "perhaps you're not aware of all the social evils, such as juvenile delinquency, drug addiction, the problems of drop-outs from schools, the spread of

133

the rebels, the beatniks, the hippies, all the harm done to the children of broken homes, and so forth. . . ."

"I think we know all that. We've seen enough of it. As a matter of fact, we all know that our friend Edward used to be, and not so long ago, a kind of a rebel. . . . However, I wouldn't say that the exclusive cause of your social evils is the disintegration of the family as a unit. Suppose I reverse your position and say that a great deal of harm is imbedded and built into the very nature of that institution? What do you say to this hypothesis? And please try to look at the facts objectively."

"Are you trying to say, in other words, that you look upon the institution of family and marriage as something bad, perhaps even evil, and the cause of all our troubles?" Marisa was really upset by this thought that offended many of her higher feelings. Gynea smiled at her excitement and replied with calm and composure:

"I can fully understand and sympathize with you, because of the novelty of these ideas. But let me hasten to add this note: we do not consider marriage and family as either bad or evil. As a matter of fact, it is the best institution you can have on your level of cultural development. We are only stating that it's neither the best nor the last step in the evolutionary process."

"I'd like to listen to your criticism of family and to learn what better solution you can offer," Marisa challenged Gynea to expound her ideas. She had gotten really worked up by that time.

"We already mentioned tonight the undignified situation of the children during the periods of agricultural societies. They were regarded and used as commodities, or, at best, objects owned for their parents' benefit, not as free, independent persons existing for their own sake. But let's turn now to the present situation and let's examine the problem from the children's point of view. Then we'll consider the blessings of happy parenthood."

"Let's hear it . . ." Marisa prompted.

"First, I'll point out the strong element of resentment that is present in all children, all appearances notwithstanding. You may recall that many of your modern psychologists, especially

134

Freud and Adler, were the first ones to document this fact clinically."

"Are you referring to the famous Oedipus and Electra complexes?"

"No, not necessarily . . . I had in mind first of all the phenomena of repressed feelings of resentment and even hatred in children against their parents, that manifest themselves in the disguised, symbolic forms of the dream work. . . . Are you ready to deny that evidence?"

"No, I wouldn't . . ." Marisa said hesitantly.

"Then ask yourself this question: what do they resent or hate? And why? Isn't their situation of physical, psychic or mental and social inferiority, dependence and helplessness what they dislike? Aren't most children always dreaming about the day when they'll be free, emancipated, on their own, independent and self-sufficient? Isn't the constant desire of every healthy child to learn as soon as possible to satisfy his own needs—to dress alone, to feed himself, to do things his own way—thus setting himself free from the painful and frustrating condition of constant subservience and obedience? Don't they always try to provoke, to defy, to disobey, to contradict? But you call them naughty, unruly, or even downright bad. . . . And one more thing, before I forget. Wouldn't you say that this drive and fight for freedom remains with every human person throughout his lifetime, discounting of course those who were made into insecure and impotent neurotics by their parents and teachers?"

"What is the main point you're developing?" Marisa asked with less antagonism, for she had to remember her own frustrations and sufferings, especially at the hands of her domineering and all-too-authoritarian, possessive father.

"It's the most important question which makes its impact felt in all aspects of human life, not in the family only. . . ."

Before Gynea could finish her statement, Knox jumped to his feet, full of enthusiasm, and cried out:

"I know what it is! It's man's quest for freedom and his constant fight for it!"

135

"It couldn't be stated in any briefer or better form," Noesis remarked, then he went on: "I would call it though the *will to freedom,* and I would regard it as more powerful a drive than the sex motive or the will to power put together. As a matter of fact, there are innumerable cases which prove that man is willing to risk and sacrifice even his life for the sake of his freedom. I'm quite positive that this is what Aristotle meant by saying that life is not worth living under any condition. And the first, the most important and the highest condition and value is that of freedom."

"What do you mean by freedom?" Marisa asked.

"Freedom is the most basic, the all-pervasive, the most powerful drive and value that makes a human being be a person, an autonomous subject, a prime mover, the only legitimate master and owner of his own existence. Freedom gives man the right to determine by his choice the contents, the direction and the meaning of his life. Man acquired an identity of his own making, an essence he himself gives to his own existence. But that involves also the freedom *from* all kinds of coercing forces, people, governments, and parents included. Thus man and freedom are coextensive."

"It's beautifully put, Noesis, and it gave me an opportunity to know you better. For my part," Knox went on, "I would venture the following corollary: I believe that if the will to freedom is man's essential attribute as a person—unlike any other object or thing—then I'd submit that the greatest and most fundamental evil is the quest for power over other persons. That's the greatest crime on earth, man's 'original sin,' if you allow me to use this expression."

"What you now have in your hands, Edward," Noesis said in a slow and measured voice, "is the one and only key you need to understand not only the truth about your past history, but also to anticipate the direction of its future evolutionary process. I'd say that evolution itself—even on the level of the biosphere, but much more so on the cultural level—is just this will to freedom, as its basic drive and force. It's only through

136

freedom that the higher and higher stages of the ascending line of life can be achieved."

"But children need a home, a mother and a father!" Marisa still objected, almost in despair. She understood the truth in her friends' remarks, but felt lost as to the problem of what to do with the children.

"What children actually need most," Gynea came to her help, "are those conditions which are best suited to satisfy their needs, physical, mental and social. Let me add that I'm not sure whether every so-called mother or father is really qualified to provide such conditions. I'll remind you only of the many harms done to children first of all by their ill-qualified parents. Look for the evidence in any standard text on child-psychology."

"Then you're implying," commented Marisa, "that not everybody is qualified to become a parent!"

"And I mean it in the full sense of what your remark implies. Not everybody is qualified bio-genetically and/or psychologically to procreate. By the latter I mean their mental health, their personal qualities and the inevitable impact on the child who is helplessly delivered to the influence of whatever adult happens to be, by sheer chance, perhaps his future executioner."

"You sound awful . . . I mean too tragic and pessimistic!" Marisa criticized Gynea's opinion. "You wouldn't allow, for anything in the world, would you, that there are at least some persons who're well qualified to procreate and to rear their own children! Would you rather take the children away from their legitimate parents by force? Nobody has or can claim to have such a right! Is this the outcome of the glorification of freedom I've heard just a while ago from Noesis' mouth?"

"You said a lot of things, Marisa," Noesis answered seriously. "And you implied much more, including a few hidden accusations. I'll try to correct the wrong impression we might have given you."

"Yes, I'd like to hear what you've got to say in your own defense!"

"If I understood Gynea's remarks correctly, she didn't imply that nobody is qualified to be a parent. Probably she meant that only a few are qualified, which means that the majority isn't. And that means also that much more harm than good is done on your earth through the institution of family to the coming generations. This becomes even more evident if you consider what I already discussed with Edward, namely, the creation of the conditions which will make the coming of the superior man possible and real. Procreation should not be limited simply to producing a new life. One should also think of the quality of the life one wants to procreate. Do you understand me so far?"

"I think I do, though it sounds discriminatory and anti-democratic."

"Then let me tell you the rest of what I have to say: Gynea didn't mean to suggest or imply that children should be taken away by force from their parents. In fact, Edward could tell you a lot about this point. We discussed already the problem of genetics, so I won't repeat that again. Besides, I'm convinced that parenthood as such doesn't confer instant holiness and perfection to anyone who happens to have a child. There's too much sentimentality and groundless glorification in the moral and religious image of parenthood. The facts, however, are different and they point to the opposite direction. Finally, I think that you share the conviction of the many who believe that the children belong to their parents."

"To whom do they belong then, if not to them . . .? To a collective, perhaps, to a party, to the government, to everybody else, except the parents, right?"

"Wrong!"

"Then I don't know what to think any more!"

"Why don't you rather say the only thing which makes sense: every human being—children included—belongs to himself only. He exists for his own sake."

"You do realize, don't you, that you're proposing and defending the most radical and ruthless form of egoism or selfishness. Your position is devoid of any trace of concern for others, the people at large, and mankind as a whole!"

"I knew you'd say that. . . . You had to. . . . You were raised and fed on the creed of the altruistic gospel."

"Then you are defending egoism?"

"Yes, I am, but neither a radical nor a ruthless one."

"Explain yourself!"

"I'm quite willing to oblige. In fact, the ideas I'm proposing are not new. Many of your philosophers expressed their conviction that man is a free, autonomous subject, a person, not a thing. Man is a value in himself, wanted for his own sake, not to be subordinated to anything or anyone else, to be used a means for the attainment of some other goal but his own perfection and happiness. For this same reason, slavery was condemned and abolished as an institution that deprives man of his dignity as a free person, as a moral subject, who exists for his own sake and belongs to himself only. The only difference between their position and my own is that, while proposing these ideas, they still claimed some supernatural and ultimate frame of reference, whereas I believe that there is no need to go beyond the natural knowledge of man's identity as a person."

"I still don't see where egoism fits into this picture . . ." Marisa said.

"But it's simple! Egoism, self-love and related terms express in different words the implications of the fact that man exists for his own sake. The pursuit of his own happiness is his most fundamental right and objective. Perhaps, I should also say that every act of the living is self-contained, self-directed, private and performed for the exclusive benefit of the organism. The same truth applies also to man's psychic activities. For example, you can't breathe for me, just as I can't think, learn, choose and act for you. All these acts must be of necessity performed by the individual person alone and for his own benefit. In one word, Marisa, nobody can live your life for you or in your stead. You'll never find your own self and the meaning of your life in somebody else. These things are self-contained, your life is yours alone and can never become somebody else's. It's not outside you, it's within you. Do you understand the meaning of my words?"

"I guess I'll have to do some thinking on this. I confess we've always been taught that one finds his own true self in others,

I mean, when one dedicates oneself or even sacrifices one's goals for the sake of others. Self-love has always been presented to us as something base and immoral, whereas the love of our neighbors was extolled as the *non-plus-ultra* of virtue incarnate. But, tell me, in what way does this apply to the situation of children in the family?"

"Doesn't everybody refer to children as born egoists, devoid of any concern with others? Doesn't the child always act on the premise of his own wants, desires and pleasures? Don't parents and teachers always complain about the hard work and patient persistence needed to teach children how to 'share,' to become considerate of others, to conform, to submit and obey? You may consider these efforts on the part of the adults as beneficial for the child. Certainly, but I have to point out also the hidden and unconfessed motives behind their efforts to domesticate, to civilize and to educate them, which is not at all beneficial for them."

"I guess you must have some unkind things in your mind," Marisa remarked.

"I can't help it for the time being, if you look upon me as an individual who is prejudiced against family and parents. I only hope that you'll come to a better insight later on. It's neither resentment nor hatred which makes me defend the position I hold. It's my respect for truth as represented by the facts of life. Now as to those hidden motives, I call your attention to the most significant ones only, that is, the parents' unconfessed desire to rule, dominate and possess or own their children. The best way to achieve their will to power is to brand egotism as immoral, to dress up so-called unselfishness as a virtue in the name of the fourth commandment, to capitalize on the children's dependent situation, to make them feel guilty for the mere fact of their existence, being forced to accept their parents' sacrifices, who, incidentally, like to adorn themselves with the virtues of self-sacrifice, in order to have a right to claim later on the same thing from their children. But that cannot be done! It never works!"

"What makes you so sure of that?"

"The facts and the results teach me that. Let's have the courage to look into them and see what the parents and other persons in authority, I mean all those who hold power over other persons, accomplish. They accomplish only one thing. They succeed in creating through their efforts the fac-simile or the carbon copy of their own image. They force those children to become little hypocrites, to develop the art of lying, hiding and cheating, in order to give the semblance of what they are supposed and expected to do. Children know very well that they are helplessly delivered to the privileged situation of the adults for quite a number of years and that disobedience means only punishment, not only psychic frustrations, but also physical pain. . . . All the while, however, they know, without having the courage to confess it to themselves, that it's resentment and hatred that they actually feel toward their parents, and can't wait for the hour when they can slam the door of their sweet homes for good. You never heard of such things before? You never saw such things really happen? Parents would learn a great deal about the true situation if they could hear all that which children say about them when out of their sight and reach."

"In other words, you would not allow for a relationship of true love between parent and child?" Marisa fell back again on her old question.

Gynea had kept silent so far, watching the development of the whole situation. She knew that Noesis would welcome a break, therefore she took over.

"Have you ever asked yourself the question of what love means and what are the necessary conditions for it to become real, not just a romantic longing for the unreachable?" She addressed her question to Marisa mainly.

"Well, you love your parents simply because they're your parents, and they love their children for the same reason. . . ."

"Why don't you also say that you love your parents because you were told that you're supposed to, it's your sacred obligation, your foremost duty, the first virtue you must have in the name of filial piety? And that similar obligations befall also the parents, regarding their children, which means that one loves out of sheer obligation, because one has to?"

141

"Well, I don't see anything wrong with that either!" Marisa snapped back self-righteously.

"In that case, allow me to point out the contradiction and the psychological impossibility of paradox present in your position." Gynea continued.

"You're giving me the impression that whatever I think or feel makes no sense, that in your eyes I'm primitive, ignorant and even stupid. That it's only your privilege to know the truth and everybody else, me in particular, is necessarily wrong!" Marisa couldn't control herself and her remarks sounded rather offensive.

Knox became really worried as to the final outcome of his painful situation, fearing also its consequences for the whole undertaking. He felt that he must try to correct the situation, so he said to Marisa:

"I don't think, Marisa, that we came together for the purpose of exchanging accusations and offending our friends. I don't think that you have any reason or right to become disagreeable simply because you happen to disagree with certain ideas. I'd suggest, therefore, that we assume a more rational attitude, not burdening Noesis and Gynea with our emotions. And I mean no offense to you by saying this. It's . . . It's embarrassing, you know. . . ."

"I'm sorry, Ed, but there's only so much one can take . . . I hate to be made to feel stupid! If you want me to, I'll leave."

Noesis perceived the bad turn in their conversation, and he hurried to remedy the situation:

"Edward, if you think that we are or feel offended, don't worry about that. In fact, we're not, for we undestand why Marisa feels as she does." He sounded sincere and reconciliatory. There was no trace of artificial affectation or simple acting in his manner, and that was enough to disarm his opponent. Then he added: "Let's go back to our problem, if we may. . . ."

Knox was very anxious to see things normalized again, so he agreed to this enthusiastically and said:

"I think Gynea wanted to lead us to the insight that feelings cannot be forced or dictated, that it's a contradiction to say

142

that one loves only out of duty and responsibility. There must be something else to such a feeling. Right, Gynea?"

"What would you say that 'something else' is?" Gynea asked.

"They must be the conditions that make love possible."

"Such as?"

"Let me see: First of all, you must be a person of a certain kind. . . ."

"What 'certain kind' are you thinking of?"

"I mean a person of certain qualities, both physical and psychic."

"You mean the possession of definite values?"

"Yes!"

"But which is man's highest value?"

"In the light of what we've discussed so far—and I happen to agree with all of it—it must be freedom, as man's highest perfection."

"In other words, freedom is the first condition for love. There can be no such thing as forced, demanded or imposed love, and you cannot claim it as a duty."

"That makes sense!"

"Then love and freedom are almost the same thing. Love is by its very nature free, but not in the sense it is understood by the promoters of licence!"

"I have to agree once more."

"Then let's put the pieces together and draw our conclusions," Gynea suggested. "The conditions for love are only two—the presence of values in a person and freedom."

"Yes, that's true. But how can this be applied to the parent-child relationship?"

"Love between parents and children can arise and develop only if the condition of freedom is present. However, the fact remains that neither the parents nor the children are free from each other. Both live in a situation of mutual dependence. It's a form of glamorized slavery. But no slave truly loves his master, neither does the master admire and respect his slaves. He just owns them."

"But this situation of mutual dependence belongs to the very

143

nature of the family as an institution!" Knox remarked with astonishment.

"Draw your own conclusions," Gynea invited him to proceed.

"You want me to say that the family as an institution must go?"

"Not right away, for you lack something better to replace it. Unless you favor a total communal reorganization of society which would lead to universal slavery where everybody belongs to everybody else and nobody is free to be and to belong to himself."

"No, I wouldn't like to see that happen! But then what?"

"The only possible thing that can be done at this stage of your socio-economic development is to liberalize the institution as much as possible."

"What would you do toward such a liberalization? What steps would you take?"

"A lot can be done right now, if we try to educate the parents, teaching them the ideas we have proposed so far, thus qualifying them to assume the true and right attitude toward their children."

"I see that we're going to consider the parents' side now and their condition and relation toward their children."

"Not only that. First of all we should say something on the meaning of marriage, then on procreation and only after that consider the parents' proper attitude toward the offspring."

"I go along with your proposal, since we've said already a great deal about the last topic. So let's start with marriage. I meant to ask you whether you're married or not? I know that you don't have families as we have it here, but that doesn't exclude the possibility of being married. As you know, we have many childless couples even on earth." Since Knox addressed this question to Noesis, he replied:

"No, I'm not married, neither is Gynea, nor is anybody else in our own world."

"But what do you have instead? There must be something?"

"Remember, Edward," Noesis remarked, "that we agreed to leave the discussion of our own way of life for last. So be patient for a while. . . . As for yourself, I know that you're a bachelor and am I correct in assuming that Marisa is single too?"

144

"Yes, I'm single . . ." Marisa broke her long silence, while she kept on sulking.

"May I also ask whether you intend to get married? I know that this question is a personal one, but perhaps we can look at it 'philosophically,' shall we say?"

"I can speak only for myself," Knox replied. "To tell you the truth, I'm not decided to go either way as yet. . . . There are many pros and cons, and I haven't hit the right balance."

"The reason I asked this personal question is because we were amazed at first seeing how many very young people, even before they reach legal age, seem to be in a hurry to rush into the state of married life, especially the girls."

"There are a few exceptions, you know," Marisa remarked ruefully. "And if the majority of girls appear to be anxious to get married, that's not altogether their fault, if we're to look upon such a decision as a fault."

"I'd like to learn how you think on this problem," Gynea said invitingly. There was no hint or trace of uneasiness on her part.

"I had in mind the general situation of the woman in our society. Our identity is equated with our sex only. We're regarded as females, as potential wives and mothers. . . . Our place in life was assigned to be the bedroom, the nursery and the kitchen. Of course it's beautified, glamorized and embellished beyond proportion. We're given the impression that a woman can find her personal fulfillment only in marriage and through her children. And it's even more offensive when they refer to the man as the head, the mind, while to be a woman stands for the heart, as if we were mindless females only. . . . We're also told that 'anatomy is destiny,' that we can never rise above our ovaries and uterus, that our whole being is destined to be only a means to procreate. . . . I don't know much about the situation in other countries, but right here only a small percentage of girls get a higher education—college I mean—and much fewer go on to graduate studies to obtain professional training. Even those who do, sooner or later, usually sooner, give up their dreams about a career and degenerate into diapers. . . . Their only reading seems to be women's magazines, the literature on happy home-

145

making, and the bible of young mothers, the books on baby care. It follows that we still look upon an unmarried woman with the same old prejudice of former generations, as an old maid, a spinster, and the subject of suspicion and ridicule. . . . Add to it that all the agents and manipulators of the feminine cult identify a woman's worth with her looks and measurements. The mind is either not mentioned at all or if it's there, it should be kept decently hidden. They suggest that femininity, the ideal of womanhood, goes hand in hand with ignorance and shallow sentimentalism. They even forgive our hysteria and discount it as a matter of fact. . . . Because, they say, we're ruled by our hormones and maternal instincts. Finally, consider the double standard of morality, one code for men, a different and stricter one for women. Then you have, in a rough outline, the full picture of the problem. Is it any wonder that our girls are so eager and willing to get married, the marriage certificate being their only and the best life-insurance policy, signed by the generous male-society?"

"You sound very critical, even disillusioned and bitter . . ." Knox remarked timidly.

"Well, since everybody here insisted on intellectual integrity and honesty, I thought I'd put down my own contribution. But I don't like it, even though it's true."

"Truth and feelings are not necessarily coextensive," Noesis remarked. "Truth can be also an unpleasant revelation about the negative aspects of life. Nevertheless, it's always to be preferred to evasions and beautiful lies."

"But if we keep on looking always straight into the facts of reality, one ends up by losing one's cherished beliefs, illusions, hopes, one after the other. . . . Despair and nausea, perhaps even nihilistic pessimism and anarchy are the results, and these round off one's total existential bankruptcy," Marisa complained.

"I still maintain that it's better and wiser to live in reality than outside of it. Besides, disease doesn't necessarily equal death, if there are means to cure it. However, the first condition of successful treatment is a thorough diagnosis, no matter how serious and gruesome it appears to be at first sight. Consequently, I wouldn't give up all hopes and resign to the inevitable."

"What are the things which give you the right to believe?" Knox insisted.

"Well, with regard to the condition of woman in countries you're not familiar with, I have reasons to say that the process of emancipation is very promising. The percentage of women holding professional jobs—in medicine, engineering and research —is much higher than in your country. The majority of working women here hold only service jobs as factory workers, office secretaries and teachers. In this respect you're trailing behind, because of the undue emphasis put on the blessings of marriage, family and children. But it's not a final stage and as everything else, is bound to change."

"In fact it's already changing, though very slowly in our own country too," Knox remarked with enthusiasm. "There are more girls in our institutions of higher learning than ever before, and that trend is bound to keep up and continue. But let's go back to the business of marriage. . . . I'd like to hear your objections and criticisms, Noesis."

"I'll be glad to state them. Then you'll say what you think of my views. Let me start, as usual, with a question, and I'm sure that I can expect an honest answer."

"Formulate your question," Knox readied himself in expectation.

"If someone succeeded in taking a nationwide poll of the married people, asking them whether they had found in marriage the promised fulfillment of their desire for happiness, whether they still would want to get married or to stay that way, if they were given another chance, what do you think the statistics would prove?"

"I can't give you the exact percentage, of course," Knox answered, "but I'd say that, according to what I've seen, observed and read about this problem, far more than fifty or sixty percent of the married people would have to answer in the negative."

"I don't think yours is a wild guess," Marisa interposed, "especially if you look into the available statistics. The rate of divorce,

147

for example, is increasing year after year. They say that one out of every four—now it could be even every third—marriages ends in divorce. That's already one third of all those who are or were married. Add to this all the cases of separation, not recorded statistically and also those who would get a divorce were it not for their moral-religious beliefs or the number of children they procreated and have to support, and, finally, the similarly unrecorded cases of adultery, then you could safely increase your percentage to sixty or seventy percent."

"Independently of statistics," Knox continued the same trend of thought, "a close observation of the true picture of the husband-wife relationship, in itself, is a rich source for further insights. With the passing of the years in their married state, along with the increase in the number of their children, there seems to be just the opposite of so-called happiness and bliss. Most of the time, their relationship is only tolerated with unconfessed resentment, for not being a wanted or welcome companionship. The frequency of their conflicts, quarrelings, suspicions, mutual blamings and accusations appear to be the order of the day. The upsurge in the demand for marriage counselors, social workers, etc., indirectly substantiates the same point. I often wonder why? Is it a necessary outcome, something built into the very nature of the institution of marriage as such, or, perhaps, it's due to man's wrong attitude, the lack of proper preparation and knowledge, or what? What do you think, Noesis?"

"I wouldn't try to find the answer in the direction of man's ignorance on the subject. Walk into any bookstore or library and you'll be amazed by the number of books on the market dealing with this problem. In fact, you find at least one book on any conceivable aspect of the married life. One to be read before you get married, a second for the success of your honeymoon, a third to increase your bedroom efficiency, a fourth on how to make your later married years a success, a fifth on sex after sixty-five. I even saw in a record shop an album with the following title: 'How to Strip Before Your Husband.' Therefore, the problem must lie somewhere else. Perhaps Gynea wants to say something too."

"It's all right, if you wish to hear my opinion. First, referring to the abundance of literature on marriage, I have the impression that most of the books deal mainly with the more prurient aspects of marriage, I mean with sex. The authors and the publishers seem to be concerned solely with the number of copies to be sold. That must be the reason for their appeal to the sexually excited imagination of the readers, building up romantic hopes and unfulfillable promises. To that extent, they do more harm than good."

"That's true," Knox remarked casually.

"Then I'll come to the main point," Gynea continued. "I believe that the institution of marriage is such that, no matter how much you read on it, how well you prepare yourself for it, how carefully you choose your partner, it brings along the amount of frustration and boredom built into that arrangement."

"I'd appreciate it if you spoke in more concrete terms," Marisa said.

"I was going to . . . Let's take the causes responsible for the failure of marriage one by one. In the first place, I call your attention to the amount of man's ignorance and naiveté. No amount of study will suffice to eliminate the element of risk and gambling involved even in the most careful and best reasoned choices. There's no way to foresee or to predict how, when and in what way the human person will change his mode of thinking, feeling, his preferences and tastes, his future behavior. And changes must occur, because any living being, by virtue of his own nature, is in a constant process of development. Total stability and stagnation—the image of unchangeability—runs contrary to the law of life. That's my first point."

"Suppose I agree with you," Marisa said, "but then it follows that no one can trust anybody and there's no such thing as a lasting relationship of any kind, the stability of which would be based upon firm principles and values. It would also follow that mutual mistrust and suspicion should be the normal state of things. But that would destroy the very possibility of any human association, it would wreck the very foundation of the whole social system. . . ."

"Your difficulty is very well expressed, and it seems to be logical too. Nevertheless, I wouldn't draw the conclusions you did, for the following reasons: I think that whenever we appeal to somebody's confidence, or when we speak of how much others can trust us, we're trying to look for some guarantee, some security or insurance. We don't hesitate to think of it even in terms of a whole lifetime commitment, as it happens in marriage, till death separates the partners, perhaps too late. . . . But there are no such leak-proof guarantees in reality, as the evidence from the statistics discussed before proves it. I think that to ask for somebody's lifelong loyalty, faithfulness or consistency, we're asking for something of which man is not capable. All the amount of hypocrisy, faking, lying and cheating gives sufficient evidence of this. It's no use to moralize and sermonize by branding it immoral, sinful, base and what not. One's goals should never be placed beyond one's reach and grasp. Besides, consider this further point; it's very important, I believe. The claim or the demand we put on somebody's lifelong loyalty amounts to the loss and sacrifice of one's freedom. Isn't this, I ask you, the cause and the source of the most frequent complaints, resentments and hostilities among married couples? We agreed tonight that the will to freedom is man's highest and most cherished value, belonging to his very identity as a person. This is the reason also for the amount of fear, hesitation and indecision that characterizes the state of mind of the partners during the period of their engagement, debating whether to get married or to stay single, especially in the case of men. To be bound for a lifetime to another person, to one person only, even if it be a superior type of individual, is the negation of freedom. A golden cage is still a prison. . . ."

"But it's not so bad and awful," Marisa tried to defend her position. "And should it become unbearable, well, there's still the possibility to regain one's freedom through separation or divorce."

"Only to repeat the same mistake all over again, going through a second, even a third divorce. This would appear rather comical, you know, were it not also tragic, because of the children who're damaged by this constant change of the partners. Wouldn't

150

it be much wiser and practical, if people—knowing all the risks and losses involved in a lifetime commitment—rather abstained from such a dangerous move for their own benefit?"

"If everyone went along with your daring suggestion, no children could be born, and the human race would die out in one generation . . ." Marisa objected again.

"Such a thing could only happen on the assumption that children can be born and raised only within the bonds of marriage and family."

"But that's our situation!"

"Which is not ours. But, obeying Noesis' wish, we'll come to that at the end of our discussion."

"Are there any other objections you'd like to present?" Knox stepped in.

"Yes, I have. So far I've mentioned only three, that is, man's ignorance, his changing personality and character throughout his lifetime, and the loss of his freedom. The other objections refer to the fallacies in the justifications put forth for the defense of marriage."

"Such as?"

"The best known of all is the worn cliché that one gets married in order to find in it or through it one's personal fulfillment and identity. It's just another form of what we've already mentioned, under the name of otherdirectedness or something similar. We also pointed out that it's sheer nonsense, because it's simply impossible for any person to find his self-contained self in somebody else. It's just not there!"

"Granted that such a thing cannot happen," Knox spoke up again. "On the other hand, you wouldn't go so far as to deny that we're social beings and through social intercourses—whatever forms they may assume—we do learn, gain and also offer some values in return to others, by exchanging and sharing our ideas when communicating them. For instance, I have to acknowledge that right now and throughout these meetings I've gained a lot of insight myself."

"But you don't really want to equate this kind of association and relationship with marriage?" Noesis commented.

151

"No, I wasn't trying to do that. I just wanted to point to the obvious similarities, that's all."

"I'd say that sometimes—such as in the present case—the differences are much more significant than the similarities. I mean to say, first, that our relationship is based on the free agreement of all participants. Second, it's only a temporary arrangement, and not a commitment for the rest of our days. If it had been of such a nature—no offense meant—I wouldn't have entered it at all! It would, of necessity, become boring for everyone. The third and most important point I want to make is the type of the relationship. Unlike in marriage, nobody is limited to the resourcefulness of one person only, especially now that we have Gynea and Marisa present."

"I don't quite understand how this last remark of yours is related to marriage in any way . . ." Knox said.

"I wanted to call your attention to one more objection against marriage. I'm sure Gynea would have mentioned it herself, had I not interrupted her. The point in question is that in the monogamic marriage—polygamy being ruled out by law and non-existent, at least in legalized form—one individual man is bound to one individual woman . . . for good!"

"Excuse me, Noesis, for interrupting you again, but tell me, is the reason for your objection against monogamy the fact that it rules out—at least officially—sexual promiscuity? Perhaps my question sounds somewhat silly. . . ."

Noesis and Gynea exchange a rapid glance and smiled at Knox's question. Then Noesis resumed his explanation pleasantly:

"Your question wasn't silly, but it tells us a lot about the way you look upon sex. We'll discuss that in due time. However, let me assure you that we're not advocates of indiscriminate sex at all. On the other hand, we don't share all the taboos on this matter. Besides, we don't put such a tremendous emphasis on it as you do. But more of this later on. When I referred a minute ago to the limitations involved in monogamy, I had in mind, first and foremost, psychic and personal limitations."

"I wish you were more specific. I still can't understand you."

"Of course. Let me put it this way. You'll agree with me that

152

every individual as an individual, a single and only one representative of his species, is limited in his dispositions, powers, abilities and knowledge. He possesses only a small portion of the total perfections belonging to human nature taken as a whole, true?"

"That's true indeed . . ." Knox asserted.

"It follows then that if one individual is tied to another individual for the rest of his life, he becomes short-changed and cut off from partaking in the values proper to other individuals."

"Sorry, Noesis, but I have to disagree for these reasons. A married man or woman is not prevented from having social intercourse with others, as a matter of fact, most people do. Besides, they can assimilate the values of the other individuals through learning, education, reading and what not."

"This is so. But I had something else in mind."

"What? Since it's not sex, what else could it be?"

"It's the same idea of limitation, necessarily leading to boredom. Let me give you an example and use it only as an analogy. What is your favorite dish, Edward, the one you like best of all?"

"Well, I'm not a gourmet, but let's assume it's roast-beef."

"Fine. Now try to imagine that from now on, till the hour of your death, you'll have to be eating roast-beef for breakfast, lunch and dinner, for snacks or any other occasion. Nothing else but roast-beef, always, all the time, with no exception, day after day, year in, year out. . . . Could you take it?"

"I'd rather starve! The very idea makes me shudder!"

"Which means that at first you'd love it, then you'd like it, then you'd just tolerate it, then you'd get bored and fed up with it, then you'd start hating it, till the very sight of it would drive you out of your mind. . . . As you said, you'd rather starve at that point."

"You're not trying to equate people with roast-beef, are you?"

"No, I'm not, but I still have to insist on the truth contained in this analogy. Let me ask you this: don't you ever get 'fed up' with people? Don't you ever get used to them to the point where you get tired of them? Have you never felt that their simple presence is a burden to you? Never got bored and nauseated, felt like running away? Not so long ago you were downright sick of them, even though you weren't tied to them by any solemn oath or vow. . . . You ran away from your group and you preferred to be alone, left alone, not to be bothered. You learned the value of loneliness and you began to love it. Solitude was welcome as a much needed refuge and relief. And, mind you, there were many whom you couldn't stand, not only one single individual."

"That's true. I'm not going to deny it. However, would you say that this should also apply to marriage?"

"I wish you took that secret poll we spoke of a while ago to convince yourself. But if you keep your eyes open and observe what's going on in the lives of married people—although a great deal of it is carefully hidden from public sight—you'll learn a great deal more."

"Aren't you generalizing again?" Knox insisted stubbornly.

"The limitation of the individual is a universal phenomenon. The psychological phenomenon described before—ignorance, fear, resentment, will to freedom and boredom—are also true, because they are dictated by the laws of our own nature. Therefore, if I'm generalizing, I'm doing it on the grounds of the evidence available. Let me add this one more point, lest I forget it. Since every individual is bound to be with his own self every minute of his conscious life, he gets bored even with himself rather often, doesn't he?"

"Yes, he does, unfortunately."

"Then he starts wanting to escape and runs away from his own self, hoping to find some boredom-chaser, other people, who're equally bored with themselves, and all sorts of pleasures, especially those which reduce one's level of self-awareness."

"Then what's your final conclusion regarding marriage? Do you condemn it altogether?"

"I'm afraid I have to!"

"Even if you do that, you still haven't found a solution for boredom. You can't get rid of your own boring self."

"I'd like to make clear that the amount of boredom varies from one individual to the next, depending on their intelligence and ability to provide a life program for themselves, I mean activities that yield some lasting value, meaning and pleasure. Such people are far less bored than the others who're not capable of this. At any rate, I'd still prefer to be bored and have my freedom than be bored together and being tied to another's boredom. It's against man's will to freedom."

"No doubt, there is something in what you say, but I'll have to do some thinking on it before I draw my own conclusions."

"Please do that . . ." Noesis said almost indifferently. He didn't seem to be eager or anxious to get people's agreement or to force his views on them.

There was a rather long silence, following Noesis' remark. Marisa took this opportunity to make a practical suggestion. Apparently, she had gotten bored either with herself or with the others. Perhaps even both. . . .

"I'd like to suggest that we continue our conversation next time when we meet again. . . ." She sounded tired and rather disappointed.

"But we haven't discussed the parents' attitude toward their children as we had planned. . . ." Knox protested, seemingly anxious to keep on the conversation.

"It's very late again, Edward, and I believe we ought to accept Marisa's suggestion and break up today's meeting. Would you like to have something to eat before you leave?"

"Please, don't inconvenience yourselves," Marisa hurried to prevent any further delay in their leaving. She got up from her chair and added: "We'll be home in no time. Unless Edward would prefer to have something. . . ."

Knox thought it wouldn't be wise to go against Marisa's wish to leave, so he followed her example. Getting up from his seat, he reached for the memory cell and put it in his pocket. By this time also Gynea and Noesis got to their feet. They extended their hands in a silent greeting.

155

CHAPTER EIGHT

CHILDREN ARE INDIVIDUALS,
THEY BELONG TO THEMSELVES
PROBLEMS OF LOVE AND SEX

Leaving the hotel, Marisa and Knox stepped back into their own world, made by their own kind, after their own image. It must have been very late, close to daybreak. The streets were empty and deserted. The world was sleeping off the burdens of the day, gathering strength for a new round in the fight for . . . what? For their lives, whatever that term meant or could mean. Only the bright patches of the street lights kept silent watch over the nothing enveloped in darkness. Nothing stirred, moved or lived, everything was reduced to a deadly standstill. The monotonous sound of their footsteps, hitting the cold cement of the sidewalks, was echoed by the walls of the buildings, as they filed past them, one by one. Empty windows stretched toward the sky, rectangular holes of darkness, reflecting nothing and saying less. The cars parked on both sides of the street told nothing about themselves or their owners. They were lined up, one behind the other, ready to obey the will and the whims of their drivers, who would be starting them in a few hours. Here and there a turned-over trash-can could be seen, its contents spilled on the side-walk. People called this 'refuse,' perhaps because of their desire to refuse the trash that filled up their own lives. A cab dashed by, rushing some latecomer to an unknown destination for untold purposes. The traffic lights alternated with mechanical regularity and uniformity—green, yellow, red, back to green again. But there was nobody to warn, to direct, to stop

157

or to guide. Its simple existence at the intersection seemed meaningless, almost absurd. From a distance, the shrill and nervous sound of a screaming siren could be heard, coming, who knows, from a police car, an ambulance or a fire-engine, filling, for a few moments, the void of silent nothingness, then swallowed by the distant darkness.

They had been walking silently side by side for more than a quarter of an hour. Knox offered Marisa the protection and security of his arm, but she took no notice of it. Both of them felt the oppressing weight of the absence of words, heightened by the depressing sight of the dead city, but neither could bring themselves to talk. With every passing minute the tension of their uneasiness mounted, the strain reaching the point of becoming almost intolerable. Knox was desperately searching his mind for something to say, to start a conversation, to ask Marisa's opinion about what they had just experienced, but the fear of something he couldn't pinpoint inhibited him. He wasn't ready, or perhaps couldn't face the obvious conclusion that their meeting at Noesis' apartment had been a complete failure, at least with regard to Marisa. He had hoped and expected that she would immediately be won over to their side and become an enthusiastic advocate of their cause. But apparently he'd been wrong. Everything in her rigid, reserved, almost hostile attitude revealed the very opposite. Perhaps, he thought, he had overestimated Marisa's intelligence, her ability and readiness to face new ideas. He reluctantly admitted to himself that he regretted having taken her to Noesis's place. After all, the ideas they had debated that night were true and had contained nothing offensive or personal. Maybe he should have prepared Marisa not to expect anything spectacular. Or was Marisa too narrow-minded, too conservative in spite of everything, unwilling to give up certain of her, perhaps secretly cherished beliefs and opinions. Noesis had dissected and analyzed them until they appeared as obviously futile and valueless, yet Marisa clung to them obstinately. Maybe her difficulty was rather emotional than rational, Knox went on musing to himself. But why? What emotional block or complexes prevented her from seeing the truth? Was there some resentment or fear or a sense of loss, or what? He couldn't tell. And it wouldn't be prudent to pry into her feelings now. This wasn't the time or the place. So he kept on walking silently at her side.

Fortunately he spotted a taxi parked at the corner. The driver was dozing when Knox called him. They got into the cab, and after a short while they were at Marisa's apartment building. He told the cabbie to wait, while he helped Marisa out of the car. He wanted desperately to say something, but the only words he managed to utter were:

"I'll call you up tomorrow."

"Do that, if you want to. . . ." She turned abruptly and walked up the entrance steps of the building lobby. Knox waited till she disappeared into the elevator. Then he gave his address to the driver. He anticipated with pleasure the prospect of a long sleep.

He must have slept for many long hours, for it was late in the afternoon when he regained consciousness. The first thing that came to his mind was last night. An uneasy feeling took hold of him at once. The thought of Marisa's strange behavior both disquieted and irritated him, and he resented his loss of tranquility. Marisa had stolen his peace of mind. She had destroyed the quiet joy he had gained from his work and lonely walks. He knew that he needed all his time and energy to cope with his work, and that could be accomplished only if his old disposition of calm and undisturbed state of mind returned to him. It was this selfish concern that made him reach for the phone. He wanted to put an end to this condition of uncertainty, face reality, whatever it might be, get this problem out of his way at any cost.

Marisa must have been up already, for she answered the phone right away. She agreed to come to Knox's apartment without asking any further questions. Apparently she had been waiting for his call, and was anxious to talk to him. In less than half an hour she was there, seated in his room, watching him straighten up the place and to make himself a much wanted breakfast, late in the afternoon.

"If you're ready to talk," Marisa started, "you could start by telling me why you called me over?"

"I wanted you to start the editing and typing . . . if you didn't change your mind," Knox remarked carefully.

"What makes you assume that I changed my mind?"

"Well, to tell you the truth, I had the impression that you weren't very impressed with my friends last night. Perhaps you expected something different?"

"That has nothing to do with my work. . . ." Marisa retorted evasively.

"I realize that, but still. . . ."

"It takes something away from its beauty, is that it?"

"No, it's not a matter of beauty. It's rather the psychological disposition you'll need to do it with pleasure and satisfaction."

"My English won't be any more or less efficient, regardless of whether I like what I edit or not. . . ."

"That's true again . . . but there's no reason to do something unless you really enjoy doing it, especially since it's not a question of money."

"In other words, you don't want me to do it. That's what you're trying to get to so cautiously. Isn't that right, Edward?"

"I wasn't thinking of that, Marisa."

"Not yet, but you might. . . . Perhaps you can find someone who'd have the right psychological motivation. Perhaps Gynea should be the one to do it, because she's better qualified, due to her superior intelligence and other things like that."

"What . . . what are you talking about?" Knox asked genuinely puzzled. Then he said, rather to himself than to Marisa: "Oh . . . I see. . . . Now I understand. . . . Everything seems to fall into its proper place. . . . I see!"

"What's that tremendous insight you've just gained?" Marisa inquired in a measured tone.

"It's not tremendous at all. As a matter of fact, it's very simple! I should've thought of it right then and there."

"What do you mean. . . .? Don't play the mysterious omniscient! I had quite a share of that kind of stuff anyway! Say it!" Marisa was becoming more and more nervous and agitated.

"Are you sure you won't blow your top if I say what I think?"

"Yes, I'm sure. . . . Go ahead!"

"Number one: I think that you weren't favorably impressed by them, especially Gynea."

Marisa had to control herself not to jump to her feet and start screaming at the top of her lungs. She held herself back by clutching the arms of her chair. The tendons on her hands were distended by the effort she made, her lips twitching and trembling. Knox went on:

"Number two: you disliked most of the ideas you heard, though you couldn't prove them wrong."

"Is there a number three?" Marisa asked almost inaudibly.

"Yes, there is. . . . Number three: since you couldn't refute those ideas, the reasons behind your disagreement must be purely emotional. . . ."

In spite of her promise, Marisa couldn't take Knox's remarks any longer. She jumped to her feet and cried, on the verge of tears:

"In other words, I'm a stupid, hysterical, jealous bitch!"

Knox kept his calm and composure and added: "My dear Marisa, you're somewhat stupid, somewhat hysterical and also somewhat jealous. But not a bitch. Just a woman. Perhaps even a woman in love, that's all."

Marisa regained some of her self-control and went on in a more sedate tone:

"So I'm stupid. . . ."

"I meant only your present performance."

"And hysterical. . . ."

"Not always, just now."

"And jealous. . . ."

"Yes."

"And a woman in love too. . . ."

"I hope so! Otherwise you wouldn't be jealous."

"And whom do I love?"

"I'd like to think it's me. . . ."

"You're a conceited bastard!"

"Whom you nevertheless love. . . ."

161

Knox got up, pulled Marisa close to him, and stopped her helpless protests by kissing her lips each time she wanted to say something. Then she stopped resisting and gave herself up totally to Knox. . . .

From then on they avoided that topic completely. There was no need to talk about the obvious, something both of them knew only too well and could express much better in action than in words. . . . Their friendship, their mutual confidence was rehabilitated and sealed through the celebration of love. Marisa's attitude was totally different from that time on. She needed no further motivation. . . . She was ready and eager to start the work for Knox, which she now regarded as her own.

Several days later, as they were working together in Knox's apartment, Marisa brought up the question of marriage, while listening to the 'memory cell.'

"Do you really believe, Ed, that marriage is for the proles only?"

"Why do you ask me that question? You heard me say that I agree with Noesis' position."

"I was thinking of your future. . . ."

"And yours too, I guess."

"Why, yes."

"You'd like to get married, right?"

"I'm not proposing to you!"

"But I should propose to you, shouldn't I?"

"Sometimes I feel that way, but then I don't. . . . It's funny. . . ."

"Well, let me tell you that I feel the same way. . . . But then I start thinking, and the more I think of it, the less I feel like going through with it."

"I'd like to hear your reasons."

"Well, without repeating all the things we already discussed with Noesis and Gynea, I wonder what we could gain with that legal formality."

"Only one thing. We'd get legal recognition. . . ."

"And permission to sleep together legally. . . . But that's stupid, you know. All that meaningless ceremony and that piece of paper you get at the end, don't add anything to our relationship. Neither does the absence of it all take anything away from its value and meaning."

"I know, Ed, you're right. On the other hand, something seems to be missing, though."

"I hope you're not thinking of children. . . ."

"No, that's not it. . . . By the way, you don't have to worry that I'll get pregnant again. I'm much more careful now after that experience."

"But then what is it?"

"Well, I'll tell you. First of all, you realize that we don't live in the kind of society Noesis talks about."

"You mean to say that it's much safer to conform. Then let me ask you this: if everybody at all times—past, present and future—conforms, adapts and adjusts to that which already is, how could there have been any change and progress, anything new?"

"And you want to be one of those who won't conform and adjust to the old?"

"I'd like to be one of the first. Though I'm fully aware of the legal, social and moral difficulties one has to face. Especially the moral prejudices, which'll hurt you even more, for being a woman."

"So you see the problem yourself?"

"Of course I do, but I'd much rather think of you as being my girl, my friend, my. . . ."

"Mistress? Can't you see that we don't even have a decent word for the kind of relationship that exists between us? Only the tag names of husband and wife are legally and morally acceptable. Being a mistress to a lover is almost the same as being a whore."

"Yes, that's how most of the 'good and just' people think of any non-legalized form of relationship between man and woman, regardless of what values and meanings there are in their relationship. But this doesn't seem to matter too much. What matters is that piece of paper which immediately confers upon those who received it a cloak of moral dignity, no matter how base and low, meaningless or poor their motives for having legalized their affair might have been."

"Nevertheless, that's how it works in the society we live in and shall have to continue living in. Unless you have some wild hopes that Noesis'll take us away from here to his world?"

"Don't talk nonsense!"

"Please, don't take my remarks as a pleading for a marriage certificate. As a matter of fact, I feel perfectly fine and happy the way we are together, right now."

"I didn't think of that at all. I realize that the most important and fundamental thing in any kind of human relationship, ours included, of course, is the free and responsible agreement between two adults. Any other form of togetherness is devoid of all meaning, no matter how many pieces of paper you collect from the authorities. Especially in our relationship. It's a personal and private thing which concerns only you and me, and I feel that it should be kept this way."

"But this isn't how the majority of people think."

"I know. But I don't know what else I could say right now. Certainly I would go through with the legal formalities, but only if absolutely necessary, if forced by circumstances. But I don't have to tell you how much I hate every kind of so-called moral coercion, that famous 'Thou shalt,' and the rest of it."

"It demands the sacrifice of your freedom, nothing less. . . ."

"Be it as it may, as I told you, I haven't reached a final decision on this matter, but I consider it only an accident and an insignificant detail. What matters is that we get along well together."

"For how long?"

"If I had put that question to you, Marise, in all honesty, could you have given me a precise answer? All you could do, most probably, is to tell me how you feel now, hoping that your feelings wouldn't change. But you'd be unable to give me a guarantee for that. And this is all I can tell you now, as far as I'm concerned, if we want to be completely truthful about it."

Marisa became pensive for a few moments, then she said: "You know something, Edward? I'm glad that we can talk openly on any topic we choose to, because we have nothing to fear or to conceal from each other."

"This is the way it ought to be! And I like to think of it as the only commandment that makes sense, and man should keep it in mind all the time."

"What commandment?"

"The commandment of truth, Marisa. This is not a commandment brought down to people by some prophet, as a revelation given by a God, shrouded in mystery. It's the commandment of reason, that which always conforms to and respects the facts of reality. It's self-chosen, self-imposed and self-fulfilled. It requires no superior sanction and justification. It requires no threats of punishment in an ever lasting holocaust. Its consequences are reaped right here and now for all those who abide by it or fail to do so. And I hope to live in total agreement with my own mind, whose only measure is reality and truth."

"That sounds very solemn and sublime, Ed. I wish life were like that . . . but it isn't. You say that 'reality' is the only measure of your mind and you respect it above everything else. Why are you unwilling, than, to accept and to conform to the existing facts of our social and moral reality as we have it? You're making an exception and to that extent you're not consistent with your highest principles."

"By 'reality,' Marisa, I meant only the facts of nature and its unchanging laws, not the ever-changing events and phenomena of culture and civilization which are man-made and therefore must, of necessity, evolve and develop. For this reason I see no contradiction in my position."

"And you refuse to adjust yourself to the given facts of our socio-economic and moral way of life? You're still a rebel, Ed, no matter what!"

"Yes, I want to stay a so-called rebel. But an intelligent and rational one, who doesn't kick everything aside just because it's the fad. . . . Rather one who proceeds selectively, by intelligent choice. There's no meaning to or justification for turning the whole value system upside down. That would identify the rebel as a vandal. I oppose only those values which have lost their

165

intrinsic validity and meaning, thus becoming hollow shells of empty ostentation and hypocrisy."

"What are the values you still retain, Ed?"

"I couldn't give you, right off hand, a structured and integrated hierarchy of my values, because I'm still working on it. . . . Nevertheless, I find a great deal of meaning in truth, knowledge, beauty, justice, creativity, love, freedom, ability and so forth."

"You realize that you said nothing about society, politics, economics, ethics and religion. Don't you?"

"I implied ethics when I mentioned knowledge, freedom and justice, which I consider as its foundations. As to the other things you mentioned, frankly, I don't care much. I consider our social, political and economic organization only as a means to create the conditions required by man for the pursuit of his philosophic, scientific and artistic goals and ideals. Besides, looking at those so-called socio-political values, one turns away with contempt, disgust and nausea, especially when one sees the ugly mess we're plodding through right now! I'm sick of the amount of hypocrisy, lying, cheating, maneuvering machinations and pandering, the dirty pulls and tricks these politicians pull, even among each other! I've lost my respect for them a long time ago, no matter how shamelessly they parade as the redeemers of humanity, at the expense of the hard-working citizens. If I could afford it, I'd buy myself an island and live there alone, in self-exile, glad to be rid of our loving and lovable neighbors. Perhaps some day I'll be able to do it, if my plans work out the way I'd like them to."

"You mean, of course, your anticipated success as a writer?"

"That's correct. Haven't you noticed, when reading or hearing about them, that many of the best creative minds lived in solitude, far removed from the market place, the many, the crowd, the ruck? Did you ask yourself the question why?"

"I think that it's because man, as he's now, is not very lovable and attractive. . . . On the contrary, it's very seldom that you find a human being at whom you can look upon with respect, admiration and love. Most of the time you have to look down, and since we don't like doing that, we rather look away. Is this why you consider Noesis your only true friend?"

"Yes, Marisa."

"The only one? . . ."

"Let's not be silly again, all right? You know very well what I feel and how I feel about you."

"What and how?"

"If you don't know it yet, then you'll have to wait till we discuss and write down the chapter on man, woman, love and sex. . . ."

"That should be interesting. . . ."

"I wonder what Noesis and Gynea think about these questions?"

"We'll find out soon enough. But this reminds me of a problem I kept thinking of since our last meeting. Do you think that they would object if I came to the future sessions?"

"I'm sure they wouldn't. Why should they?"

"Because . . . of my stupid performance there the last time. . . ."

"Come on, it wasn't that bad! And this time you'll be able to assume a more objective and less emotional attitude."

Knox's work progressed at a more rapid pace with Marisa's help in editing and typing. Sometimes he'd get tired of writing, and then he'd ask Marisa to read the material that had been already typed back to him. Seated comfortably in his armchair or stretched out on his bed, he listened, interrupting her whenever some correction or addition was needed. Sometimes they'd disagree on what words would best be suited in a certain passage, Knox being rather stubborn and impregnable to Marisa's suggestions.

Noesis made his appearance after three weeks, to set the date of their next meeting. He wanted it to be on the following week-end, at his own apartment. As soon as Knox agreed, he hung up, leaving no opportunity for Knox to inquire about Marisa's presence. Apparently Noesis had taken it for granted, on account of their previous agreement. Sometimes Knox found it rather strange that Noesis always maintained an abrupt and reserved manner toward him. He never said anything more than the absolutely necessary, never inquired after Knox's life. Similarly he never disclosed anything about his own, how he spent his days, where he went, what he did, how he felt. Nothing at all, just an impersonal, restrained, cautious and secretive detachment. He held his distance carefully at all times, without being cold, arrogant or offensive. At times Knox felt tempted to inquire about these details, but he was afraid to do so—apparently, with good reason, he thought that Noesis would politely refuse to talk about such matters. The truth was that there wasn't even an opportunity provided for such venture. Evidently Noesis had no desire to create such an opportunity either. Therefore, Knox considered this matter as closed.

Before they left for Noesis' place, Marisa reminded Knox to take along the finished chapters and at least one of the 'memory cells.' She was somewhat apprehensive and nervous lest she make another mistake. They were welcomed with sincere openness, without the artificiality of strained affectation and socially required friendliness. Marisa felt immediately at ease. She couldn't discover any sign of hidden resentment or regret in their behavior. Noesis saw to it that they were comfortably seated. Gynea had prepared some refreshments for them perhaps in anticipation of a long session. She then tuned the volume of the music coming from a radio that looked like none of the makes familiar to Knox and Marisa. They must have been listening to some musical performance directly broadcast from a concert hall.

Knox started the conversation by handing over to Noesis the manuscript:

"I have some material ready for you." There was satisfaction in his voice.

Noesis looked into it briefly and said: "If you don't mind, I'd like to keep it till our next meeting. I'd like to read it more thoroughly and so would Gynea."

"You can keep it. Marisa went through it before she typed it out. I hope you'll approve of it."

"It's not a matter of approving or disapproving. This sounds too much like censorship, which is another means to curtail the freedom of thought."

"Which is unknown to you, I guess. . . ." Knox remarked.

"Most certainly!" Noesis agreed. "Thinking is man's highest faculty and by its very nature it's free. There's no such thing as guided or directed thinking. Once it's guided, it's not free, therefore it's not thinking."

"I can imagine what you must think of the techniques of conditioning, manipulating, coaxing, enticing, persuading, and worst of all, brainwashing!"

"We don't think of it at all," Noesis replied with contempt. Then he continued with a smile: "I hope you have your secretary with you. Turn it on and put it on the table, so we can start our discussion."

Knox complied with this request, and Noesis asked, in the manner of a professor readying himself for his lecture:

"Now let's see where did we stop the last time?"

"We said we were going to consider the parents' attitude toward their children . . ." volunteered Marisa.

"Oh, yes! I remember. However, before we go into that, do you have any questions concerning the material covered already?"

"I feel like a student who hasn't prepared his homework," Knox replied with a broad smile, "but we were busy with the stuff we just handed over to you for your inspection."

"I don't like this term, I mean the inspection," Noesis said. "But anyway, the reason why I asked this question was that neither of you seemed fully convinced about the ideas proposed the last time. . . ."

"That's true," Marisa felt she had to speak up. "I wonder whether it's part of the agreement between you and Ed that he has to agree always, no matter what. Even if he should happen not to, he can still fulfill his commitment as a writer."

"Nothing is farther from us than to force our views on anybody! The only thing I want is that my ideas should be presented in their original form and meaning, and in that respect I'm sure I don't have anything to fear."

"All right, then," Gynea proposed, "let's go straight to our questions for today. Perhaps as we go on, our ideas will be

169

understood in their full context, making it easier for you and your future readers to comprehend their true significance."

"Speaking of the parents' attitude toward their children," Knox started, "we've already mentioned, from an historical point of view, that they were regarded by their parents as welcome additions to the available man-power, as working force in the agricultural societies."

"Then let's move on to the present situation," Noesis said.

"In this respect we already discussed the child's over-all dependent situation and the ensuing psychological reactions, such as resentment, hidden hatred, and the desire to emancipate."

'That's fine, but let's look into the psychological make-up of the parents."

"Well, idealistically speaking," Marisa tried to guess, "every parent is supposed to love his children. . . ."

"Which is not the case. Not by far!" Gynea remarked emphatically.

"But they ought to! I mean they should, they must! After all, it's their obligation!" Marisa insisted.

"But they don't, at least not all of them, and even those who do, don't feel that way about it all the time," Gynea retorted.

"However, that's their fault!" Marisa continued.

"I'm not so sure that the parents should be loaded with the whole guilt in this respect," Gynea suggested.

"Who else should be held responsible if not the parents?" Marisa went on stubbornly. "Are you going to blame society in general, the environment or what?"

"To blame either society or the environment for anything," Gynea replied, "means to move from the concrete facts of reality into abstractions. It serves only one purpose, that is, the desire to evade responsibility of the individual human beings, who're the only real carriers of life."

'Then you have to go back to the parents."

"Are you sure that there's no other alternative left?" Gynea asked.

"I think I have it," Knox interposed with enthusiasm. "It's the institution of marriage and family that you have in mind as the responsible cause, I mean, the concrete individuals who make up that institution."

"Here we go again . . ." Marisa remarked rather mordantly.

"I'm sorry to disappoint you, Marisa," said Gynea, "but that's the way it is! And I'll try to prove it to you."

"I'm ready to be convinced," Marisa challenged.

"I don't want to convince you. You have to convince yourself by going through the required process of analysis and conclusion. In other words, you have to think it through."

"All right then, I'm ready to think."

"Then let's start with this question: why is it that people have children?"

"Sorry to interrupt," Knox intervened, "but we already answered a similar question. It was stated, I think, that people want to have children because usually they consider them as the most important meaning in their lives. We also said that this identification with one's children doesn't work. No one can find the meaning and happiness for one's existence in someone else's person. Perhaps I should also add, though it may sound cynical, that a great many children are born simply by accident and miscalculation."

"All the things you mentioned so far are true," Noesis observed, "however, you seem to have forgotten one important aspect."

"Which one?"

"The necessary outcome of their desire to procreate, that is, the parents' loss of freedom. And this brings about a serious conflict for them, the one ensuing from their desire to have children, on the one hand, and the resentment coming afterwards from the loss of their independence, on the other. And what's worst of all, this conflict is deepened by the obvious contrast between the idealized and glamorized picture of parenthood and the crude realities of everyday life, which never match their illusory expectations."

"I wonder how they manage to solve this conflict?" Knox inquired.

"Most of them never solve it, or else, if they try to do so, very soon they give up, they give in, they put up, and resign, with a deep feeling of personal frustration, which they don't like to admit even to themselves. They feel guilty about it, so they repress it."

"But repression, as I recall it from psychology, is no solution at all. It only leads to the formation of secondary and substitute forms of behavior," Knox tried to recall his lessons in college.

"Such as the symptoms of irritability, tension, nervousness, the lack of patience and even worse reactions."

"What for instance?" Knox wanted to know.

"I'm sure you must have heard of situations where the children are rejected. By this I mean, right now, only the psychological aspect of it, although cases of physical rejection, brutal beatings, total neglect and abandonment are not to be forgotten either. Whenever one sees such cases, which aren't as rare as one would like to assume, one wonders about the truth and honesty of the claims loudly voiced by almost everybody—at least officially— concerning the unconditional love of the parents for their children, as well as the appeals to maternal instincts as their source and cause. . . ."

"I'm sure, however," Marisa commented, "that you're not ready to generalize. After all, one should also recognize the solicitous care many parents have for their children, sometimes even an exaggerated concern and worry about their safety and well being. As a matter of fact, I have noticed that most parents seem to be anxious to attend to all the needs of their children, they are ready to deprive themselves of many things as long as they know they gave their children all that which they feel they owe to them. Many children even become spoiled and overprotected."

"And you want to tell me that all this is done because of only one motive, love?"

"Certainly not because of their hatred!" Marisa said with conviction.

"Couldn't there be some other hidden motives?" Noesis suggested.

"What are you thinking of?" Knox asked.

"Well, let me mention just a few, briefly. . . . We can't go into every detail for lack of time. Take the following cases, how-

ever: Suppose that a child gets everything as far as the satisfaction of his organic needs are concerned, but practically nothing regarding his psychic needs for approval, acceptance, belonging, security, attention, and a truly person to person relationship. Can that happen?"

"In fact, it happens far too often," Knox remarked pensively.

"Certainly, this attitude isn't inspired by love, correct?"

"By what then?" Marisa injected her question.

"One possible cause could be the feeling of guilt. But let me
explain what I mean by this. Take, for example, the case of a
parent—mother, father or both—who know that their children
came to them without being wanted, by accident. But they had
to accept the inevitable. They were against abortion because it's
considered a crime, immoral and inhuman, besides being sinful.
Nevertheless, they could never manage to change their feeling of
resentment toward them. For that reason, they felt guilty of
omission for not fulfilling part of their parental duties as it had
been preached to them. Then, in order to reduce the tension
created by their guilt, they did the only things they could have
done; they exaggerated in matters of satisfying the organic needs
of the child. Does this makes sense to you?"

"As an isolated case, it can happen. . . . But I wouldn't generalize," Marisa doubted.

"I'll give you other examples," Noesis went on. "Let's look
closely and critically into the well known cases of overprotection. Certainly best proof of the parents' overflowing love for
their children. But I disagree on this point too, for the simple
reason that I never take appearances for reality. That's the first
and most important lesson in the methods of scientific and philosophic inquiry. One should always keep in mind that while the
phenomena or the effects are easily perceived, it's much more
difficult to go beyond them in order to find their hidden causes."

"But doesn't the nature of the cause determine the nature of
the effect?" Knox objected.

"It does, certainly. But the point is to find the true cause and
motive which is not so easy, if you realize that for any given
effect or phenomenon there can be not only one, but a variety

173

of causes, and, similarly, one cause can produce more then one effect or phenomenon. So, I repeat again, don't make the mistake of taking appearance for reality."

"How does this apply to the business at hand?" Knox questioned.

"It's simple. We're dealing now with psychological phenomena and their causes, that of overprotection, for instance. I wouldn't say that love and only love is at the root of such an attitude as its true cause."

"What would you suggest as an alternative?" Marisa asked.

"The neurotic traits of the mother's or father's personality. Their poor adjustment in the world of reality, their own feelings of insecurity, fear, indecision, helplessness, and the necessary overreaction to these in the form of overprotection, understood as their exaggerated need for security, safety and protection, projected onto their children. This should sound at least as plausible an explanation as that of love. . . ."

"But some amount of love could well coexist with the things you just described, couldn't it?" Marisa went on.

"No doubt about that, but I'd still regard insecurity as the main cause. And I have a good reason to maintain this. It comes from the effects of this attitude on the children."

"I'd like to guess what you meant by your last sentence," Knox said.

"Well, go ahead. It's simple. . . ."

"I remember the lessons I got on how children learn by imitation the pattern of behavior displayed by the adults around them. So by the effects you probably meant that the children catch on, they become contaminated by exposure, they'll internalize the neurotic traits of their parents. They become conditioned to think, feel, act, and react within the same frame of reference."

"That's the first step only. Think also in terms of the further effects on the development of those children. If they develop and mature at all, it'll be in the wrong direction. They'll only perpetuate the same pattern of fear, insecurity, dependence, and the demand for all sorts of security and guarantees."

"But that's a shame!" Marisa remarked with spontaneous sincerity.

"Nonetheless, it's a fact," Noesis continued. "Then you should raise the question whether parents should be regarded unconditionally as the loving benefactors of their children, or perhaps, as their malefactors, without consciously wanting to be such. Moreover, you should also conclude that in your family-centered social system, a child's development and future—his whole life— are simply a matter of sheer luck. . . . Since no one can pick his own parents, it's a matter of blind chance whether you'll be born in an environment that meets the conditions of a normal and healthy development or, unfortunately, just its opposite."

"How true!" Knox agreed gravely.

"But this isn't the end of the story. First, you should conclude that not every person is qualified—biologically and psychologically —to fulfill the responsibilities belonging to procreation. Second, procreation shouldn't be left to mere chance only."

"Which is another reason why you object to the institution of marriage and family," Knox suggested.

"Of course. But allow me to continue and call your attention to another consequence of this unfortunate situation. You complain a lot, as I can see it from reading your books and magazine articles, about the embarrassing increase of juvenile delinquency, drop-outs, all kinds of rebellions and crimes. The first thing you propose, with sermonizing setentiousness, is the tightening of the family ties, stricter laws and prohibitions, clamoring for more parental authority, and the like. You've been doing this for quite a long time and you're getting nowhere. Your statistics fill you with dread, worry and fear. Then you move to the other extreme. You clamor for more freedom, a more understanding and permissive attitude toward the children, you promote lectures, discussion groups, workshops, courses in psychology and a host of other 'solutions,' thus betraying your helplessness and also the fear you've developed in front of your own children. You're afraid to take any definite stand, because you fear that you may damage and harm them even more. Then somebody starts preaching on the miraculous, omnipotent power of the limitless, unconditional love which understands, allows and forgives everything, hoping that you can escape the worst. Thus you move in the closed circle of constant experimentation, trying one thing, then dropping it as soon as somebody comes along with any wild idea that sounds 'interesting,' not realizing that you reached the end of your resourcefulness. Some of you may have a dark and uneasy feeling that perhaps there could be something basically wrong with marriage, family and children, but as soon as the idea emerges in your mind, you banish it in strict obedience to the moral-religious dogmas, taboos and prejudices which you blindly obey. And the harm keeps on being perpetuated."

"You must realize, Noesis," Knox said very seriously, "that it's simply impossible, I mean, it would be pure and sheer insanity to start campaigning against marriage in our society, asking for its dissolution or abolition. I don't have to describe the total chaos and anarchy which would result from that."

"I agree with you fully, Edward," Noesis replied. "In fact, you must remember that on several occasions I insisted that every stage in the process of evolution is a necessary one. Therefore, it's not a matter of starting an irresponsible revolution against your present institutions, but you can do two things at least. You can try to improve what you have right now, and in the meantime, you can prepare your people to think of the new ideas and possibilities open to them. The ideological change must preceed its physical embodiment. In this sense, I'd say that *Logos* comes before *Bios*. . . ."

"Before we get off the subject," Gynea suggested, "I want to point to another possible cause and motive for overprotection. I'm thinking of certain parents' hidden desire to own, possess and dominate their children. They want to turn them into helpless, impotent and dependent neurotics. Through overprotection, they don't provide their children the necessary opportunities to learn by doing, through their own experience, by trial and error. Consequently, they remain immature and underdeveloped. They can never fulfill their desire to emancipate from their condition of dependence on their parents. They can't develop the traits or qualities of self-confidence, self-esteem, self-love, self-respect, but suffer under their unwelcome feelings of inferiority. Of course, the parents always claim prudence, safety, security and love as the motives underlying their wholy performance."

"It's hard for me to believe that parents can become so base, so immoral, so selfishly motivated!" Marisa exclaimed indignantly.

"Of course you must feel this way, since you must have been raised on the gospel of universal love," Gynea answered. "But let me finish. Take, for example, the method of enslaving children in the name of martyrdom and self-sacrifice of the parents. Many of them don't hesitate to assume that role and to act it out with unfailing consistency. They seem to be the incarnation of selfless dedication, service and sacrifice of all kinds. They even talk about it when they assure their children that they are ready to become sacrificial animals on the altars of love. . . . They speak of their sufferings, frustrations, worries, sleepless nights, deprivations and self-denials that they offered up for the benefit of the children. They confess to have lived for one unselfish purpose only—to become the slaves in the service of their children. Their only meaning in life is their children's happiness, they say with a sorrowful sigh. . . . But ask yourselves, how do children feel about it and what does this sacrificial role-acting accomplish?"

"I should say that such children react or should react with limitless gratitude and love," Marisa prompted immediately.

"You don't really mean it!" Knox looked at her with utter surprise.

"That's what they're supposed to feel anyway," insisted Marisa.

"But that doesn't mean that they actually feel it," Gynea remarked. "Let me ask you this. If you were given a choice between helping someone or being helped, which alternative would you prefer?"

"Certainly I'd rather help than be helped!"

"Why?"

"Because I feel better that way! It gives me more pleasure."

"But, I must insist, why? What's your specific reason for this preference?"

177

"Well. . . . I don't know. . . . What do you mean to say?" Marisa was confused.

"All right, then, I'll tell you. Whenever you help somebody, you experience the pleasure coming from the knowledge that you're able to help. You enjoy your position of superiority. Conversely, when you're being helped, you resent your condition of helpless inferiority, as well as the superior position of the person who helps you. It offends your pride. And this is how children feel about the self-sacrifice and martyrdom of their parents."

Marisa didn't know what to say to this right away. She thought for a while and then remarked:

"You know, Gynea, you seem to derive some kind of pleasure in turning all our values and ideals inside out and upside down! If one followed your turn of mind, one would end up, in no time with nothing to hold on to."

"Do I really give you the impression of a cynical, sarcastic, malicious, ill-disposed, bankrupt nihilist and pessimist?" As Gynea asked this pointed question, a faint smile played at the corners of her mouth.

"No, I didn't mean that!" Marisa answered quickly and a little apprehensive. "You must have other values you live by . . . but what about us? Have you thought of that?"

"I know that this must be a painful experience. You must have a terrible sense of loss, seeing your cherished beliefs shown for what they are," said Gynea in a conciliatory manner. "Truth can be unpleasant, I know, and that's why people often give preference to their illusions. But, you see, it's only truth that can set you free for the acquisition of new values as you progress and mature. For instance, I'm sure you do not entertain and worship any more the hopes, ideas and values which were so dear to you, so close to your person, when you were, say, twelve years old?"

"I should hope not!" Marisa replied.

"Well, the same applies also to the crisis you're experiencing now."

"But when am I going to reach the final stage of complete serenity, peace of mind and happiness . . .?"

"There's no such thing," Gynea went on. "Instead of dreaming with such non-existent nirvana, you should take pleasure from the very feeling and experience that you're growing and reaching ever higher levels of insight!"

"I'm afraid we're digressing from our main objective again," Noesis interrupted the dialogue of the women. "Let's go back to our present issue. I still would like to mention one or two more cases typical of the parents' attitude toward their children. There isn't much to say on the possessive and domineering type who always insists on his God-given authority and infallibility. Everyone can see the obvious goals which such an attitude serves as a means. It's equally easy to guess what the children's feelings and reactions are to this kind of treatment. Let's rather concentrate on the so-called normal and average cases, those in which the extreme elements we've considered so far are missing. We have to do this, in order to avoid any possible accusations that we're building our case on the exceptions rather than the rule, right, Edward?"

"I remember having said something like this before. . . ." Knox admitted.

"Therefore let's take a 'regular' case. There's an average family consisting of the parents and five children. I could increase or decrease the number of children, but that's irrelevant, as you'll see. Let's assume that they belong to the middle-class or perhaps even to 'upper upper of the higher middle.' Consequently, this family is rather well off economically, socially and culturally. Let's also suppose that the parents like each other and their children, who are healthy and intelligent. No major catastrophe or tragedy ever befell them. . . ."

"What's the point you're trying to develop?" interrupted Knox with impatience.

"Just a minute and you'll see," Noesis said soothing him. "In conformity with the expected standards of values, the parents consider themselves very fortunate and many times blessed by God, who sent them those fine children. Occasionally they have

179

to admit certain burdens of life in general, the normal problems involved in raising their children, but all in all, they can't complain. . . ."

"I know what you're going to do next," Knox interrupted again. "You're going to apply your methodical distinction between false appearances and true reality, correct?"

"Well said, Edward! That's it! But why don't you do this yourself? I'd enjoy listening to it. . . ." Noesis suggested.

"All right, Noesis, with pleasure!" Knox accepted the challenge. "You want me to talk about those hidden thoughts and feelings that the parents dare not confess and talk about in the clear, right?"

"Consider only the parents' side right now, if you don't mind."

"Fine. It can be stated in one short sentence: at the end of their road, or perhaps even while still on it, the parents regretfully resent their loss of freedom."

"Be more specific, please," Noesis insisted.

"I'll be glad to. The parents must realize, even if they guiltily conceal this fact even from their own selves, that they spent the best years of their lives, their youthful energies, for one purpose only: the benefit of their children. They remember with some hidden bitterness that the welfare of their children very often demanded the sacrifice of their own projects, plans, goals and ideals. They accomplished only one thing, they raised a family. But what was the price they had to pay for it? The fact that with all their energies directed toward this effort, they could never make something worthwhile of themselves. . . . The man became and remained only a husband and a father; the woman became and remained only a wife and a mother. They dedicated their lives to others, namely to their children, but never to themselves. And for what purpose? What did they personally profit by it? Their children, once grown, will follow their own paths. At best they'll be on friendly terms with their parents. But their real dedication will be some place else, in their own lives, perhaps many hundreds of miles away from them. And the parents, elderly now, will be glad to be at least financially self-sufficient and independent, all too worn out and tired to pursue any higher ideals. If the children should get married and start a family, they'll be repeating the same routine, a life of small pleasures and even smaller virtues, and the same cycle of untold frustrations and losses will continue. . . ." Knox seemed to have finished his discourse.

"There's one more small detail you haven't mentioned, Edward," Noesis commented.

"What is it?" Knox inquired.

"The particularly frustrating condition of the mother."

"In what sense?"

"You apparently never listened to the well known complaints of the housewives," Noesis reminded him.

"Oh, yes! I remember now! They always complain about being shut in and shut up, tied down to their children, day in, day out, without much variety or lasting change. Often they confess that there are times when they're pretty close to losing their wits and their patience. They feel like slamming the door behind them for good, because they're constantly chained to the crib and to the sink. They haven't one single moment of peace, when they have a little time which they could claim as their own. Then there are the boring, repetitious, meaningless but necessary household chores, which, in spite of all the modern facilities and the glamorized advertisements, add more to their over-all feeling of frustration, nervousness, sometimes leading to fits of hysteria."

"Very well put, Edward," Noesis approved. "But let's say something about the husband's situation too. . . . Marisa, would you like to take up this part?"

"I'll try, though I'm not a man. What I'll say will perhaps betray my feminine bias. . . . Anyway, I think that husbands are much better off then their wives. . . ."

"Now, do you really think so?" said Knox somewhat provoked.

"Yes, I do. Perhaps you want to impress me with the tremendous burden that weighs on the shoulders of the breadwinner, the provider, who must assume the final responsibility for the lives of the whole family. This is true, no one wants to deny this fact. On the other hand, he has some fringe benefits the wife never gets. For one thing, he isn't, as you yourself said, Ed, chained to his children the way the mother is. He spends the greater part of his time away from the tribe, looking after his profession, which he can pursue, and not give it up like the mother. If he's any good at it, he must derive pleasures from it. Besides, he meets a lot of interesting people, he goes places, sometimes on extended trips, which he welcomes as a wonderful break. He only spends his evenings and week-ends with his wife and children. He also expects his wife to manage the whole household rather efficiently, for, after all, he thinks he has a right to demand it, because he's the one who pays the bills. He's the one who supports everybody. They live off him and that gives him an added right to assume an air of importance and authority. In the name of his many responsibilities, he doesn't want to be bothered with the trivial questions and the petty little problems of the set-up. He's willing even to pay for the children's piano lessons, as long as they practice while he's away. Besides, as a woman, I believe I can safely mention that the man is better off even biologically. He isn't handicapped by monthly discomforts the way we are, not speaking of the delights of pregnancy and childbirth. Finally, he lives in a man-made world, where he makes the laws. He fixes the rules of the game, making sure that he allows himself certain privileges—such as the double standard in morals—and expects the woman to conform and to obey, or else!" Here Marisa paused for a second, then asked Knox defiantly: "Well, Ed, what do you have to say for yourself? Is all this right or wrong?"

"You win, Marisa. Your analysis is well done. Congratulations," Knox replied, then he added: "I'm glad you see all this so clearly. It's good for both of us."

"But tell me, Noesis," Marisa addressed him directly, "what can be done about all this? We agreed that it's impossible and unwise to start a war on our institution of marriage and family at the present stage of our evolution. What do you say?"

"Since we know by now that the will to freedom is man's strongest drive and need, I'd do everything to safeguard it, even within the rather narrow limits of your present institutions. I'd

182

like to believe that at least the more educated individuals will recognize the falsity of the attitudes we discussed so far, and will abandon their quest for power, their desires to rule and to dominate. Perhaps they'll learn to love in freedom and respect the same value in other people's lives."

"This sounds very edifying, Noesis," Marisa remarked, "but it doesn't seem to amount to more than daydreaming and wishful thinking. I'd appreciate if you gave certain concrete suggestions as to how to attain it."

"Of course. I understand. Therefore, think of the following possibilities. Can you imagine a husband who doesn't want to dominate the lives of his wife and children?"

"Yes, I can. . . . You can imagine anything, you know. . . ." Marisa sounded skeptical.

"Then also try to think of a wife and mother who doesn't do any of those wrong things we analyzed before."

"If there were such things as perfect wives and mothers. . . . But there aren't," Marisa persisted.

"Can you imagine," Noesis continued, apparently unperturbed by Marisa's negative attitude, "that parents could educate their children in freedom and for freedom, respecting the one simple truth that children—as every human being—exist for their own sake. That they belong to themselves, that their lives are their own and that the attainment of their own happiness is their first and highest purpose?"

"Ideally speaking, you're right again. But the ideal is never the real, and the real isn't the ideal," Marisa continued.

"Then let me ask you this, Marisa," Noesis made his last attempt, "do you deny the facts of development, evolution and progress altogether? Have you lost your faith, based on historical evidence, in the very possibility of improving man's life on earth? Wouldn't you allow a future for man? Don't you think, for example, that the present level and stage of your civilization is better and superior to the mode of life of the bushman? Finally, if you're so firmly convinced that man on earth is doomed to move downward, from disaster to disaster, you'll have to prove and document your pessimistic outlook."

"What about the possibility of man destroying life on earth by mere accident or miscalculation?" persisted Marisa stubbornly. "They say that man is quite capable to accomplish total destruction with one stroke, should he choose to use the atomic bombs kept in readiness for any eventuality?"

"We're quite aware of that danger ourselves. I recall though, that we discussed this problem at the very beginning of our conversation, isn't that correct, Ed?"

"Yes, we did indeed," Knox agreed.

"I have one more comment to add to this," Noesis continued. "The proper and rational attitude toward life and the future shouldn't be based on a distorted view, dictated by one's fear of possible disasters and emergencies, which ought to be regarded as the exceptions rather than the rule. I think, moreover, that man would refrain from using his power of total annihilation if for no other reason than because he understands that there would be no victors in such a case, only the total loss of everything. I mean, man isn't ready to commit race suicide."

"That's exactly how I feel too!" Knox reassured Noesis.

"Do you think we still have time to go into another topic tonight?" Gynea suggested. "If you aren't in a hurry I'd propose that we eat something and then return to the second part of our session."

"What would we discuss?" inquired Knox, full of animation.

"It's the rather involved question about man's relation to woman, and of course, the ensuing problems of love and sex," Noesis declared.

"Do you think we can finish it tonight?" Knox asked doubtfully.

"If we can't cover every aspect of this complex problem," Gynea went on with her proposal, "we could finish it during our next session. Unless, of course, you feel tired and would prefer to leave." She addressed her last sentence to Marisa in particular.

"I don't want to be the one who spoils other people's games and pleasures. If Ed would rather stay, I might as well. But I'd welcome a break, though," she concluded.

Gynea got up from the sofa and walked into the kitchenette, followed by Marisa who had offered to help her. Noesis picked out a few records from his collection. They were operatic high-lights from Bizet's Carmen, Boito's Mephistopheles and Wagner's Tristan and Isolde. He let Knox make his choice. He picked Carmen, saying:

"Don't you think it would be a good preparation for our discussion on love and sex?"

"Certainly it's better than a requiem mass. . . ." Noesis answered with a smile. The passionate sounds of the orchestra and Carmen's voice filled the whole apartment. They sat in silence, eating their sandwiches and listening to the tragic denouement of that love story set to music. At the end of the first side of the record, Knox commented with obvious excitement.

"Do you know what I like in this music?"

"What?" asked Gynea with curiosity.

"It's the free, uninhibited, daring and passionate affirmation of life, the celebration of love and its meaning, even at the cost of one's existence."

"I fully agree with the first half of your opinion, that is, the affirmation of life and the courageous saying Yes to love," Gynea answered. "But I wouldn't subscribe to the tragic finale, Carmen's death at the hands of her lover Don José."

"Why?" interposed Marisa eagerly.

"Because it makes no sense at all!"

"What do you mean?"

"I don't see why the tragic element should be always and necessarily associated with the beautiful phenomenon of love. It simply doesn't belong there!" Gynea went on, as though thinking aloud.

"But it tells a lot about the way people on this planet think of love," Noesis manifested his view.

"Please, explain what you mean," Knox asked him.

"To my mind, the tragic outcome betrays the presence of the old feelings of sin, guilt and punishment usually associated with love and sex, as the residue of the original idiosyncrasy of the 'forbidden fruit,'" Noesis submitted cautiously.

"I've never thought of it in this context!" Knox reacted with surprise.

"But therein lies the origin and the cause of all the difficulties and problems implicit in your conception of love and sex," Noesis continued. "It's the case of your conscience being saddled with an unwanted burden."

"Come to think of it, I have to agree with you," Knox conceded. "In fact, our way of looking at love and sex is still caught in the web of our inhibited moral and religious prejudices. Sex is still an unsolved problem. At best, it's only tolerated with uneasiness and a lot of hypocrisy to it. It's still a taboo, a 'forbidden fruit,' as you put it."

"But that's not so!" Marisa objected. "Not for the more enlightened and liberal minded people, at least! The whole picture of the old puritanic tradition has changed considerably due to the revolutionary ideas of Freud and his associates."

"That's true," Gynea had to admit. "However, Freud's ideas on the *Id*, the libido, infantile sexuality, its development through the oral, anal and Narcissistic stages toward the goal of heterosexual experiences, moreover, his doctrine on repression, complex formation, sublimation, dream analysis and the rest of it, met with the most vehement opposition and denunciation coming from the enemies of the body, of love and sex. And there's still a great deal of the old inhibitions present even among the educated people. Love and sex is either not mentioned at all, or else it becomes an object of jokes, some of which in a very low and bad taste."

"Do you agree with Freud's ideas?" Knox directed his question at Gynea.

"I can't answer you with a straight Yes or No. . . . I certainly don't agree with Freud that the sexual instinct, drive or need represents man's most basic and the only motive pervading and directing all aspects of his conscious or unconscious behavior. That's unsubstantiated generalization, an oversimplification."

"This is how I think too," Knox agreed.

"Furthermore, Freud accomplished only the negative part of the work to be done. He broke some of the restrictions and prohibitions prevailing in the society of his generation. Since then, it became permissible, though not always welcome, to discuss the topic of sex and love in society, in schools, not mentioning the proliferation of the countless books written on it, its influence on modern art, literature and the motion picture industry."

"How do you know all these things?" Marisa marveled. "You're supposed to come from another world, but you seem to be better informed about our ideas than many of us!"

"You don't have to be a Zulu to know their way of life. . . . You may have gone there to become acquainted with their way of living, or you may have read and studied it from your books. But coming back to Freud, I do agree with him that the pleasure principle or man's quest for pleasure is a fundamental and permanent need of every human person. I wouldn't, on the other hand, equate pleasure with the *Id*, the *libido* and *Eros*. . . . For there are as many pleasures as the number of activities man successfully performs. Besides, there's not only a quantitative but also a qualitative difference between the diverse sources and forms of pleasure. To consider, for instance, the scientist's quest for knowledge as the sublimation of his surplus libido, betrays a rather naive and simplistic ingenuity."

"Perhaps it also betrays Freud's own obsession with sex?" Knox ventured.

"That might well have been the case from what we know about his personal life," Gynca agreed. "But there's one more aspect I'd like to emphasize. I think that Freud's doctrine on the tripartite division of the human psyche into *Id, Ego* and *Super Ego* represents the revival, the modern version of the old opposition and conflict based on the dichotomy or dualism between body and soul. To that extent, therefore, Freud, far from placing sex on totally new foundations, only reinforced the old prejudices of Plato and his followers."

"I've never thought of that in this perspective," Knox mused. "But it makes sense, though. What has been accomplished so far is that we made the topic of sex both fashionable and respectable, but the old conflicts are still within us."

"What do you think," Noesis asked, "is at the root of this conflict?"

"Well, we mentioned the moral-religious and social taboos."

"I know that, but what is then at the root of those taboos? Why did they come into existence at all? There must have been some reasons, since the causeless cannot exist."

"That's true. Let me think. . . . Perhaps it's the conflict created between the body and the soul, the latter being extolled as the first, original, true, higher and superior part of man's nature, while the former was denied and rejected as the low, the inferior, animal, that is, only the material, instinctual and base part of man, the cause and the source of his shame and embarrassment?"

"That's not enough. . . ." Noesis insisted. "Go somewhat deeper and ask yourself the question why this doctrine was invented, for what purpose and what it has accomplished?"

"That's a hard set of questions," admitted Knox.

"Well, then, allow me to say what I think," Noesis continued. "Let's start from the last part of my question and ask again, what did the doctrine about the soul-body dichotomy accomplish in the way man was forced to look upon himself since its invention?"

"Due to the fact that man couldn't possibly live as a spirit without a body, he had to satisfy, at least occasionally, his sexual desires and needs. But he did it with the dirty conscience of a thief who appropriates something which is not his by right, feeling unclean, guilty and abject afterward, looking upon himself as a sinful, fallen, degraded, depraved creature, an immoral delinquent, a moral criminal. At the same time, he felt resentful, contemptuous toward himself. He hated himself and was ashamed, disgusted. Consequently, he lost his self-love, self-respect, self-esteem, and also his personal pride, of course. He became humble under the weight of his compunction. He was ready to submit, a penitent asking to be punished. He feared the revenge and the wrath of the gods, at the hands of 'the good and the just,' who were to mete the punishment out to him. In modern terms, he became a neurotic, a schizoid, a man divided against himself, his own worst enemy."

"Excellently worded, Edward. Where did you take it from, or is this your own conclusion?" Noesis inquired.

"In the name of the commandment of truth and of intellectual integrity, I must confess that I took a large part of it from our philosopher, Nietzsche," Knox said modestly. "But tell me, do you agree with it or don't you?"

"One hundred percent! But I'd also add that Nietzche believed that the invention of sin and the so-called 'moral world order' served only one purpose, that is, the means for the desire to rule men through their sick conscience."

"But it's awful!" Marisa voiced her indignation. "It would mean that what parades as virtue is just the disguised form of an unholy quest for power, in itself an immoral intention and deed. It's a hard truth to accept, if it's really true!"

"Since you sound rather skeptical," Gynea intervened, "I'll try to convince you without taking the better of your mind, all right?"

"Proceed at your pleasure," Marisa invited her.

"Well, then, let's go back to the foundations and first premises," Gynea proposed. "First of all, what do you think of the doctrine of the mind-body opposition? Is it true or false?"

"I have to reject it as false, in the light of the evidence coming from the science of biology and psychology, which demonstrate the opposite, that is, man's psycho-somatic unity, oneness, wholeness and integrity. They say that mind and body are only two different aspects—and inseparable ones for that matter—of that one and indivisible reality called man."

"Fine. But then if the first premise is false, what do you have to say on all the conclusions based on it and derived from it?" Gynea pressed her point.

"They stand or fall with the truth or falsity of the premise itself."

"Well then?" Gynea asked with satisfaction.

"Yes. I see now. You're right. The whole business is false and corrupt, breeding falsity and corruption."

"Well put indeed. But make the connection with our topic, sex."

"To tell you the truth, Gynea," Marisa confessed, "I could never bring myself to that level of self-abasement, where I could regard man's origin as low and sinful. But I thought that I was alone with my conviction. Therefore I kept it to myself. Besides, I lacked the right ideas to justify my position to my own self. I'm glad I have it now."

"Before we go too far with our conclusions," Noesis remarked, "I'd make one important qualification regarding the matter of sex."

"What is it?" questioned Knox.

"Just a simple and self-evident principle; sex taken as a biological fact and the means of procreation is neither high nor low, neither morally good nor bad, neither virtue nor vice. But considering its psychic component, that is, man's attitude toward it, his motivation, his intentions, whether he uses it or misuses it, sex may become all the evil things I mentioned before."

"Are you trying to put down certain restrictions by reintroducing a new set of taboos through the back door?" Knox asked critically.

"No, I'm not," Noesis replied. "Though I must confess that I'm against all sorts of indiscriminate sex and promiscuous love-making, called also licence. I look upon it as the misuse of freedom and sex, instead of being its intelligent use."

"Could you be more explicit," Knox suggested.

"Surely! I was going to. . . . So listen. Do you remember the all important principle of man's psycho-somatic unity?"

"I do. I just mentioned it a while ago!"

"Then apply it to the issue of sex. That's all I wanted to say."

"I have it!" exclaimed Knox with pleasure. "Let me say it. You mean that just as the body cannot and should not be separated from the mind—some people call the latter a soul—so sex should contain both the physical and the psychic elements in it to make it whole, one and meaningful!"

"Go into more details," Gynea coaxed him on.

"Sure! If someone separates the two components, he violates the integrity of the whole. Thus sex, devoid of its psychic components, becomes base, no better than prostitution. Conversely, a psychic element not translated into physical expression equals the impotence of a sterile mind and body."

"What would you call the psychic element?" Gynea went on.

"Love, what else?" Knox remarked with certainty.

"Would you care to elaborate on your conception of love?" Gynea pursued.

"I have no definition ready. But, speaking negatively first, I'd reject the romantic infatuation as a beautiful sickness of the imagination. Similarly, I'd oppose the attempt to associate love with any altruistic interpretation, such as attending to someone's needs, to care for those who suffer, to dedicate one's whole life to the service of the down-trodden, to sacrifice one's own goals and values, to divest oneself from every selfish concern and to become a totally selfless non-entity. One cannot sacrifice one's own self, for it would amount to self-extinction. The self is man . . . and man is his own self."

"Then would you say that love is a selfish concern?" Gynea went on with her questions.

"Yes, of course!" Knox answered. "To love and to claim, at the same time, that one isn't really interested in the object of one's love or in the person whom one loves, means to deal with contradictions. The same appears also from the effects of love: joy, pleasure and satisfaction—call it happiness, if you wish. These are personal, private and, to that extent, 'selfish' experiences of the individual self." Knox became very animated and pleased with his success in exercising the powers of his mind. Gynea added another question:

"What are the conditions which make the birth and develop ment of love possible?"

"I'll say what Ed told me the other day, all right?" Marisa broke in and looked at Knox for approval.

"Go ahead, just don't say all the things I told you!" Knox said with a smile.

"Well, you spoke of respect and admiration for the values belonging to the character of the person whom we know and learn to love."

"But if this is so, how on earth can people claim to love the imperfect, the valueless, the sick, the negation of values?" Gynea inquired further.

"They claim something which nobody can accomplish," Knox took over again. "Every normal, healthy mind is naturally attracted by the good, the beautiful and the true. Similarly, a healthy person instinctively shrinks and recoils with aversion from the bad, the deformed, the ugly, the unhealthy and the false."

"In other words, you'd never concern yourself with those who don't meet your standards?" Noesis interposed his question. "You'd never help anybody?"

"Oh, no! I didn't mean that!" Knox protested. "Certainly I'd help, but not because I consider man's misfortunes a positive value! My purpose would be identical to the desire of a medical doctor to restore the sick to health again. And that would give me pleasure. However, that's only the first step. One removes, if one can, the negative, in order to make room for the positive, which alone is the cause of one's love, understood as our respect and admiration for one's values. I'd say that the same applies also to self-love. One can love oneself only on the condition that one knows and identifies oneself as the possessor of definite values or perfections. Otherwise, one ends up by hating oneself for one's failures and impotence. And this is what Aristotle teaches in his ethics."

"If these ideas are part of your convictions," Noesis remarked addressing himself to both Marisa and Knox, "I'd like to know what you think of those who worship the value of suffering and build their so-called virtues around the shrines of self-sacrifice?"

"I think of them with contempt, disgust and aversion," Knox answered. "I consider them sick, that's why they repel me so much. They're psychological inverts."

"In what sense do you use these terms?" Gynea asked.

"Perhaps I should have identified them as either masochists or sadists, or even both. Let me explain what I mean. As you know, the masochist is the abnormal person who derives pleasure from suffering, whereas the sadist is the other abnormal type who secures his pleasures from inflicting pain and suffering on his victims. But the important point is this: both types are motivated by the desire for pleasure, and, to that extent, their motivation is legitimate and normal, I'd say. Only the means they choose to attain them are different and abnormal. This is why I used the expression 'psychological inverts.' "

"Do you realize, Edward," Gynea questioned him, "that if you take your ideas to their logical consequences, you'll have to admit that there is a great deal of abnormality present in your religious and moral beliefs? For instance, your conception of God as the one who punishes man with eternal hell-fire. The sacrifice of the Innocent, his son, for the sins of the guilty. The insistence that suffering is good for man because he deserves it and the more he suffers, the better for him. Some go even further and say that one sure way to measure God's love for someone is by weighing the amount of suffering he visits upon him. That He allows evil to exist for this purpose, though He's thought of, at the same time, as omniscient, omnipotent and all-loving. . . ."

"How true!" Noesis confirmed. "But it must be the love of a masochist and a cruel sadist coexisting in a schizo whom people worship as their god. Besides, in the field of morality or ethics, one finds the same glorification of suffering as the inner core of an inverted morality. The insistence on mortifying the flesh, self-denials of all kinds, the self-imposed sufferings and punishments for the body. The castration of all passions, the mutilation of one's nature by the repeated acts of self-violation, the hatred of all pleasure, especially those of the body, and finally, the condemnation of all of life and its values, in the name of an unwarranted hope and belief in an afterworld. All this completes the picture of an unhealthy morality."

"I agree with most of what you've just said," Knox declared. "However, I wonder whether you and your people are absolutely free of suffering. After all, I assume that, in spite of your superior stage in evolution, you're neither omniscient nor omnipotent. Limitations, therefore, and all the imperfections which they imply, must be with you in some form or another. What would you answer, Noesis?"

"I'll answer your question, though you must realize that we've wandered far away from our original problem. I'd like to get

193

back to it after this. As to your question, I'll tell you now only the essentials, leaving the details for later on, if we come to that. Certainly, I agree with you that the root of suffering lies in the limitations of our being, in our ignorance and inability to transcend these limitations. But I want to say that suffering and knowledge are inversely proportional. The ignorant suffers more, because of the many mistakes that he makes, whereas the one who knows more is better equipped to deal with the problems of existence. Medical science could serve as the best illustration. It follows, therefore, that in our world and in our lives there is less suffering than in yours, due to our superior civilization and culture."

"Nevertheless," Knox objected, "there must be some amount of suffering present even in your lives!"

"No doubt about that, but instead of putting ourselves on our knees, folding our hands in prayer, humbled by fear and guilt, we walk up to them straight, upright and with courage. We take it as a challenge and we're confident that we'll defeat it by the power of our minds!"

"Still, what do you do while you're fighting it?," Knox insisted. "I mean, victory doesn't come to you by the miraculous act of your will power! And at least for that period of time, suffering is still with you."

"That's true, but we take suffering with dignity. You see, Edward, one can suffer with dignity, without losing one's pride and courage."

"I see. . . ." Knox felt he had to agree and withdrew any further objections.

"Now let's go back to the questions on sex," Gynea proposed in compliance with Noesis' request. "I'd like to present a few more critical remarks on the topic."

"Go ahead," Marisa prompted, apparently forgetful of the late hour.

"I find a strange paradox in your world, almost the coexistence of opposites, with regard to your contradictory attitudes toward sex."

"What's your point?" Knox inquired.

194

"Just the obvious," Gynea said with a smile. "First, you have the moral-religious taboos you inherited from the primitive ages of your past that created the negative and prohibitive attitude toward sex. Then you have its opposite extreme, in the rather distasteful mystification and glorification of sex through your mass-media communication, accomplishing the state of a collective monomania, an obsession with sex, giving an undue significance and emphasis. Am I correct in my statement?"

"It's very well taken," Knox agreed.

"But that's not all," Gynea went on. "I'm thinking of the psychological effects, of the peculiar and unhealthy disposition and attitude toward sex, created in the minds of the victims. It's the perfect example and illustration of how a neurotic framework can be created on a collective basis. It's the coexistence in one of two opposite forces, pulling and tearing the individual apart, as if he were on a rack. He has, on the one hand, his natural sexual desires and needs, heightened to an abnormal degree by the peddlers of sex and pornography. On the other hand, he has to face the inhibiting power of the moral-religious code, which 'forbids,' condemns and throws filth upon it, generating the feeling of guilt, anxiety, thus creating the attitude of ambivalence, the chronic and exasperating feeling of tension, because of unsolved conflicts. Add to this the fact that, according to your moral standards, every woman and man, but especially the woman, is supposed to postpone, to deny the satisfaction of her sexual needs till the hour of marriage. Since practically nobody can live up to such an unnatural standard, all sorts of psychological and social problems arise. Most are condemned to seek sexual satisfaction in a clandestine manner, and sex crimes are not an unusual event in your society either. I could also mention the victims of both extremes, I mean those of the puritanic attitude and the others who overemphasize sex. To the first belong the frigid and emasculated impotents; to the second, the joy-makers, the pleasure seekers, the licentious, hedonists of every kind and form. To me this seems to be the whole picture of the sex situation as you have it here."

"Well, I must commend you for hitting the nail right on its

head," Knox commented. "I remember that in college the most popular topic of our bull-sessions was the issue of premarital sex, contraceptives, abortion, and so forth."

"Then you could also mention," Noesis added, "the problems of sexual adjustment in marriage, extra or co-marital sex, post-marital sex, the situation of the divorced, the widows, adultery, and finally, the variety of sexual aberrations."

"Whom are you charging with the responsibility for these facts?" Marisa asked.

"You should've said 'what' instead of 'whom,'" remarked Noesis. "Why didn't you?"

"Because I'm not ready to excuse every crime and to absolve every criminal from his guilt in the name of environmental conditioning, or as momentary insanity," Marisa retorted brusquely.

"I'm not willing to uproot the foundations of justice either," Noesis continued in his calm manner. "Still, I insist that the greater part of the problem of sexual offenses is due to your contradictory position and attitude toward sex, created through your present social, moral and religious codes and beliefs. In other words, your institutions are of such a nature that they implicitly contain, breed and invite transgression. You may recall that we already made it clear what unholy desires of power and domination lie hidden behind these codes and customs."

"What would you suggest, then, as a solution?" Knox asked.

"The perfect solution would require the abolition of your family centered social system. However, we already came to the conclusion that this would be unfeasible. Therefore, the only thing left to be done is to work in the direction of a slow transformation of your institutions in a non-violent manner by means of education, enlightenment and emancipation."

"What should be the first step toward such a goal?" Knox asked again.

"I'd propose the total revamping of your outlook on sex and its evolution within man's life. I'd cleanse it from the stain of both puritanism and licence. I'd teach that sex should be accepted for what it is, namely, as the most natural and legitimate part of man's nature. I'd avoid the senseless mystification of over-glamorized sex and, similarly, I'd reject every attempt to associate it with sin, guilt and punishment. Consider also what we've already said tonight, and you'll end up with a healthier attitude than the one you have now."

"I'm afraid," Gynea interposed, "that Noesis forgot to mention one important point. The so-called war of sexes, which I consider as another illustration of the unhealthy conception of man's relation to woman."

"That's right," Noesis agreed. "In fact, this would be the last part of our discussion for tonight and it won't take too long."

"I think Marisa already described a good part of the unfair situation in which women find themselves in our society," Knox suggested.

"I know, and I'm not going to repeat that part. I'd rather talk on the missing part, the positive elements which could translate into reality the woman's desire for emancipation," Noesis said with emphasis.

"I have the impression that you're going to talk on the old topic of the equality of sexes," Knox sounded rather disappointed.

"No, I'm not. But since you brought it up, let me say at least that in theory and in principle most of your civilized countries subscribe to woman's equality, but in practice and in reality there has been little change outside of granting them the right to be educated and to vote."

"Perhaps that's the way you put it," Marisa interjected, "but I'm not ready to defend the equality of man and woman in an absolute sense. After all, no one can deny that man and woman are different, both psychologically, and, of course, physically."

"I believe, Marisa," Noesis observed, "that you think of equality in terms of identity, and it's for this reason that you insist on the obvious differences which I'd never try to disregard. But the way I look at it is this, man and woman are equal, nevertheless, different."

"Isn't that a contradiction?" Knox expressed his astonishment.

"I don't think so," Noesis replied. "Don't you always say and never get tired of repeating that 'all men were created equal'? But that doesn't mean that they're identical. As a matter of fact, every man—considered as an individual—is different. I'd go even further and say that every individual as such is bio-genetically and psychologically only one, therefore, unique, original and exclusive. Which means, Edward, that in the whole history of mankind's evolution, from its primitive beginnings up to the present and future too, there has never been and will never be another individual such as you, for instance. . . . Nature doesn't repeat itself."

"If you meant this as a compliment, please accept my due appreciation." Knox reacted with good humor. "But I'm not overwhelmed with this revelation, because it's true also of you, of Gynea, Marisa, and of every living organism."

"I'd like to hear what Noesis has to say on the difference between man and woman," Marisa insisted with curiosity.

"What I have to say is really known to you already," Noesis started. "Perhaps my words will be different, that's all. Anyway, when I speak of the differences, I don't mean to imply any opposition and conflict, sometimes called 'the war between the sexes.' "

"I'm sure that you have nothing left for that old mythical conception of women being 'superfluous spareribs' either?" Knox remarked jokingly.

Noesis smiled in agreement and continued: "Instead of opposition, I'd rather suggest the idea of mutual complementarity of what we call the masculine and the feminine modes of being a person. There're certain traits—physical and psychic—which are more prominent in man, and we call them for this reason masculine. Similarly, the predominance of certain other characteristics in woman, identifies them as feminine."

"I hope you're not referring again to the old cliché that 'man's the head while the woman's the heart'!" Marisa remarked ironically.

"Oh, no! Not at all! In truth, as you pointed out yourself some time ago, that is a disguised offense against woman, implying that women are mindless creatures, fit only to serve as useful means for man's sexual satisfaction."

198

"Did you then refer to that other old saying that 'behind every great man there's a great woman'?" Marisa kept on.

"I wouldn't say that either. But if I were to say something to that effect, I'd rephrase it so as to read: 'At the side'—and not 'behind'—'of every great man there's a great woman.' But even this less offensive form doesn't express the truth."

"Why?" Knox asked.

"Simply because it's based on the wrong assumption that man and woman are by the necessity of nature destined to depend on each other and to live together. I don't like the implication of a dependent relationship. It's against the principle of freedom and self-sufficiency. I believe that both man and woman should first become independent, autonomous and self-sufficient persons, before they become anything else to each other."

"Aren't you asking or demanding too much, especially from a woman?" Knox doubted.

"No, he isn't," Gynea intervened. "Your question, Edward, betrays a lot. In fact, it tells me that you're convinced that the woman is meant to be a born dependent, a native appendix, a kind of parasitic being, a formless mass or matter, to be shaped after the image of the man who takes her under his protection and guidance."

"But, truly speaking," Knox insisted, "isn't this the real picture we form from the knowledge of our past history?"

"And you're ready to take it as the expression of ultimate truth?" Gynea challenged him.

"Since you force me, I'll have to say a few things which might not please you. So I present my formal apologies in advance. . . ." Knox began.

"You don't have to go to all this trouble of being nice and so tactful," Gynea remarked with severe dignity.

Knox pulled himself up and said: "I only meant to point out that all the values of our civilization and culture—our religions and philosophies, the sciences, arts, our socio-economic and political values—were created almost exclusively by men. Where are the woman philosophers, scientists, artists, leaders and creators?"

Marisa took offense by these humiliating observations, so she

199

snapped at Knox: "Do you know what really happened, you glorious and proud sons of Adam? From the beginning until now you've enslaved us, you filled our homes with the products of your creative efficiency in the bedroom and elsewhere, then you wheel around impudently and blame us for not having accomplished the work in which you wouldn't have allowed us to participate!"

"I didn't mean to hurt your feelings, Marisa," Knox apologized.

"Let's bury the war hatchet," Noesis proposed, "and let's try to set things straight. There's truth in both what Edward and Marisa said. And I interpret this in an historical perspective. Remember that every stage in the process of evolution is a necessary one. Therefore, given the primitive socio-economic conditions of your life in the past, things had to take that course of development, especially if we keep in mind that the woman has been burdened and handicapped in many ways through pregnancy and childbirth. However, the next stage of development will bring along the woman's full emancipation and her participation in the creative roles of life."

"Thank you, Noesis," Marisa sighed with relief.

"I'd like to take up again the ideas of personal autonomy and self-sufficiency," Gynea said. "I want to point to the negative and destructive consequences, especially in marriage, when these values are absent in the persons who get married."

"Let's hear it," Knox said with his usual eagerness.

"If I'm not mistaken," Gynea went on, "most people hope and believe that marrying someone will give than the solution to all their personal problems. Both partners start out with the conviction that they'll be sure to find in marriage, through each other's person, their own identity and fulfillment. They commit the same grave mistake and fallacy of trying to accomplish the impossible, that is, to find themselves in others. And, as we already agreed, this never works, because it's impossible. They speak a great deal about their needs: the need to belong, to be accepted, to be wanted, to be loved, to be useful, to be understood, to be helped, to be encouraged, and so on, endlessly. They crave for closeness, togetherness, understanding, warmth, congeniality, psychic affinity, communion, oneness, and what not. These are the things they expect to find in marriage. And then look at the results. What do you see instead? Didn't we mention the increase in the rate of divorce and separation in another context already? Should we go into the endless list of family problems that keep marriage counselors in business?"

"There's no need for that," Knox replied. "But what are you going to say next? We already heard from both of you that you don't have much left for the institution of marriage and family. On the other hand, you also know that we're stuck with it, so to speak, and for a long time to come. So then, what's there to be done?"

"Correct the mistakes that can be corected, thus improving that which you have to live with," Noesis declared.

"This is easier said than done. . . ." Marisa joined Knox in a resigned manner.

"Nevertheless, it can be done. It's not impossible. Of course, it requires a lot of work and patience," Noesis stated. "Certainly, it's much easier to depend, to be protected, to rely on each other as useful crutches, and to bandage each other's wounds. You can glamorize this as a virtue. You can call it love, charity, compassion, sympathy, pity or what you will. But let me tell you. it doesn't work in the long run. One of the partners, usually the more independent and self-sufficient one, sooner or later will get tired of the perpetual role of the good Samaritan. He'll begin to feel exploited, used and misused. He becomes aware that he has always been the giver, getting only more complaints and worries in return. His feelings of frustration will mount in intensity until he'll be ready to call it quits. . . . Perhaps not an open break, just the inevitable search for compensations, usually found outside the bonds of marriage. . . . Finally, I'd like to remind you of the inevitable loss of freedom and of the necessary conditions of love and friendship. Do you still remember them?"

"Yes, I do," Knox replied. They're two or three: freedom, respect and admiration."

"But you realize that you can't respect and admire the inferior, the low, the mediocre, the negative, the absence of values. Consequently, so-called incompatibility—which is your classic way of finding good reasons for your bad causes in marriage—has to show up its ugly face."

"The conclusion and the moral in this is simple," Gynea took over. "Before you can be anything to anybody in a constructive way, you have to become a person of value for your own sake, an independent, self-sufficient being. You can't give something you don't possess yourself. But you have something of value only if you yourself acquire it. There's no magic formula, and a marriage partner is no magician either. He cannot imbue values in your person. That's something which is self-acquired."

"Granted that what you said is true," Marisa commented, "I still didn't hear either of you express your ideas on how you see men and women as complementary. You see, my difficulty is this: if every person becomes—as you say that he ought to—totally autonomous and self-sufficient, I don't see any reason why and for what purpose they should associate at all, either in marriage or otherwise. There remains only one thing to be done, namely, to satisfy their sexual needs, which they cannot, under normal circumstances, satisfy by themselves. Is that all that's left for man and woman to hold in common?" Marisa concluded with disappointment.

"You still seem to look down on sex and consider it as something belonging to the lowest rank of your values. But we said enough about that," Gynea replied. "So let me answer the first part of your question. By complementary, we mean the exchange of values and not the exchange of problems, troubles, personal deficiencies of all sorts. Then you may recall that, in the beginning of our discussion tonight, we mentioned that every individual represents only part of all the values which the human race as a whole is capable of creating. Thus, we approach another human being with the intention of offering him or her our own values, in exchange for the values the other one possesses. And this applies not only to the man-woman relationship, but on a larger scale too."

"But then, if I understand you correctly," Marisa continued, "the man-woman relationship—apart from sex—is in no essential way different from what we generally call friendship?"

"That makes sense. And tell me why should it be any different? Isn't friendship the only true form of all human relationships? Husband and wife, shouldn't they be friends? What else would you like to find in that relationship?"

"Well, there's the business of children. . . ." Marisa tried again.

"We've said a lot about that situation from both sides. But let me ask you whether you agree or not that the only correct form of the parent-child relationship should be that of true friendship, based on the respect for the freedom of all concerned? That the whole family should be based on this friendship, between the parents themselves first, and then also with regard to their children?"

"That's true. . . ." Marisa conceded. "But you mentioned before certain different psychic traits in men and women, which we call masculine and feminine. What are they?"

"Oh, well! So much has been written and said on this question that there's hardly anything new to add to it," Gynea continued. "The image of the human male and female has undergone so many changes and interpretations, that one doesn't know any longer which one to choose. . . . You find the most romantic mystification of femininity—the eternal womanliness—and also the equally exaggerated naturalism and rationalism of the advocates of emancipation. Likewise, man has been depicted either as a demigod, the personification of all virile virtues, or else, as the ruthless tyrant who oppresses and exploits the weaker sex. I would, therefore, suggest that we abandon these distortions, and to regard both man and woman as two different individuals, whose differences shouldn't be based only on their sex characteristics. In this sense, I'd say that whatever these differences may be between man and woman, they shouldn't be emphasized to any greater degree than the differences existing between any two individuals, regardless of their sex."

"Then I'll have to conclude again that the main reason why man seeks out a woman is to satisfy his sexual appetites. . . ." Marisa insisted.

"And also the exchange of their personal values, through which they become mutually enriched," Gynea concluded. Then she added: "Certainly you'd find it easier to agree with me if you could see the women in your world standing on equal footing with the men in the creation of all cultural values. However, you can see even here and now, on your own planet, that the attitude of the few professionally educated and trained women is very different from those whose only asset so far has been their ability to get pregnant and to attend to the chores of their household. And I'm inclined to believe that this is the trend of the future."

After this last statement of Gynea, there ensued a prolonged silence, as if suggesting that they had exhausted their topic for the night.

"Well," Knox said, "I guess we discussed every possible angle of our topic for tonight, don't you think so?" As he spoke he stood up, straightening his body.

"Yes, I believe we did," answered Noesis thoughtfully. "There's a great deal of material to be thought over and prepared."

"I should say so!" agreed Marisa hastily, while gathering her things.

Gynea smiled with understanding. Noesis then saw them to the door, and they departed as usual, leaving aside all the superfluous banalities of social conventions.

CHAPTER NINE

A DIFFERENT LIFE STYLE IN THE AGE OF TOTAL
AUTOMATION IN A UNIFIED UNIVERSE

Noesis made his next appearance at Knox's apartment the following week. He had come rather early, around six o'clock in the afternoon. Knox and Marisa were just getting ready to eat dinner. They were surprised when Noesis didn't decline Marisa's invitation to join them. Oddly enough, they had roast beef for dinner that night. . . .

"I see that roast beef is your favorite dish, Edward," Noesis remarked jokingly, as he took his place at the table.

"So it appears, doesn't it?" laughed Knox remembering what they had said regarding roast beef and married life. "But I still like it," he said looking at Marisa, who became visibly embarrassed by the allusion.

"Ed told me that Gynea left," she said to steer the conversation to another direction.

"Yes, she did. She wanted to visit certain places which she hasn't yet seen on your planet," answered Noesis quite matter of factly. "She wanted to do this, because she doesn't know whether she's ever coming back here again once she returns to her place of origin."

"You must travel a lot," observed Knox, "There's no distance you couldn't reach, in no time at all, I suppose!"

"Yes, we do. We never stay too long in any place. I see no reason why one should."

"But don't you get attached to some place which you consider your home?" Marisa asked with surprise.

"We like to think that the whole of the universe is our home," Noesis replied. "We're cosmopolitans, in the strictest and truest sense of the word. This shouldn't surprise you though, for I've noticed that traveling has become one of your favorite pastimes, made possible through your improved means of transportation. Provincialism and attachment to one place is on the wane even on your planet."

"That's true," agreed Knox. "In fact, I couldn't imagine myself living out the days of my life sitting still in the same narrow spot, when I know of the many places that there are. . . . Open and inviting me! I hope some day I'll be able to afford to go around the world. It helps to widen one's narrow horizons of existence and to acquire new ideas, to learn about the ways how other people live. . . . But I guess I'll have to wait a long while before this dream of mine can materialize. It's always the same thing . . . money!"

"Which is no problem to us," remarked Noesis indifferently.

"Then everybody in your world must be a millionaire!" exclaimed Marisa.

"We don't have one single millionaire."

"I know!" Knox broke in. "You mean that money's unknown to you!"

"It's known to us, but we don't use it. We don't need it."

"What do you mean?" questioned Knox in utter amazement.

"I'm sure you must think that I'm joking or something like that, but I'm not!" answered Noesis serenely. "I really mean what I said. Of course, it must be really very hard, almost beyond the limits of your imagination, to think of a social and economic system in which money is non-existent, for the simple reason that it became superfluous."

"Then, what do you do?" Knox tried to figure out the answer. "Probably you trade in goods as we did here on our planet before money was invented, as a more direct means of exchange, correct?"

"No, that's not right either! I suppose we'll have to discuss this subject in more detail. Should we consider it as our topic for tonight?"

"Why not?" Knox agreed promptly. "I was thinking on our next subject of discussion anyway. Allow me then to set up the recorder, yes?"

Noesis nodded in a gesture of assent, and said: "Let's then proceed methodically, from the beginning."

"Of course," assented Knox, then added: "I know what you meant by saying that money is of no use to you!"

"What?" Noesis showed amused curiosity.

"It's only a guess, of course. I was thinking of the way the problem is solved in religious communities, in the monasteries, cloisters, convents, and all sorts of congregations. The members of these societies take certain vows, poverty being one of them. They own nothing as individuals. Everything belongs to the order, which provides for the needs of all the members, who, in their turn, need no money. They don't have to worry about their meals, clothing, shelter, education, medical care, and so on. So, even if they had money, they couldn't use it. They'd have nothing to spend it on. It's kind of a holy communism, they own everything in common. . . ."

"And nothing as their own, not even their freedom. Remember their vow of obedience?" added Noesis critically.

"In other words," Knox said, "I'm wrong again. My example's no good."

"It's not the best, because in addition to the flaws I already hinted to, the community as a whole still needs money in order to trade. The only difference is that the supply of goods is done collectively, not individually. It's only a shift or a transfer of the same function from the members to the superiors of the order. You find actually the same situation also in the families. In most cases the wife and the children are supported by the father as the bread-winner or provider. They receive the goods needed for their subsistence, but the father needs money to pay for them. It's another form of communitarian organization, in which the members of the family are and remain in a situation of dependence, which is the opposite of freedom."

"Then I give up! I don't know what to think any more! Will you please explain how it can be done?" pleaded Knox.

"All right, then. Let's go back to the beginning, and let's follow up the evolutionary stages of the economic process with a view toward the future."

"That's asking for too much!" Knox expressed his doubt. "I don't think we can cover that much material in even two or three sessions!"

"No, I don't agree with you, if we think only in principles and concentrate on the few fundamental ideas upon which the whole system of economic life depends."

"I hope you're right!"

"The first thing we must think of is the relationship between man's needs and the means to satisfy them. Need satisfaction is the key concept. Then we think of man as a producer and a consumer. After that, we speak of him as a trader."

"This sounds very interesting!" Marisa remarked.

"In addition to all this," Noesis continued, "we have to think of man both as an individual and as a member of a group. If he were alone, the only thing he'd have to succeed at would be to provide for his own needs. But this has never been the case, because man very soon discovered the advantages of living in society. The plurality of members made the organization of all economic activities not only necessary, but also desirable. It's the division or distribution of the many forms of production among the members for one common purpose. Each one performed the role of the producer, but only in one specific function. Specialization started and with that also the mutual dependence of the members on each other. The ideal of total self-sufficiency was abandoned. Some of the freedom was sacrificed in exchange for the greater amount of comfort and security achieved through organized labor."

"At this point, I believe," Knox observed, "trading came into being on a larger scale."

"That's correct," Noesis agreed. "First, man exchanged goods; then, they also exchanged services useful for the production of goods. They may have paid for each other's services in goods, up to the point where money was preferred as the means to simplify the ever increasing complexity of exchange. Money became the good par excellence, by which man could buy any goods he needed. Money had been desired for the benefits it confers. It sets one free and independent, increases the security and comfort of the individual, and also gives him a great deal of power he can use for either good or evil purposes."

"Unfortunately it has been more often misused than used," Marisa observed. "I think that it's because of its misuse that people still regard it as something evil."

"I'm glad that you see it in the right perspective, because taken in itself and for what it was meant to serve, money isn't evil, quite the contrary. But there are still a few more principles I want to mention. The all important law of supply and demand which causes the fluctuation of the prices on the market, making the value of money relative. Then there's the problem of private property or private ownership of both the means of production and its sources."

"Why do you label it as a problem?" Knox inquired eagerly.

"Because of the many and conflicting ideas and feelings associated with it. As you know, there're those, like Marx, who defined private property as a theft. . . . Then you have the advocates of the old liberalism in economics, the defenders of free enterprise and the profit motive, giving rise to laissez-faire capitalism. The latter believe that private property is man's inalienable, natural birth-right which becomes the human person as a producer. As a matter of fact, your present world is divided into two opposite camps, each defending one of these opposite ideologies, and they're ready to start bloody revolutions and wars for its sake too. . . . "

"You're saying what Marx taught a century ago, namely that the whole of life—man's civilization and culture—should be regarded as the direct and indirect upshot of his economic needs and concerns."

"Why does that upset you?" Noesis asked calmly. "Certainly, I wouldn't subscribe to it on the whole, because as such it is just another example of hasty generalizations. On the other hand, however, there is no way to deny that man's material needs come first and that upon their satisfaction depends the rise of

209

his cultural needs and interests. Man is neither a disembodied ghost nor a brute. Remember that *Bios* comes before *Logos*. . . . You cannot preach anything to empty stomachs. The most you can do is to induce them to attack those whose stomachs are full. . . ."

"Speaking of stomachs," Marisa interposed, "would you like to have anything else?"

"Thank you, Marisa, but I can't. My stomach's full, so I'm ready and qualified to engage in more philosophising," Noesis answered playfully.

"Let me ask you this," Knox took the opportunity of the break, "are you for or against private property?"

"You should have asked me also whether I'm a capitalist or a communist," Noesis replied with a smile.

"Well, what's wrong with those questions?" Knox retorted curtly.

"One thing only. They lack the all important evolutionary and historical perspective. That's all. If you remember that every stage of evolution is a necessary one, you'll be ready to accept also that our ideas, principles and values are true only within their own historical perspective, neither before nor beyond that."

"But are you defending relativism and denying the existence of absolute truths?" Marisa exclaimed with astonishment.

"It would take me too long and away from our topic if I engaged in discussing the merits of absolutes, relativism, subjectivism and the rest of those involved problems. But to satisfy your curiosity, let me at least say the following: there're certain constants or permanent elements expressed in the laws of nature, but the forms in which they appear vary. It's the idea of the eternal recurrence of the same under different forms. You weren't present when I discussed it with Edward."

"How would you apply that to the business of economics?" Knox challenged his friend.

"It's rather simple, I'd say. The constants would be the ever recurring needs of the human being, dictated by the functional laws of his nature and identity. But the forms of their satisfaction vary and evolve. You have outgrown the old tribal and patriarchal systems. Slavery also belongs to the past, together with feudalism. Right now you're experimenting, with varying success, with capitalism and communism or welfare statism. And so on, into the future. . . ."

"You still haven't told me point blank whether you're for or against private property," Knox reminded him.

"Suppose I tell you," Noesis replied, "that I'm both for it and against it, but not from the same point of view and at the same time and place."

"I'm sorry, but I don't understand you at all," said Knox visibly frustrated. "Would you please speak more clearly?"

"Certainly. Let's go back once more to the beginning, as I've suggested twice already. Try to think of the conditions which made the rise of private ownership necessary, because of its usefulness. Of course, you'd say that the word 'mine' is as old as mankind, and you'd also predict, I assume, that it'll never disappear from man's language."

"And I assume that you believe that it will, or else be replaced by the possessive 'ours'?"

"It'll disappear only as far as the possession of objects is concerned, and it won't be replaced by anything else," Noesis affirmed with conviction.

"Why this new qualification, pray?"

"Because there's one instance, and only one, which is a unique exception. It's my own existence, my own being, my own life, which does not and cannot belong to anybody or anything else but to the sole carrier of life, to the individual. If you want to call it man's first and most intimate private property, you can do that, because it's true. In this sense, the word 'mine' will never disappear from the lips of men."

"If you defend and extoll the principles of individualism, how can you, at the same time, be against private property?" Knox wondered. "I understand that private property is the one and indispensable condition and guarantee of man's independence, freedom, self-sufficiency and privacy. It's almost the natural consequence of being a human person, its natural extension, so to say."

211

"All the things you said, Edward, are true in every respect, but only within the framework of your present social and economic system which you shouldn't consider the last stage in the process of evolution."

"But I don't!" Knox replied impatiently. "Remember that I already mentioned with regret the imminent triumph of collectivism which I take as the death sentence for everything individual and private."

"You should also remember that we didn't consider that so-called thiumph as final and ultimate," Noesis emphasized his point.

"I haven't forgotten that either, but I can't imagine what new socio-economic system could take its place. Are you thinking of a return to or a resurgence of individualism?"

"No, I'm not, and for the simple reason that there is no way to return to the past. Past is past, neither present nor future. . . ."

"But everybody says that 'history repeats itself,' that 'there is nothing new under the sun,' and this seems to fit very well with the idea of eternal recurrence."

"You seem to make very little of those three words I emphasized so much, remember?"

"Oh, yes," Knox said indifferently. "They were 'under different forms,' but I would put more weight on the word 'same.' . . ."

"Not realizing that your emphasis would make evolution either impossible or reduce it to the insignificance of an illusion, no better than wishful thinking and daydreaming."

"Sometimes, you know, I feel that way, especially when I become fully aware of the unglorious record of our past and present history."

"Which comprises only a few thousand years, an insignificant moment in the endless duration of time," Noesis tried to bring Knox to better understanding. Then he continued: "Let's go back again to the problem of private property. I hope to remove your objections or misunderstanding if we look into it more closely. I propose that the origin and the establishment of the right to private possession was due to the special economic conditions man had to solve."

"What conditions do you have in mind?" Knox inquired.

"I'm thinking of the law of survival in a rather adverse situation, when the scarcity of material goods was the general rule. And I want to establish a direct proportion between mans' insistence on his right to private ownership and the quantity of good available. The greater the demand for the goods which cannot be easily secured, the greater the insistence on the right to exclusive ownership, and vice-versa. It's just another consequence of the law of supply and demand."

"You mean to deny man's right to keep as his own the results of his own efforts? You seem to defend and justify the right of others to dispose of those goods at random will. . . ." Knox objected again.

"I would never deny the working man's right to keep the fruit of his labor. After all, he invested his own intelligence, energy and time. Neither do I want to sanction looting for I regard it as a violation of man's freedom."

"Then what?" asked Knox, totally confused.

"Perhaps it'll be better if I illustrate my thoughts with an example. Suppose that there is a man who has only one piece of bread that he needs for his survival. He realizes that his life and survival depend on that piece of bread. Naturally, he will be ready to fight with tooth and nail to defend it against any unwelcome aggressor. He is ready to risk even his life in the combat to keep his only means of survival, right?"

"That's only natural. But what does that prove?"

"Be more patient, and let me finish my example," Noesis answered to Knox's interruption. "Suppose now that another man is fortunate enough to dispose over such a large quantity of food that his survival is guaranteed for the rest of his living days. Do you think that this second fellow would be ready to risk his life for a piece of bread?"

"No, of course he wouldn't, but he would still regard his whole food supply as his own. He wouldn't fight over a piece of bread, he might even give some of it to the poor as charity, but he wouldn't give up his right of ownership, he regards it as his own and he would fight for that."

213

"That's true, although there is a third part to my example," Noesis went on patiently. "Imagine that every man is in this same fortunate situation. Unlimited quantities of food are available for all. In what way would that new situation change man's attitude toward private property?"

"Before I think of those changes, let me tell you that the third part of your example doesn't impress me at all, because I take it for what it is: a utopia!"

"I don't hold that against you, Edward. Your past and present economic situation forbids you to consider it seriously. Nevertheless, may I point out to you a few facts that you seem to have forgotten?"

"Yes, such as? . . ."

"The vast quantities of surplus food stored up by your government at a tremendous cost. They have to do that because production or supply surpasses the demand of the population. They are caught in a dilemma. . . . If they stop or control production, they have to pay people for not producing, which, incidentally, does happen; it is part of your farm subsidy program. If they do not control it, the surplus goods that will flood the market will create a chaos, bringing about a violent shake up in the prices, threatening the stability of the whole market. For one thing, the farmer would get practically nothing for his products, thus becoming unable to compete with those in other fields of production who are not yet threatened by overproduction, and so on."

"What's the point you are trying to develop?" Knox inquired anxiously.

"Right now I only wanted to point out to you the changes, rather the problems, you're facing, because of the improved methods of production which require less people, less time and less energy than ever before. This also means that man's labor is becoming less and less needed and significant for the production of goods. The machine is taking over. There is a shift from the value of physical labor and skill over to the demand for the powers of the mind. The process of full automation, for instance, is being held back for two reasons only: one, there is the threat of unemployment as a consequence of the machinery taking over the human labor. Then there is a lack of persons trained to perform intellectual work. Now, if you put all these pieces together, thinking in terms of the future, perhaps you will not dismiss the third point of my example as a simple utopia. . . ."

"I meant no offense with that observation," said Knox apologetically. "Neither am I denying all those facts which you pointed out. Still, I do not see how it will change man's way of thinking about private property. We have quite a number of millionaires and not one of them is willing to part with his 'surplus' money! On the contrary, it seems to become a compulsive mental obsession with them!"

"I agree with you, but theirs is rather a psychological case and not a matter of economics. They act in that way because it's through their wealth that they try to establish their privileged position of authority and power, their sense of superiority as a compensation for some hidden feeling of inferiority. Or, if you prefer another explanation, I would say that the competitive pattern of your economic system based on the profit motive, accounts for this rather strange condition."

"Take away the profit motive," Knox observed, "and man will produce only the bare minimum required by those who rule over him and punish him if he fails to put up that minimum quota."

"That is the situation which prevails especially in the centrally directed and controlled system of production in the socialist countries, I'm aware of that. I also know that, seeing that this system doesn't work, they are slowly reverting to the old method of free enterprise and personal profit."

"Apparently you don't regard this as a welcome sign of progress though," Knox remarked.

"No, I don't, because I can't call regression as equal to progression."

"In that case, what's the solution?"

"Look, Edward, let me add another point to my example. Perhaps then you'll see the idea I'm driving at. . . . You may as well regard it as another utopian dream from your own limited point of view."

"Let's hear it!" Knox prompted him.

"Suppose that all men have all the goods in unlimited quantity available to them. How would that affect their thinking, their motivation, their relationship to each other?"

"You're indirectly suggesting, I guess, that in that state, the desire for private possession will not exist. Man will not be required to provide for himself, to build up his present and future security, since—as you assume—everything is there for their taking, with no end and no restrictions. Suppose that this could happen. Still, who is going to do the work? Who is going to produce, to supply, to provide?" Knox persisted.

"Can you think of a stage of total and complete automation of all the steps and aspects of the production line? It shouldn't be hard for you to do that! Your own economists point out that there has been a steady decrease in the working hours—from sixty to fifty and less. They predict a four day working week, then even less than that. It takes less and less time and effort to produce more and more."

"But that would put man out of work! He would cease to be a worker, a producer, and would become just a consumer! And if that should happen, what will man do with his leisure time? This is presenting problems even now, in our present society! Idle people become restless and dangerous! There are only so many hours a day that one can watch television, or pursue some other kind of boredom chaser. In other words, the solution of the economic problem will give rise to an even more complex and serious social problem, that of excessive leisure. . . ."

"Undoubtedly, every change brings along with itself a necessary period of crisis and requires new ways of adjustment to the new conditions in one's enviroment. As it has occurred in the past, many will not have the required resilience and adaptability. Those will be the real trouble makers, but only for a while. They will fall aside and life will continue its ascending climb."

"You still owe me the answer as to how people will live in such a society. . . ." Knox reminded Noesis.

"First, I'll talk about the things which will not exist any more,

216

such as man's daily worries and concern with the necessities for keeping himself alive. Second, there will be no opportunity left for ruthless competition and exploitation. People won't crave after privileged positions to outdo their neighbors, to secure power over them through their wealth and to subject and control them through their stomachs. This also means that there will be no sense in displaying one's private possessions, mainly to arouse the neighbors' envy, jealousy and resentment. I mean to say that there will be no need for and no purpose behind private property. It will become meaningless, because it'll be useless. Then there will be no social stratification into the many—often very ridiculous—classifications of people according to their affluence, position, profession, and so forth. . . . Finally and most important, many of the crimes which are being commited in your society now shall become extinct. There will be no reason for them, because there will be no need or desire to rob, to lie, to cheat, to murder, to persecute, to attack. Wars and revolutions will belong to the past."

"This sounds too good to be true!" Marisa finally spoke up after a long silence. "I meant to ask you for quite a while," she continued, "whether the things you were talking about actually represent the conditions of life in your world?"

"Yes, Marisa, they do. I realize, though, how difficult it must be for both of you to rely upon my word only as the expression of truth. Maybe if you accustom yourselves to think in terms of thousands of years from now, into the future, my statements will not sound as fantastic and unbelievable."

"The main difficulty I have," Knox observed, "comes not so much from my lack of imagination with regard to what science and technology can accomplish in the future for man's material welfare. My problem is more of a moral nature, because it concerns man and his nature. I'm not ready to believe that the economic and social conditions alone—in one word, environment— is the main cause for man's moral and cultural decadence. After all, man has achieved a great many things as far as his civilization or material progress goes, but I do not see a parallel improvement in man as a person. As a matter of fact, you pointed to this yourself, Noesis, when you called us motorized barbarians, remember? On the other hand, I'm not ready to blame technology for man's cultural decadence either. I know we settled these questions already. Therefore, I believe there must be something else to it. Material progress doesn't equal cultural progress."

"We agreed on that," Noesis assented. "However, I want to clarify my position from another angle. I didn't mean to imply that there is or there should be a direct relationship of causality between economic progress and culture. In fact, I regard material security and comfort only as a necessary condition—not the cause —for the possible rise of a cultured state of being. I know only too well that a wealthy man is not necessarily a highly cultured person, perhaps even the opposite. Nevertheless, I maintain that leisure is the first condition for the birth of culture, because man has to become free from material concerns in order to engage in any creative work, if he has the ability to do so. This is the reason I insisted repeatedly on the principle that *Bios* comes before *Logos*. Besides, going back to your remark, Edward, to the effect that your material well being has not produced cultural progress, the reason is simple. There is a gap between your advanced technology and your beliefs which date back to the pre-industrial and pre-scientific ages. Your science has progressed, but your philosophy and ethics are still lagging behind, caught in the web of mythical ideas and prejudices. I shall say more about that when we come to the discussion on ethics and religion."

"You mentioned so far only the negative aspects of the outcomes due to the future development of economics," Knox reminded Noesis. "I'd like to hear also the positive side of your predictions."

"I will summarize them by using the slogans of your revolutionary ideas of the past. I think the French revolution started as a fight for freedom, equality and brotherhood under the banner of reason, am I correct?"

"You are well informed," Knox consented. "But those ideals never became part of man's life on earth."

"They couldn't have, because the required economic conditions were non-existent. We agreed that the will to freedom is man's most basic and highest need and value. But let's analyze, so to say, the dimensions of freedom or its different forms. First, I think there is freedom *from* things and people."

"Do you mean to say that in your world nobody works?" Knox inquired with surprise. "Even if one assumes that most of the work can be done by machines and automation, there is still need to create these machines, to plan, to calculate, to control, to direct and to design. . . . Unless you have a perfect fac-simile of a human brain, a super-computer, with a built in I.Q. that surpasses that of the first rank genius. . . ."

"There is no physical labor to be performed by man in our world. We have also relegated most of the administration and supervising jobs to our computers. But there is one thing no computer can do, no matter how complex its structure and functioning—it cannot think for itself, it can't create or act on its own initiative. It only manipulates the variables fed into by a living intelligence. Therefore, there is work to be done, but only intellectual and creative work."

"Who performs that work? What for? Out of duty? To whom? You told me that money and profit are non-existent in your world."

"You ask too many things at once." Noesis answered pleasantly. "Let me answer your questions one by one. First, let me explain to you what we mean by work. We don't look upon it with mixed feelings of resentment as a burden because of its necessity. This attitude applies rather to your mode of thinking. Let me ask you this: do you remember our gardener? He did not grow his beautiful flowers because he was forced by need, because he had to make a living, because of a profit motive or in the name of a duty he owed to some authority above him. No, pleasure and joy were his only motives, and his success was the proof of his ability. His work was self-chosen, self-imposed, self-directed, and performed for a personal reason only, his own satisfaction. . . . Whatever other benefits came from his work, he regarded them as secondary and insignificant. In other words, the exercise of one's creative ability is the only justification and sanction for the work we are doing. I should mention on the side that nobody is required to work any definite amount of time for any given period, and yet all the work gets done, because every creative mind has to express himself of necessity. Even in your world the great philosophers, scientists and artists worked in obedience to their personal desire to express themselves creatively. They thought, studied, discovered and created for their own sake and satisfaction. And that would take care of your many questions concerning work."

Knox felt that he had to agree with this. Then he went on with his questions: "Before I interrupted you, you were talking about freedom from things and people. What did you mean by freedom *from* people?"

"The same thing you mean!" Noesis replied bluntly.

"I don't believe you mean solitude, do you? You don't live like hermits! Although you don't have our institutions of marriage and family, you must have some kind of social organization, true?"

"That's correct, but one which is based on freedom! Perhaps if I introduce the ideas of individuality and equality, it would help you to understand. Nobody belongs to anybody."

"But everybody could belong to everybody else . . ." Knox interposed again.

"How can you say such a thing?" Noesis asked with genuine surprise. "I think I better tell you once and for all that our social organization does not by far resemble any form of socialistic, collectivist, communist and totalitarian system! Freedom and equality cannot exist side by side with those forms of radical government. When we use the terms of freedom and equality we mean just that, and we respect them instead of making a shameful farce, a travesty of them. . . ."

"In other words, you don't have anyone in authority, no kings, no queens, no emperors, no heads of states, presidents, governors, and. . . ."

"Nothing. No politicians whatsoever. That kind of a being is unknown to us. It's a specimen that must have died out a very long time ago."

"And nobody holds power over anybody? There are no masters and no slaves? Nobody tells anybody what to do, how to live? . . .

220

You have no laws, no tribunals of justice, no government at all?"

"You're asking too many questions again," Noesis observed with a smile. "But this time I can answer all those questions with one simple No. We don't have them, because we don't need them."

"But . . . but how?" Knox insisted with astonishment.

"Because all those jobs can be performed better by computers, with the added advantage that computers have no will to dominate, to rule, to dictate, to enslave, to subject and to exploit. They don't display themselves indecently in public, posing as the saviors of mankind, while everybody knows that they are paranoiacs, blinded by their will to power over men, or perhaps just cheap little mediocrities and opportunists."

"However, that presupposes that everybody acts according to reason and nobody makes mistakes, or even worse, violates the laws of your country . . ." Knox interposed.

"We have no written code of laws, as I told you."

"Then everybody does as he pleases! Doesn't that necessarily create a conflict of interests?"

"No, it doesn't, because we don't live as we we 'please.' . . . We don't live by following our irrational whims and impulses. We are rational beings! We always obey our own reason, in accordance to our own knowledge. Remember that even Socrates taught that no one does the wrong or evil thing unless he is an ignorant."

"I know that. But it never worked that way in our own world. And if it works for you, it must be only on account of your superior intelligence and knowledge."

"I'm glad that you came to the right conclusion by yourself. I'll say more on that when we come to the question of ethics."

"What name would you give to the kind of society you live in?" Knox inquired further.

"Do we need a name to label it? We dislike high flying slogans. . . ."

"So you don't have a name for it because government, as we have it here, is unknown to you. Nevertheless, how would you describe it for our benefit and understanding?"

"Call it by the name of a 'communitarian democracy,' although I am afraid that you or your readers will misinterpret it in many ways. First, they wouldn't know what to do with the term 'communitarian.' They would immediately associate it with some kind of communism! Then, the term 'democracy' has been misused in so many ways, for so many unholy purposes, that by now it means nothing at all."

"So far you mentioned freedom from things and people. . . . I believe I understand some of it. On the other hand, you admitted that you live in society. Then I also remember that you mentioned once that you don't have racial differences and nationalities. Does this mean that you all belong to the same race?"

"This term presupposes again the conditions which exist only on your planet. You have your races because of the long process of inbreeding, made possible through the geographical isolation of certain segments of the population. However, such things do not exist in my world. Besides, procreation is not based on the random mating of whoever chooses to do so, as you must recall from our discussion on genetics."

"May I interrupt you for a minute, Noesis, for one question?" Marisa asked timidly. "I know I missed your discussion on eugenics. . . . Still, I want to ask you who is going to prohibit or to allow any man or woman to procreate or not? Who gives them the right to impose their will on others?"

"You consider the problem in the wrong perspective, Marisa," Noesis observed. "This is not a matter of a few dictating the terms upon which others are allowed to live. Neither is it a conflict or a clash of contending wills. It's only man's voluntary consent, based on his rational acceptance of the facts of reality. Man does not obey the will of his equals, he is not subject to their arbitrary authority. He obeys and respects only the evidence and the facts of reality as the final authority, which ought to be accepted by any rational being."

"I'm glad that you made it so explicit, Noesis, because I was afraid that on writing down that passage, if I don't make it clear enough, someone could raise the objections Marisa just brought up. However, since we are allowing ourselves a small digression, could you also clarify the issue of private property, if you don't mind?"

"Of course," Noesis agreed graciously. "I read somewhere in your books that private property is defined as the right to use and to dispose of things *(ius uti et abuti)*. I'm going to use this definition to clarify my ideas on this subject. But please keep in mind two things I've already alluded to today—the universal abundance of all goods and the strictly rational—not emotional— attitude of our people. Consequently, I must say that we have the right of the exclusive use of all things for as long as we need them. In this sense I may call them 'mine.' Therefore, the only thing we don't have is the possession, the accumulation and the disposal of things—I mean destroying them or selling them— because there is no need and no reason to do that. There is nobody to sell to or to buy. Besides, we consider it rather childish and primitive to insist on a piece of paper which gives you the legal right to call certain things as 'yours' only."

"Excuse my insistence," Knox went on, "but couldn't there be a conflict of interests? Let's suppose that two individuals want to occupy the same flat because they happen to have the same preference for its location, the view of the surroundings and the rest of it. What happens then? One of them has to give up and give in, and the other one wins."

Noesis could hardly restrain himself from laughing. There was a shade of amused surprise on his face when he answered: "I'm sorry, but I have to dismiss your question as being very childish, based on a mediocre person's emotions and whims. It's no better than the case of children fighting over the same lollipop just because one happens to be purple."

"You seem to dismiss man's emotions as the proof of his primitivity, his immature condition and inferiority," Marisa remarked critically. "I wonder whether you are the absolute incarnation of pure reason and transcendental logic. . . . Should this be the case, your life must be rather arid, I mean, similar to endless syllogisms and mathematical equations. But that's not human!"

"That is not so, Marisa," Noesis disagreed. "In fact, Edward could tell you that we regard man as an indivisible unity of body and mind, giving even more significance to his biological quality and outfit than you do. Therefore, there is no such thing as 'pure reason.' As to your insistence on man's feelings, sentiments and emotions, I have to say that I don't regard emotions as absolute dictates or primary causes one should accept unconditionally. As a matter of fact, psychology tells you that our feelings are only responses or reactions to what we experience by our senses and interpret by our intellect. But this means that knowledge comes first as the cause and feelings, second, as the effect. First we know, then we feel. Moreover, the nature of the knowledge determines the nature of the emotions that follow. What I object to is the worship of any emotion, regardless of its causes or nature. A human being is human only because of his reason and only to the extent that he guides his life by his intelligent choices and does not indulge in any irrational whim or fit. But that doesn't makes life 'arid,' empty or devoid of joy and pleasures. . . . The fact is that the man, whose thought reaches the highest limits of his quest for knowledge, experiences the deepest and most rewarding feelings. As you must know from the lives of your great geniuses, all of them were passionate men. However, their passions were caused by their quest for more knowledge. You define philosophy as 'love of wisdom,' as an intellectual love of knowledge. Finally, our love for our fellow men should be derived from our knowledge about their values, qualities and perfection we respect and admire."

"I've never thought of emotions in this light," Marisa admitted seriously.

"Suppose we go back to our unfinished matter," Noesis motioned. "What was the last thing we were considering?"

"It was your remarks on races and nationalities," Knox informed him. "I would also presume, as a natural consequence, that you must speak one language only?"

"You guessed it right. The plurality of languages and the unfortunate barriers it creates in the field of communication, could develop only because of the geographical isolation of peoples for a considerable length of time. But you know from linguistics that the many living languages can be reduced to a few original ones."

"You've mentioned a few things about your way of life from a negative point of view so far," remarked Knox. "You mentioned the things you don't have, such as poverty, ignorance, the will to power, senseless competition, social classes, races, nationalities, crime, armed conflicts and so on. . . . Would you care, at this point, to speak in positive terms and give us at least a glimpse into your own way of life, how it's organized and how it works?"

"There is nothing to prevent me from doing so," Noesis answered with a smile. "But I'm afraid you'll end up rather frustrated, especially if you expect to hear the kind of fantastic and spectacular things invented by your fiction writers. I grant, it's very entertaining, but only that!" Noesis paused for a minute as if reflecting, then continued: "First of all, the population on our planet is limited, and it's kept that way. There is no population explosion. The reason is obvious: there is no pleasure in being crowded together with too many people, it would only give rise to many social problems as you have it here. For the same reason, the existing population is also well distributed all around the globe. The density of the population is almost constant and invariable. Of course, we don't have uninhabited or uncivilized areas. Similarly, there are no big cities such as your New York, for instance. Most of us live in well spaced and distributed buildings, each one being equipped with all the facilities and provisions—material and cultural—so as to make it completely self-sufficient and independent from the rest. This applies also to the apartment units themselves. If one wanted to, one could be born, raised and live one's whole life without leaving that autonomous unit. However, this never happens. No building is occupied to its full capacity, in order to allow for the many visitors who keep coming, while others are leaving. I would say that there are approximately one hundred units altogether in each building, but no more than three on each floor. The lower stories contain all the provisions which are automatically, I mean, mechanically delivered to the apartment by simply pressing the proper button or lever. The supply is never exhausted because of the watchful eyes of our computers. The upper stories contain our cultural facilities."

"This is fantastic!" Marisa exclaimed. "According to what you just said, each building has its own stores, school, hospital, recreational facilities, its bank . . ."

"Sorry, no banks, no fire departments, no police stations either," Noesis halted the flight of Marisa's imagination. "We have no need or use for money, there are no fires and no disorderly people either."

"Where are the production centers or your factories?" Knox wanted to know.

"You're right," Noesis replied. "I forgot to say that certain areas are reserved for that purpose, rather remote from the residential sections. The reason is self-evident, although our factory buildings and their surroundings are far from unsightly!"

"What do you use for transportation?" Marisa inquired. "Do you have cars or does everybody own his small . . . 'space scout,' or, shall I say, his little 'flying saucer?' "

"You may call them by those names," Noesis smiled again.

"Then everybody must be flying around, your skies must be full of those luminous bugs," Marisa tried to picture for herself an unseen reality. "Don't you have accidents and collisions?"

"Since every craft operates on its own magnetic and gravitational energy," Noesis explained, "collisions can never occur. The field of energy around the craft serves also as a protective shield and automatically alters its course or the direction of the flight whenever necessary."

"Do you stay long in one place?" Marisa questioned on.

"Whenever there's some new project to be worked out, we do. Otherwise, we're almost always on the move, so to say, exploring the vastness of the universe. This is, you see, another reason why we cannot get attached to one place, much less to any one object."

"Are there many populated planets in the universe?" Knox inquired.

"I remember that you asked something similar during our first meeting," Noesis reminded him. "But we don't know the exact

226

number, because we haven't explored every corner of the cosmos."

"On what level of civilization and culture do people exist on those planets unknown to us? I assume that there may be some that are even more advanced than yours. . . ." Knox continued.

"That's a fact, but there's the free exchange of ideas on an interplanetary basis, so the differences are soon levelled off whenever the biological and physical conditions are favorable. . . ."

"Let me ask you a question on another topic," Marisa said. "How many people live in one apartment or do you live alone, by yourself?"

"Our way of life provides for both privacy and social contacts," Noesis answered, realizing that Marisa couldn't imagine that way of life at all. "Of course, we don't like to be crammed together with many people. Our need for privacy is far greater than our desire for togetherness."

"Then I assume that most of your contacts must be rather superficial, accidental and of short duration. . . ."

"I have to disagree with you, Marisa," Noesis replied. "We most certainly respect every person's freedom, therefore we never impose our presence on them beyond the necessary limit of time. Besides, there's no need for a long span of time to know another person rather thoroughly, and it may also lead, in the opposite direction, to frustration and boredom. On the other hand, our friendships are neither superficial nor short lived. Our respect and admiration for our friends isn't based on the changing and unstable moods and whims of the moment. As I told you before, our emotions are caused by our knowledge."

"Do you like or love everybody in your world in just the same way?" Marisa kept on her questioning.

"I suppose that you must think of us as if we were all absolutely identical, not allowing for individual differences. You're imagining a production line for human beings, total uniformity and equality. But this is far from the truth."

"I imagined," Marisa clarified, "that all of you are equally superior men and women, geniuses all, possessing the same intelligence, the same dispositions, tendencies, abilities."

"You seem to forget what you must have heard in your psychology classes, namely, that equality in the general level of intelligence doesn't exclude the presence of individual differences, known as personal attributes and abilities," Noesis informed.

"Then if you have those individual differences, there must be some discrimination going on. . . . You must prefer the company of some to that of others. Perhaps there are even some for whom you don't care at all, or even dislike them."

"Of course we have our own preferences and proceed selectively," Noesis explained. "But I wouldn't imply that this circumstance leads necessarily to social conflicts! We're neither children nor barbarians!"

"How long have you known Gynea, if you don't mind this personal question?" Marisa asked abruptly.

Noesis smiled at her ingenious question and replied: "For quite a long time, I'd say. And are you also going to ask whether she's my only friend, the first one and the last one?"

"No, I'm not!" Marisa retreated quickly.

"Speaking of time," Knox changed the subject, "I assume that your lifespan must be much longer than ours. . . ."

"Several times longer," Noesis consented. "We also learned how to control the problems of aging, although we haven't reached immortality."

"Then you'll be dead some day!" Marisa cried out with her usual naiveté.

"But of course! That's the natural course of life!" Noesis replied.

"And how do you feel about death?" Marisa continued.

"We're getting off our subjects as usual," Noesis observed. "That should be the last of our discussion. But let me tell you this much, we don't consider death a tragedy."

"I have one more question," Knox broke in. "It's really nothing important, just a matter of idle curiosity. Your existence must be recorded some place. I know you have no citizenship papers, but you may have something similar to a birth certificate, as a necessary means of identification. I assume that your real name isn't Noesis. . . ."

"You're thinking in the right direction. Our so-called birth certificates record the date of our birth and the genetic code only. There's no mention of parents or relatives. Through the genetic code, we prevent the dangers of long inbreeding. Then as to my real name, of course, I have one, but why attach so much importance to an arbitrary combination of vowels and consonants? Rather keep on calling me Noesis. I like that name."

"I meant to ask you also about your profession," Knox ventured timidly.

"I'd suggest that we leave that for the next time we meet. I was thinking of discussing the topic of education anyway. Then I'll give you the answer." Noesis paused for a moment, them he added: "I would suggest to reconsider the whole problem of social and economic life from a new perspective. I would do that only if you're not too exhausted," Noesis said, looking at both Marisa and Knox.

"I'm willing to listen," Knox answered. "What about you, Marisa? Can you take more of this discussion?"

"I'll try not to fall asleep, all right?" Marisa observed rather stoically.

"Well then," Noesis picked up the conversation again, "do you remember what was said about the different modes of looking at life, I mean more specifically, the departmentalization of knowledge versus its integration?"

"If my memory doesn't fail me, that topic was discussed to some length during our third meeting." Knox tried to recall.

"I think you're correct," Noesis said. "I would like though to enlarge on these topics by exposing a doctrine on the dialectics of evolution, embracing all regions of reality, time and space, as a process of historical development on a cosmic scale."

"What I gather from your introductory words, Noesis, this is going to be rather heavy stuff, involving perhaps some form of methaphysical or ontological discussion," Knox intervened. "But I find it rather strange to engage ourselves in this speculative and abstract theoretizing when we have to deal with the concrete and practical problems of our social and economic life. I mean, I don't see the relevance of your proposed cosmological discussion of your life and ours. It could have been right for Hegel to accomplish that feat of logical gymnastics, being the man he was."

"I expected this critical remark of yours," Noesis observed. "On the other hand, you could agree with me that a theoretical foundation and a comprehensive view of the whole is necessary even for the radical pragmatist to solve his concrete and practical problems. Besides, I'll use only the dialectical method of Hegel without ending up with his monistic panlogism or absolute idealism," Noesis explained.

"I wonder what will come out of it," Knox mused.

"I would beg you to be somewhat patient with me for the sake of the insight I'll try to create," Noesis continued. "The three moments of the dialectical method involve, first, the thesis or original position, that is, in our case, the basic idea of the unity of the cosmos; second, comes the antithesis, the power of the negative, that is, the fundamental limitation of our own being. Man is limited in his individuality, in his knowledge, his power and action, in time and space. The necessary consequence of this ontological limitation is the emergence of the fragmentation of the original unity into plurality or multiplicity, the appearance of the famous dualisms or dichotomies in life, leading to conflict situation; the third moment of dialectics is called, as you know, the synthesis, the reconciliation of the opposites, leading back to the fullness of more being. The driving force of this triad is, of course, the dynamic, creative nature of being, embracing higher levels of integration and unity, preserving, at the same time, the principle of continuity in complexity." Noesis paused for a moment, giving Knox the opportunity for his next remark:

"It appears to me that evolution seems to be the crucial element in the whole process. But what is the meaning and the direction of this ascending line of evolution anyway?"

"It is the quest for more being in order to overcome the limitations in individuation and to achieve the goal of the unification of the universe," Noesis replied. Then he continued: "Let me become more specific in the description of the triadic moments which I consider the universal law of the cosmos. As you recall, the original position, the thesis, represents the unity of whatever is. The idea of unity implies, by association, the concepts of oneness, wholeness, entirety, universality, completeness, harmony, measure, fullness, perfection, equilibrium, simplicity and beauty. I surmise that there is only one law, only one rule or norm, only one code or blue print, pervading all regions of reality from the simplest element to the remotest distance of the galaxies. What that law is we only can guess at as the copenetration, the fusion of the two co-principles of any being, called by Aristotle the coexistence in one of so-called matter and form. The best illustration we could get for this principle comes from biology. Any organism displays to the observer two aspects of its reality, that is, the formal principle of organization, Aristotle's *entelecheia,* responsible for the coordination of all the chemical processes for the purpose of the preservation and growth of the living, and, naturally, the stuff, the so-called matter. Other examples could be taken from everyday experiences. If you lift the hood of your car and take a look at the engine, what do you see? Matter, parts, disposed according to a formal principle of organization, the physical theory and the idea of a motor of explosion. Or take our simplest element, the hydrogen atom, the father of all other elements. What does the careful observer see? According to the model, there is the stuff, let's call it matter or energy, and the organization of that energy according to the nucleus and its only electron. But be careful now and don't violate the basic unity of being; don't try to divide, separate that which is fundamentally the same; don't call it matter versus the form, or body versus the soul, matter versus consciousness, the higher in opposition to the lower. In any existent, from the simplest to the most complex, we find the unity of being, the coexistence of the intrinsically necessary principles as a condition for existence as such. To be, to be real and existent, anything must be something, must possess an identity, a definite nature of its own, and this identity consists in the conjugation of the material and formal principle of organization. That applies to all regions of reality, regardless of the labels attached to them, such as physical, material, living, psychic, spiritual, and what not."

231

"Could I interrupt you for a moment?" Knox asked.

"Go ahead, since I realize the many problems this doctrine poses."

"Well, for the time being, I have only two questions. First, what is the ultimate nature of reality? Second, if you start with the first moment of the dialectical process, the original unity of being, why is there a need and a justification for disturbing that ideal harmony and perfection through the advent of the antithesis, the principle of limitation?"

"As to your first question, the ultimate nature of reality, I have no final answer," Noesis confessed. "I know of the various attempts of the past, identifying reality with matter, with Newton's mechanical clock-work, then the theories of A. Whitehead and Theilhard de Chardin, viewing the universe as an animated organism with different degrees of consciousness. Finally, the principle of indeterminism of Heisenberg, and so forth. The trouble with these theories is that they take only one aspect of reality, either matter or consciousness, as standing for the whole of being. I have to confess to you than even in our superior science, we do not have the final answer."

"It is the very first time, Noesis, that you allowed some imperfections even in your own world," Knox remarked with great satisfaction.

"We never claimed omniscience," Noesis replied and went forth: "I take your second question, regarding the justification of dialectics in nature, as an attempt on my part to try to answer the first one too. My answer would be in viewing the nature of the universe in the light of a dynamic energy which has to expand, explicate or empty itself through the process of evolution even if this leads to limitations in implicit conflicts. It is in this sense we talk about cosmogenesis, biogenesis and logogenesis, without implying any fragmentation of the unity of the universe. There is unity in complexity and in diversity, and complexity itself presupposes the continuity of the whole, directed by the only principle or law of existence I referred to just before. So it appears to me that the ultimate purpose of the whole dialectical genesis consists in the quest for self-realization of the being of the universe."

"This is a very nice way to put it, for it also could serve, by implication, as a justification for suffering, pain, injustice and the existence of the evil," Knox retorted with emphatic voice. Noesis could not let this remark go by, so he replied: "I'll have more to say on suffering and evil when we shall discuss the matters of ethics and religion."

"I can wait for the information, but I can't hold back another observation I have to make. On repeated occasions, you called us 'mechanized barbarians.' But now it turns out that our barbaric condition could be easily justified by the necessary steps in the dialectical march of our history. Quoting your own words, 'It is a necessity to go through the stages of evolution.' It had to happen according to the law of dialectics. So we are not the responsible agents of it, only the subservient tools subjected to it." Knox said all these things with a remarkable resentment in his voice. Noesis took his remarks with unflinching eyes, and added his own:

"I have to agree with part of your observation as far the stages of evolution are concerned. But I might also add the part your race took in disturbing the process of evolution. I have in mind that long standing stain on your history, the outspoken hostility and persecution of science and the men of the enlightenment. For more than one thousand years you lived under the reign of darkness and superstitions. Part of it is still with you in your outmoded views on ethics and religion, turning your modern man into a schizoid individual, unable to use properly and integrate your scientific progress with the moral codes you pretend to live by. It is in this sense I meant to use the term of 'modern barbarians.'"

"Isn't this just a lot of hogwash?" Knox retorted.

"Call it what you want, it doesn't upset me in the least," Noesis answered calmly. "On the other hand, I can defend my position, if you allow me a few more minutes to finish our discussion on dialectics. This time I turn to the second moment of

233

dialectics, the power of the negative, the basic limitation of the human being."

"Is there more to it than what you already said?" Knox observed impatiently.

"I'm afraid there is a lot more to it. I'm thinking of a rather famous list of dualisms or dichotomies through which your race accomplished the fragmentation and division of the unity of your being. Do you want to hear it?"

"Let's have it out!" Knox replied with resignation.

"I'll group these dualisms into two categories, applying the distinction made by your philosopher William James between the "tough minded" and the "tender minded" attitudes toward reality. The tough minded is a believer in the material, physical, natural, quantitative, measurable, extended and this-worldly traits of reality, reached by sense knowledge, observation of facts, experiments, inductive reasoning, geared toward the application of knowledge in scientific, social, political and economic problem solving. It is the frame of the mind of a radical empiricist, pragmatist, the basic extrovert or other-directed disposition of this type of a person, with a rather liberal, democratic and collectivist creed added to it. In matters of morality and religion, the tough minded approach defends naturalism, with a secular, profane, all-too-human point of view, emphasizing the temporal, limited, finite and imperfect nature of man. Then we have the opposite world view, that of the tender minded people. They believe in the transcendent, metaphysical, idealistic, eternal, logical essences, spiritual in nature, to be reached by the famous tool of intuition. Intuition posits a priori, direct, immediate apprehension of eternal verities, unlimited, infinite and all perfect, residing in the God head. The supernatural, the sacred, holy, immaterial, divine or godly, receive the absolute priority in their value system, professed as a rather dogmatic, conservative, stagnant, passive attitude toward life in general, especially when they talk about the "lower" regions of the natural world, labelled as a "vale of tears" and sufferings of all sorts. Following the lead of Plato and Augustine, they propose the purification, mortification, the castration of all base instincts of man, represented by the body of man, urging everybody to engage in contemplation and meditation, in the disinterested detachment of the mind from this world. Introversion or inner-directedness is the best term to identify this tender frame of mind."

"What is the point in presenting this rather accurate description of the two categories of the mind?" Knox asked Noesis.

"If you take a moment to reflect on the consequences of these ideas in shaping the cultural climate of the world in action, you'll find immediately its relevance to the concrete problems of your social, political and economic life," Noesis urged Knox.

"Let me see. We have two classes of opposite ideas," Knox started his analysis. "Then, if we believe in the primacy of the ideas, dictating a certain life-style, we end up with two opposite camps, accomplishing the division and fragmentation of the unity of being," he concluded.

"If you also add the power intrinsic to ideas, you're very close to the root of all limitations, conflicts, discord, strife and war," Noesis added. "Let me give you some concrete illustrations pertaining to man's social and economic life, in addition to the long bloody history of revolutions and wars," Noesis continued. "We have to recall only the classical conflict of today between capitalism and communism. In capitalism, based upon the sacredness of property and free enterprise, with a view toward profits, we have the source of man's competitive, aggressive and cruel behavior. The will to power over people through the acquisition of goods and money, is responsible for the alienation of the laborer from his work, for the social stratification of the rich versus the poor, the ruthless exploitation of the producer, the rise of trusts and monopolies, the ongoing war between the labor force and management, the repeated economic crisis of recessions, depressions, inflation and the artificial means to create work by starting a new armed conflict, and so forth. On the other hand, we have the communist manifesto, which boils down to one simple formula: instead of many capitalists, they have only one capitalist, namely the totalitarian state, the communist party, who owns everything, including the soul and the body

235

of the laborer who continues in the same state of economic, social and political alienation."

"Your diagnosis of the conflicting forces is to the point." Knox finally seemed to agree. "But my question is still a practical one: what do you have to offer as a solution? Is there a third way to solve the problems in our planet?"

"For the advent of the third way or the third world, you'll have to wait till the obstacles are removed," Noesis said. "The main obstacle, in addition to the conflicting ideologies, is your condition of dividedness, living in your 'schizoid' world."

Knox was ready to interfere again but Noesis continued: "Let me finish what I meant by the 'dividedness' of your world, then I'll attend to your objections. Your world is divided into many countries, some small, others rather large, by natural and artificial boundaries. Some countries are rich in resources, they have developed to a great degree the tools of industrialization and technology, while other are still labelled as 'underdeveloped.' In addition to this division, you have your world divided into different nations, with different languages, different history, traditions and customs, different races, and so on. The third class of division comes in on the international scene: there is competition within the economic and political systems of the disunited nations, instead of cooperation. Cooperation is stalled not only because of different ideologies, but also on account of the balance of trade. Now, my dear Edward, if you add up all that I said so far, there is not much hope and room for a peaceful integration of your economic and political interests. As long as you live in this "schizoid" world of yours, divided and fragmented in all these ways, there is not much to hope for," Noesis concluded.

"Perhaps there is a distant hope if we include now the third moment of dialectics, that is, the synthesis, the reconciliation of the opposites, the unification of the parts into a whole," Knox ventured this idea with more conviction.

"There are signs that the divisions will be slowly eliminated," Noesis remarked. "Through the progress of science, technology, transportation and the process of automation, plus the interdependence of the various countries in their respective facilities and resources—for instance, the oil of the Arab countries—there will be the slow emancipation from your rather provincial and narrow perspective. If this trend continues, the idea of a unified, integrated world, one united planet and the planetary man will become a reality as is the case in my world. Then you'll have also the opportunity to foster the unification of the cosmos by engaging yourselves in the inter-planetary exchange of your cultural and material goods."

Noesis's last remark indicated that he considered this long session ended. He soon left. Marisa and Knox were still under the spell of the many new ideas they had learned about a higher form of life as it could be. Nevertheless, Marisa thought to herself that she wouldn't like to live in Noesis' world. It didn't seem human to her, as she understood that term.

CHAPTER TEN

THE FUTURE OF EDUCATION AS A CREATIVE PROCESS

After a whole week of relentless work, Knox and Marisa decided to take one evening off and to allow themselves a much needed break. Knox proposed that they spend a few hours in a rather exclusive and quiet cocktail lounge, whose main attraction was an excellent pianist whom Knox used to listen to with great pleasure. He not only liked his style and technique in rendering the best known French and Italian chansons, but also the man himself. One could see that he was one of those rare persons for whom playing the piano was much more than a means to make a living. . . . Although he was willing to oblige by playing tunes that the customers requested, he played them as though he was doing it exclusively for his own pleasure. He had an air of being completely forgetful and unaware of his surroundings, as if the only thing that existed and mattered for him was his instrument and his nimble fingers running up and down on the keyboard, possessing a will of their own as they flourished on any given theme. When applauded, he'd mechanically turn halfway around on his stool and acknowledge it with a brief nod with his head. His face remained impassible, showing neither pleasure nor annoyance . . . just indifference. He'd then turn back to his only friend, the piano, empty his glass with one gulp, light a cigarette, and go on playing, totally aloof of everything else.

Marisa accepted Knox's suggestion with delight. She rushed over to her own living quarters, promising to be ready in no time. But women seem to suffer a partial amnesia of time when it comes to dressing up. After half an hour of patient waiting, Knox threatened to leave by himself unless she made haste.

When she finally made her appearance in Knox's apartment, he immediately forgave her to annoyance of futile waiting—she looked elegant and attractive.

A short cab ride brought them to their destination. They chose a table in the far corner and ordered their first drink, thus acquiring the right to be there. In answer to Knox's question, the waiter informed that the pianist would be back in an hour. They decided to wait, sipping their drinks and smoking.

Knox looked unusually tired, almost exhausted. He just sat there silently, gazing fixedly into the space before him at nothing in particular. He seemed to be absorbed in some thoughts of his own, but judging from the melancholy expression of his face, those ideas weren't an exercise in the power of positive thinking. Marisa immediately perceived Knox's gloominess. It made her feel uneasy, anxious and somewhat frustrated, for she had anticipated an evening of joyful intimacy and pleasure.

"What are you thinking of so seriously?" she ventured her first question, just to break the long silence.

Knox looked at her with bewilderment, as if he had just woken up. Then he recollected himself, lit another cigarette and said in an unnerving voice:

"A lot of nonsense, I guess. . . ." After a pause he added: "But come to think of it, it isn't nonsense, it's true. And I can't help it. . . ."

"Why do you have to be mysterious about it?" Marisa asked in an irritated manner. "Can't you put it into words? That is, if you want to talk at all. . . . If not, say so, and I won't bother you with my questions any more."

"I'm sorry, Marisa. . . . I didn't mean to hurt you. Forget it! It's nothing, really. Let's have another drink." And he signaled to the nearest waiter. But Marisa, who was determined to make Knox speak up, went on:

"If it's something personal or something you want to keep from me, it's all right," and she looked nervously at her watch.

"I have nothing, no secrets to hide from you. I didn't want to talk about it out of consideration toward your person only. . . .

I don't want to contaminate you, so to say, with my ideas," Knox mumbled.

"That's very considerate of you," Marisa observed. "But put your mind at ease. You're not talking to an innocent little girl out on her first date."

"I guess you won't give up until I tell you," Knox capitulated with a forced smile. "It's rather difficult to explain it briefly. . . . Perhaps if I tell you that I'm sick, disgusted, weary of the way we live here in this world of ours, you can guess the rest. . . ."

"It's your old disease, Ed," Marisa interpreted. "Remember you used to feel this way, even during your period of rebellion?"

"No, no! It's not that," Knox protested. "You've got it wrong. At first I thought so myself, then I saw that it's something else, perhaps something much worse. . . . It started after I met Noesis, and it's getting worse, sometimes it's almost unbearable. . . ."

"I had a feeling, a premonition that this whole business would end badly!" Marisa remarked seriously.

"No it's not Noesis' fault at all," Knox spoke rather to himself. "His ideas are true. . . . Nevertheless, they're almost deadly, in the sense that they destroy almost everything, every principle, idea, value or conviction I used to have faith in. . . . As a result, I feel only contempt and disgust for our whole way of living. I always knew that there was something utterly wrong with this whole thing, and now I know what it is. Now I know what life could be! And it actually exists, but it's so remote as to be completely out of my reach. So I've become totally uprooted, displaced, maladjusted, almost bankrupt. The more I realize how primitive, shallow and wanting our way of life is, the more frustrated, angry and resentful I grow within myself. . . . Sometimes I feel as though I were living in a strange world that only fills me with dread and nausea. It's worse right after the session with Noesis, because then I'm even more aware of the existence of another world, immeasurably superior to our own. I feel like an expatriate in my own country, as though living as a refugee in a strange world, which isn't to my taste at all. Tell me, Marisa, if you please, how can you keep on loving something, after you've seen how imperfect that object of your love is? You can't go on pretending indefinitely. You have to accept reality for what it is, even if its true face fills you with aversion and hatred. In other words, I've become alienated and estranged from my own life and existence. All values devalue themselves in the light of what I've heard from Noesis."

"Perhaps you're exaggerating somewhat," Marisa suggested, trying to be helpful. "You become too serious, too involved, even tragic about it. And you shouldn't. . . ."

"I wish I could stop it, but there's no use faking reality, ignoring the evidence and leading a life of constant evasions. It doesn't work. . . . Even if you try it, you know all the while, within yourself, that you're lying, rationalizing, escaping, running away."

"Are you implying that there's nothing, absolutely nothing at all, that makes sense, that has value or meaning to it, that still binds you? That the whole of life is just a big lie, a dirty joke played on us?"

"No, it's not quite the way you put it, Marisa," Knox went on thinking aloud. "There's some meaning, some value, some sense, no doubt. But not enough, you see. Let me give you an example: suppose that up till now you've been riding an old fashioned buggy, pulled by a lifeless nag. . . . Then, one day, you're given a ride in a splendid automobile, racing at top speed on the highways, enjoying the comfort and the smoothness of the ride. Then imagine that you have to put up again with the old buggy and the slow motion of the poor old horse. . . . Do you see the point I'm driving at?"

"You've been spoiled, that's all!" Marisa pronounced tersely.

"It's not that simple, though. . . ." Knox kept on reflecting. "I wish I could settle it that easily! But it doesn't work! I can't! I'm not saying—to return to my example—that the old buggy and the horse are nothing at all. In fact, for those who've never known anything better, it's a wonderful thing! They like it. . . . Because of their ignorance, they have no means to discover the real dimension of the thing they have. They have nothing better to compare it with. Their ignorance and poverty is a blessing, a bliss. . . . They're the people whom the holy ones call 'the poor in spirit.' Believe me, they're much better off. . . . They're happy, satisfied and contended with their small lives, their small pleasures, their small virtues. They're like little children, and the kingdom of heaven belongs to them. They're humble, pious and meek."

"And you feel utterly miserable, almost crushed and bankrupt. . . ." Marisa interposed.

"That's how I feel, unfortunately. . . ." Knox agreed.

"But you can't go on living like that!" Marisa exclaimed alarmed. You'll either end up in a madhouse or you'll kill yourself! There must be a way out, an exit, a solution, something!"

"There's no exit," Knox said gravely. "We're trapped, locked up, imprisoned. And it's unfair, a rotten deal, a rigged game, a dirty trick, a curse and you end up as the loser anyway. . . . It's stupid, it's absurd, it's . . . maddening, as you said."

"Why don't you kick it all?" Marisa said rapidly. "You said that it all started with your Noesis, and it got worse ever since. If you still have a will to live, you should kick it and fast. Give it up! Forget it! Look at it as a stupid incident, as a nightmare. . . . Dump it all and come back to life! You've still got a life to live which is worth much more than the highbrow, learned sophistication of those queer fellows, about whom we know nothing certain. . . ."

"I wish it were as simple as you'd have it, but it isn't! I can't do it! Even if I tried, I know it wouldn't work, because it can't. . . ."

"Because you don't want it to. . . ." Marisa reproached him.

"Listen, Marisa," Knox tried to explain, "do you remember Plato's allegory of the cave?"

"Yes, and what of it?" she snapped angrily. "It's the product of another star-gazer, of a deluded mystic and philosopher in one!"

"I didn't ask you to start worshiping Plato," Knox said patiently. "But his example's good and true. It gives you a lot. . . . Remember the fellow who succeeded in freeing himself from his chains, got on his own feet for the first time, turned his back to the shadows on the wall and walked out of the dark cave into the blinding light of the sun, discovering another world, endlessly more real and beautiful than the images he was used to take as the whole of life. . . . Can you imagine, Marisa, that this fellow could have given up his new vision, in exchange for a miserable existence, spent as a chained prisoner in the mud of a cave?"

"I remember that he walked back into the cave once. . . ."

"Just to break the good news to his fellow prisoners."

"Who didn't give a damn, didn't stir, didn't even listen. . . . Perhaps because they were wiser, more practical, and wouldn't give up what they had—no matter how imperfect—for something they knew nothing about, for the story of a visionary. And you're the visionary, Ed."

"Remember the commandment of truth?" Knox asked emphatically.

"There you go again with your sermonizing. . . ." Marisa observed, visibly displeased.

"But Marisa! You surprise me!" Knox exclaimed astonished.

Marisa looked at his face and saw the confusion and frustration that was taking place within him, then she said:

"All right, Ed. In the name of that commandment of truth, I have something important to tell you. You may not like it. . . . But as you said, one cannot keep on pretending forever. . . ." Marisa's words sounded heavy, charged with emotions.

"But I thought all this while. . . ." Knox started to say something, but Marisa completed the sentence for him:

". . . that I'm totally taken in as you seem to be by your friend from nowhere."

"And you aren't?"

"No, I'm not. . . . Perhaps this is an unexpected blow to you, Ed, unpleasant and very frustrating and all that. . . . However, truth shall liberate us, no matter what." Marisa had to stop to catch her breath and to control her violent emotions. She was unusually pale, and her contorted lips twitched nervously. She was shaking all over and she could hardly manage to reach for her glass and lift it to her lips. She lit a cigarette with trembling hands, and went on:

"Perhaps I'm only one of those mediocrities and sluggards who vegetate in the darkness of the cave. . . . That could very well be. . . . But then, if it's so, I accept it, though you may look upon me, from now on, only with contempt and disgust." She paused again and looked at Knox's face, twisted painfully, then she continued mercilessly:

"From the beginning, as soon as I met them, I have felt an almost instinctive dislike for them, I mean Noesis and Gynea. You interpreted it as jealousy on my part for that super-woman. Well, that was only partially true . . . and also understandable at that. But this is only part of the whole truth. As for the other part . . . well, you may call it resentment of the inferior toward the superior types, knowing that he could never match those so far above him. . . . If that's what you're going to conclude, go ahead! Let it be so!"

"But . . ." Knox tried to break in. Marisa cut him short, saying,

"Don't interrupt me now, hear me out to the end. . . . I'm not sure that I'll ever be capable of doing what I've just started, so let me go on. I don't know what you think of me, as a person, but I want to help you dispell all your possible doubts. So listen: I'm not a philosopher and I don't intend to become one. . . . Neither am I a scientist nor any kind of a creative genius. . . . I'm not an idealist, I don't worship eternal absolutes and infallible truths. I'm not an impractical daydreamer, a visionary with an exalted mind. My turn of mind is very practical. I'm a pragmatist, Ed. I want to live. . . . I want to live here and now. . . . I want to live my life the best I can . . . , I'm not willing to give up this life, this existence of my own, I don't want to sacrifice my youth, my desires, my passions, my goals. Of course, you may always consider them middle-class, low, petty, too pedestrian, highly imperfect and limited, fit to satisfy the wishes of only an average or below average person. You're free to do that. . . . And I, on my part, am free to choose what I want as the contents, meaning and direction of my life. I'm not as sick, disillusioned and despaired as you are. I won't give it up. Just because two individuals filled up your brains with certain ideas that—by their own admission—do more harm than good to us. . . . No, I haven't as yet lost my common sense!"

Marisa stopped abruptly, as if she had presented all her arguments. She leaned back on her chair, stretched her arm to reach for her glass, which she emptied, placing it back on the table again. She felt exhausted and, at the same time, strangely relieved, as if she had finally gotten rid of something which had been choking her for a long time. She looked at Knox's bewildered face, waiting for his reaction. There followed a long silence, that grew more and more painful with every moment that elapsed. . . . Finally Knox leaned forward toward Marisa and said in a hoarse voice:

"You must have planned this in advance. . . . Tell me, what are you up to? What do you want to do?"

"That depends on what you have to say to my little speech."

"Did you really mean what you just said? Every word of it? Do you stand by it?"

"I mean every single vowel and consonant in every single world!" said Marisa resolutely.

Knox paused again, collecting his thoughts. He then asked: "Then can I ask you this question?"

"You may ask me as many questions as you wish. . . . Your pianist hasn't arrived yet anyway."

"What is it that you hate in Noesis and Gynea?"

"Just what they did to you and almost succeeded in doing to me also. It so happens that I react to it in a different way than you do. You said it yourself, a few minutes ago, that you lost your will to live because they made you see how imperfect, limited and narrow our values are here on this earth. That's the great thing they have accomplished so far. You ought to feel very grateful to them, and consider this an added reason for your blind worship for them. But they haven't got me, and they aren't going to either!"

"Could there be any other reason?" Knox insisted.

"Come on, Ed! Let's not ride on my being jealous again, please! It won't work this time!" Marisa dismissed Knox's idea.

"Then what is it?"

"They're inhuman or worse, that's all!" Marisa blurted out. "Apart from their ideas, take, for instance, their awful behavior. Last time, remember, Noesis came to our place and condescended to eat with us. It may sound trivial to you, but his boundless dignity and pride prevented him to comply with the minimum of good manners. He just kept on eating without a word about the food, or even a thank you at the end, as common decency would require it. Of course, you're going to excuse him by claiming that he's so much taken up with his lofty ideas that he simply wouldn't lower himself to be concerned with the meaningless acts of animal vegetation. Now even if I could believe this, I'd still consider it non-human. Then there's their totally strange behavior and attitude. They're always so solemn, so deadly serious, so aloof from everything and everybody that it becomes offensive, even if they don't mean it to be! Did you notice that the last time Noesis didn't have one word to say about our apartment, about your moving or anything? He doesn't seem to live in reality, he doesn't seem to be real at all! And again, his boorish manner of leaving after his last sentence, not deigning himself to utter even a miserable good night or something to that effect! Now that to me is positively inhuman, again!"

Knox kept on looking at her in utter amazement, resembling a man who was waking up to some ugly reality after a beautiful dream. He was still in the same position, leaning forward, and resting his arms on the table. Then, as though to convince himself that what he was hearing was true, real, existent, absolute, he said:

"All right, Marisa. Go on. What else?"

"Well, if this isn't enough for you, let me tell you that their ideas are totally absurd. According to them, there's no God, no marriage, no family, no children, no money, no private property, no race, no nationality, no government, no anything! But then, what do they have left? I know what your answer's going to be —they have their superior minds, their ideas, their infinite wisdom, and so on and so forth. Well, they can have it and keep it as far as I'm concerned! I've got to live my life here and now, and on this earth, or else, never. . . . And that's all, Ed!"

Knox listened attentively to her words, trying to discover some hidden motive behind them. . . . But hard as he tried to come up with something that could dispel this nightmare, that would

247

help remedy this situation, he couldn't. She seemed to mean all what she said. So he asked calmly:

"Well, Marisa, what are your plans?"

"What are yours?" Marisa fired back the same question.

"As far as my person goes," Knox said very slowly and very earnestly, "I'm not going to follow your suggestion to 'drop and dump' my relationship with Noesis."

"I was afraid that this'd be your answer. . . . Apparently, they've got you, body and soul, and for good. . . ."

"Yes, Marisa, this is true," Knox agreed with the same seriousness.

There followed a period of silence. By then Knox had recovered enough to straighten himself out and light a cigarette.

"I feel sorry for you," Marisa interrupted the silence.

"Why? There's no reason for you to feel sorry for me! Besides, you shouldn't waste your energies on useless feelings. Remember that you need them all in order to satisfy your immense will to live."

"That's what I'm going to do," said Marisa, raising her voice to emphasize her determination. "I don't know what you're going to say next, but I've decided not to take part in your future conversations. I've had enough of them for a lifetime!"

"There'll be only two or three more sessions," Knox informed casually.

"So much the better!" Marisa observed with relief. Then she added, as though on second thought: "There's my editing and typing. . . ."

"There it is, indeed," Knox answered coolly.

"Well, if you need my help, I'll continue to do it for you, although personally it doesn't mean much to me. . . ."

"So you'd be willing to do it simply out of the goodness of your heart," Knox remarked ironically.

"Look, Ed!" Marisa retorted with impatience. "I know what you're after again. You think that you can win me over again through the magic power of my love for you. It won't work this time! Try something better!"

"I wonder," Knox said in a thoughtful mood, "whether there's any meaning left for us two in that word 'love.' . . ."

"In other words," Marisa said alarmed, "unless I think exactly as you do, unless I feel, act and live, in every small detail, the way you do, there can be no talk about love between us?"

Knox twisted his mouth in a bitter smile: "I can hardly imagine a lasting friendship between two persons whose ideas and values clash head on. . . . We'd only do what we did tonight, namely, to discuss, argue, and disagree. . . . That can't work in the long run. . . . We'd end up quarrelling, becoming disagreeable, and then finally hating each other."

"Then what? What are you going to say next?" Marisa cried almost on the verge of hysteria.

"You should know, Marisa, that for any man his work is his first love."

"I'm beginning to realize that!"

"And if one's partner in life thinks little or nothing of it, the man has to make a choice between his first love—his work—and his partner."

"And of course the choice'd be his work. . . ."

"Yes!" replied Knox firmly.

Marisa was taken aback by Knox's blunt answer. Had she obeyed her first impulse, she'd have jumped to her feet and left Knox right then and there. But something unknown to her kept her motionless in her seat, staring with unbelief at Knox's drawn face. The sound of his curt 'yes' kept on ringing in her ears, but apparently she wasn't able to fully comprehend its total meaning and fateful consequences. The thought of their final break flashed through her mind, but it appeared to have no more reality to it than a word uttered in a dream. "No, no," she told herself in panic. "It's not true, it's not real! It can't be!" She probably hadn't heard him well, there must be a terrible misunderstanding. . . . She looked at Knox who was sitting impassively across the small table, staring fixedly at her all the time, without stirring or uttering a word. She made an effort to recollect herself and said almost in a whisper:

"Are you waiting for me to get up and to leave?" Her voice

broke at this point. "So this is, in other words, the end of all we've been planning together? And you don't even seem to mind it or care too much about it! It makes no difference to you whether I stay or go! I guess it's all the same to you, just an insignificant matter, not more than a common annoyance. . . . And I hate myself now for sitting here, talking to you, instead of walking out!"

"Do you realize what you're trying to do?" Knox asked her in a subdued, measured voice.

"Say all the things you usually say on these occasions!" Marisa cried out, losing her self-control. "Go ahead and tell me that I'm a hysterical woman and all the rest of it! Come on, say it! Talk! Say something! Don't just sit there like a sadist enjoying the sight of his victim's slow torture and death!"

She took a handkerchief from her bag, lowered her head, unable to control the flood of her tears, while she fought to stifle the sobs that were shaking her body. Knox didn't move from his position, only lifted his glass and emptied it, in a slow and controlled motion. Finally he said:

"What I meant to imply with my last question was simply that you were trying, perhaps unconsciously, to put the blame on me for your perfect job in destroying everything. You panicked at the sight of the wreckage you accomplished and cried out for help." He stopped, drew a long puff from his cigarette, then added: "Where's your impassioned and self-assured attitude of a few minutes ago? Your hunger to live, no matter how? The aggressive tone of your attacks on me and my friends? Could it be, on second thought, you're not quite sure that you meant what you said under the drive of your blind impulses?"

"You're cruel, Ed! Cruel and heartless! You want to drive me to utter despair and madness!"

"You're a strange creature, Marisa!" Knox observed severely. "First you pile offense upon abuse, you debase my highest ideals, throw mud on everything I still want to keep clean and undefiled, then you start crying, because you got mud on your own hands instead. You blame those whom you made suffer for not

250

rushing to your help with sympathy and understanding. First you kill, then you fall into despair, because resurrection doesn't follow death. . . ."

"I didn't mean to hurt you, Ed, so help me, I didn't!" she muttered painfully. "I only . . . I just . . . tried to help you out of your terrible mood."

"You don't help a patient by robbing him of his last hope and faith in his recovery."

"Maybe you're right, Ed. Perhaps I'm no match for you. I'm not the type you want. I'm only a dead weight on your shoulders. I'm of no help. I just make things worse!"

"Do you expect me to jump and take you in my arms and tell you 'No, you're wonderful, you're the best girl I've ever met,' and the rest of that romantic nonsense? But that's so cheap and distasteful and melodramatic!"

"Im sorry, Ed," she said in a conciliatory manner.

"Don't be a penitent now!" Knox continued. "That's another act that fills me with revulsion. There's no dignity in starting to walk on your knees! It only arouses the ugliest of all feelings, pity!"

"What do you want me to do?" Marisa cried in exasperation. "Whatever I do or say is always wrong! There's no way to satisfy you, you're not human! I'd better realize that and go, happen what may! I don't care any more. . . ."

"Now this is the third role you're assuming," he went on impassively. "It's the role of helplessness, put on or chosen with the purpose of appealing to the so-called Christian virtue, the disposition of the good Samaritan. But that fellow should have known that there's at least as much offense in helping as there's goodness and virtue."

"I simply don't understand you. . . . Are you trying to force me to go?" Marisa snapped impatiently.

"I wouldn't do that for anything in the world," Knox answered quietly.

"Why not? It'll come to it anyway!"

"Because I don't see why I should assume the responsibility which is yours only."

"So I have to make the first step?"

"And the second too, if you so decide. . . ."

"So you wouldn't lift one finger to stop me, right?"

"I respect everybody's freedom, so that I may have the right to expect their respect for mine," he asserted with conviction. "But before you go, I'd like to ask you one question, just to satisfy my curiosity."

"Go ahead," Marisa agreed gladly, because this gave her another reason to delay the much dreaded decision.

"I'd like you to explain me what is it that you meant by your will to live. . . . Aren't you living right now? What do you expect from your life? What are your desires, your plans and goals?"

"You know that I can't answer you in one sentence. I don't have that philosophical turn of mind you and your friend Noesis have."

"You can answer me in a hundred sentences, if you wish, using just plain ordinary words," Knox explained.

"You see, Ed," she started helplessly, "I'm only a woman, and that puts me in a position different from yours. . . . Now don't start talking about the emancipation of women, their equality, and so forth. . . . That might become true and real in some distant future, but we're very far from that right now. Besides, I owe the truth even if it hurts me to say it. I have no special talents, you see, I'm an average person, neither an idiot nor a genius. I have to find the meaning of my life within the limits of my own being. To reach for the impossible is asking for frustration in advance. Consequently, the values you believe in and live for, cannot be mine. Perhaps I was meant to be just an ordinary plain housewife and mother. . . . Or maybe somebody who's learned the art of modern sophistication. But none of these things mean anything to you. As you said yourself when you were talking about the buggy and the nag, there're people who should never be given a ride in a modern car. . . . It spoils their innocent happiness, based on their ignorance. To each one according to his measure of ability." Marisa stopped waiting for Knox to say something.

"And you feel that you cannot live the way you want to as long as our friendship lasts?" Knox inquired.

"You said so yourself once before and just again tonight. As I cannot live up to your ideals the way you'd like me to, so you can't share with me pleasures I find in the values I stand for. So we'll be drifting apart anyway, living under the oppresive weight of an open secret neither will dare to discuss. . . . As I'm no match for you, Edward, you're no match for me either, but for different reasons. . . . Perhaps you'll be better off with a more intellectual type."

"Or else, which's even better, if I'll stay alone, by myself," Knox concluded.

It was Marisa who took her eyes off Knox's face, looked aside, a bitter smile on her lips. She reached for her bag, excusing herself. Knox called the waiter, paid his bill and bought a drink for the pianist. Marisa soon came back and found it only natural that Knox was ready to leave.

Very soon after their break Marisa told Knox of her decision to spend one year of college in Italy. She was accepted without difficulty, as she was able to cope with all the expenses. During the two weeks preceding her departure, she maintained a friendly relationship with Knox. She did her editing and typing just as before, took care of the needs of their daily life, but there was no trace left of their former intimacy and friendship. Cultivated friendliness was the only way to keep the situation tolerable and to reduce the mounting tension between them. On the pretext of the journey, they rearranged the two apartments into two independent units. Occasionally Marisa went out alone in the evenings, while Knox worked on his book. Though he knew exactly the time when she went and returned, he never mentioned it. On the day she left Knox was nowhere to be found. . . . He had apparently left on purpose. Marisa left him a note which contained just the usual formalities with a nice little hint at her hope of seeing him again upon her return. The real estate office rented Marisa's apartment within less then a week to some college boys. Knox had no desire to get acquainted with them, so he avoided all possible occasion for any contact.

253

Marisa's absence meant for him—among other things—an increase in the load of his daily work. When he felt exhaustion closing in, he went for a lonely walk, choosing the uninhabited parts of the countryside. Quite often, he wouldn't leave his apartment for several days, and then only to buy a new supply of provisions. During his walks he tried to analyze his own feelings and reactions toward the unexpected break with Marisa. He was surprised at himself for the relative ease with which he took their separation, even rejoicing at the idea of his freedom. On the other hand, as the days went by, he couldn't hide from himself his desire for some human contact, especially when his self-imposed loneliness weighed heaviest on him. Experience taught him that he had to pay a high price to preserve the ideals of total independence and self-sufficiency. He often doubted whether he could take this as the permanent condition of his life. He feared that he'd develop into a perfect hermit, living in total isolation in the midst of a great metropolis.

His next meeting with Noesis took place at the latter's apartment. He was alone, apparently Gynea hadn't returned from her trip yet. He could not conceal a slight feeling of disappointment, but he chided himself on this account. He also perceived that Noesis had noticed something unusual about him. What was it, he thought, that had betrayed him to Noesis? He knew, of course, that he had become more reserved and detached in his attitude, and perhaps, there could have been some traces of sadness, or maybe it was just a new trait of grave seriousness visible on his face and in his eyes. Noesis asked no questions. Marisa's absence was apparently taken as natural. Knox handed him the new pages of his manuscript and Noesis returned those he had gone through already. Knox expected to hear some comment on Noesis's part, he was even ready for some criticism or suggestion, but Noesis remembered only the payment due to him. Then Knox started the conversation by saying in an unsteady voice:

"I've been troubled lately by a strange thought, Noesis. You'll find it unusual, perhaps, but I'd still like to hear your reaction on it, if you don't mind. . . ."

"Let's have it out," Noesis invited him encouragingly.

"It's the problem of self-awareness, one's level of consciousness, that keeps rising with the appropriation of more knowledge."

"That's quite in order," Noesis answered.

"I know that, but I meant to speak of one's rather mixed feelings toward knowledge. On the one hand, there's the undeniable pleasure man experiences when his curiosity is satisfied through his new insights and discoveries. . . . On the other, there's—at least in my case—the reverse side of knowledge. It casts a long shadow. . . ."

"What are you referring to?" Noesis asked with increasing interest.

"By the shadow I meant the discovery one makes in the light of his knowledge about the true face and value of life and existence. And for this reason, I'm inclined to look upon knowledge as both a blessing and a curse. I even think sometimes that the curse is greater than the blessing. . . ."

"Why do you say that?"

"Because of the necessary limitations of our knowledge. We know so much and not more. We're learned ignorants, and ignorance is humiliating to the mind and fills man with anxiety, fear, resentment. . . ."

"You must have been reading some existentialist authors."

"No. Not lately, that is. Though I did study them before. But apart from them, don't you think that their point is well taken? If one could find all the answers, it'd be fine, fair and wonderful. But to be stopped midway, in mid-air, so to say, neither up nor down, is very frustrating to say the least. And when one gets into such a mood, one looks upon the animals with jealous envy. . . . At least they don't know, they're unaware of themselves, they possess no insight into the limitations and imperfections of their being, they've no questions to ask and live out their lives according to the dictates of their instincts. . . ."

"Would you say then," Noesis asked carefully, "that man should abandon his mind, desert the battlefield of more knowledge and revert or regress to the level of sheer animality?"

"No. Of course I know that no such thing can happen! And exactly because man is caught in the midst of both knowledge

255

and ignorance, his condition is rather absurd and pitiful."

"If you know all this, what do you propose as an alternative?" Noesis asked seriously. "Are you dreaming of reviving Rousseau's utopia, of returning to the blessedness of an uncivilized, natural state? If you knew anything about the lives of the primitive savages, you wouldn't regard their condition as enviable or better than yours. What do you prefer—a witch doctor or a medical doctor? An underground hole or this airconditioned apartment?"

"You know what my answer to these questions are," Knox replied.

"The only thing I can do for you," Noesis continued, "is to refer you back once more to the evolutionary point of view, even with regard to the problem of knowledge. I agree with you that—as you stated— you're learned ignorants. For that matter, we're ignorants too, but to a lesser degree. Perhaps man'll never reach omniscience, but that shouldn't prevent him from leading a meaningful life. Then there's another circumstance: the absurdity of your existential situation is due, not so much to the limitations of your knowledge but rather to the strange mixture and coexistence of knowledge and mythical belief. Many of your questions arise from your primitive religious outlook on life, such as its origin and end. . . . If you had organized your lives on the premises of philosophy and science only, you wouldn't be troubled by questions about the unknowable. . . ."

"I guess you're right," Knox agreed. "But we've been raised and educated in this direction."

"This last remark of yours reminds me that we meant to discuss the questions related to education," Noesis remarked. "Are you ready to go into that?"

"Of course I'm ready!" Knox answered with liveliness. "But what plan or method do you propose, in order not to get lost in the vastness and ambiguity of this issue?"

"I'd suggest that we ought to talk, first about the errors and deficiencies of your present experiments in the field of education, with the purpose of preparing the ground for the proper understanding of the principles I'm about to propose."

"I assume that these principles represent the essence of your philosophy of education and are put to practice in your own world?" Knox inquired with curiosity.

"That's correct," Noesis said. "But speaking now of education, I'd suggest again that we make a distinction between the formation of man's character and the proper training of his intellect, by formal instruction."

"That's necessary, true enough," Knox assented.

"To start the first part of our task, I'd say, as a general, introductory remark, that the education of children's left to the care of incompetents."

"Of course you have the parents in mind, when speaking of incompetents."

"No, not only the parents. I also meant your 'professional educators,' that is, your psychologists and teachers of all sorts."

"People'll say that you're prejudiced and that you exaggerate a great deal!" Knox observed.

"Perhaps they'll overcome their shock if they think further," Noesis remarked quite matter of factly. "First, let's point out the mistaken attitude of the parents."

"But we covered that rather extensively in our previous session!" Knox reminded him. "What else can be added?"

"Not much indeed," Noesis consented. "But we should look closer into the methods used by parents in order to accomplish their objectives, as well as the effects of these same methods on the child's character."

"What's your first objection?" Knox prompted him.

"It's their wrong idea about the nature and purpose of education. They start with the wrong premise, that a child is an undomesticated little animal, full of all sorts of base instincts and tendencies. Therefore, education becomes equated with domestication, taming and conditioning. In fact, however, this accomplishes nothing more than the mutilation of the child's most vital energies."

"I don't know if I quite follow you," Knox said. "Please give me more concrete evidence."

"There're only two different methods to accomplish the domestication of the child," Noesis replied, "and both of them fall within the techniques of conditioning. I have in mind, of course, two concrete and very powerful stimuli, that is, pleasure and pain. These are the most effective forces that are used to create the desired reactions in the child. Those are reinforced afterwards by the same agents—reward and punishment—that is, by manipulating the child's desires and fears. And there you have the whole story in a capsule. You can figure out the details. . . ."

"But if you oppose the techniques of conditioning and also reject all that it involves, what do you have left to use for the purpose of educating?"

"I don't take conditioning as equivalent to education," Noesis said firmly.

"For what reasons?" Knox persisted.

"Simply because the child isn't an animal, and human behavior isn't the behavior of animals. And this qualification makes the whole difference."

"I wish you'd talk in more specific terms," Knox expressed his desire.

"I'm going to, but it's both impossible and beyond the limited purpose of our discussion to debate all the problems of educational psychology. We have to limit ourselves to the essentials. First of all, the basic difference between animal and human behavior can best be stated in two brief formulae: $B = S + R$ and $B = S + I + R$, respectively, which means that, strictly speaking, an animal doesn't behave, it only reacts to the stimuli with necessity $(B = S + R)$. An animal is bound by, and is helplessly delivered to, the stimuli acting upon the sense organs, which, in their turn, react mechanically and automatically to whichever stimuli act upon them. An animal is guided through the sensations of pleasure and pain, while satisfying his organic needs. And it has no other needs whatsoever. Do you understand this much?"

"Yes, but go on to human behavior," Knox coaxed his friend.

"Certainly. You notice the new element, the letter 'I' in the formula for human behavior $(B = S + I + R)$. 'I' stands for interpretation, which means, that apart from man's innate and natural reflex reactions, man doesn't react blindly and mechanically to any given stimulus. Before he reacts, he interprets the nature of the stimulus by his intellect and can also anticipate the outcome of his reactions, if he reacts at all. For he's free, he can choose, accept and reject. Man lives selectively."

"But you don't mean to say that this is true also for children? You must have had the adult man in mind, I'm sure. . . ." Knox commented.

"I agree with you to a point," Noesis assented, "because choice presupposes the ability to estimate, to judge, and this act can be performed only by intelligent beings. Besides, man's reason or intellect develops from the state of potentiality into that of actuality, and this process of maturation, development and evolution requires time. On the other hand, I wouldn't equate man's chronological and physical age with his mental age. There's no such parallel and direct relationship. Besides, one shouldn't forget either that the most important of all these things is the innate intelligence, or, as you call it, the I.Q., which sets the limits to development. I hope you can see how these problems are related to the questions of genetics."

"But all this still doesn't put children on the level of adults," Knox persisted.

"I'm sure of that," Noesis replied. "Nevertheless, I insist that it's wrong to establish almost an essential difference between the behavior of the child and that of the adult. Such opposition would destroy or violate the principle of the organic unity and continuity of life."

"I'm sorry to disappoint you," Knox observed, "but I don't see how one can put the child and the adult on the same level. I'm not a child and a child isn't an adult."

"Your objections are valid only insofar as you refer to the level of attained intelligence, of intellectual maturity. Of course, it would make no sense to start teaching theoretical physics or metaphysics to children. . . . Although even in your world there have been a few exceptional cases of individuals who, so to say, had no childhood, because very early they were already learning

Latin, Greek, history and sciences. Such was the case of John Stuart Mill and a few others."

"Are you indirectly suggesting that, due to the success of eugenics, all the children in your world are born with such superior intelligence?" Knox asked astounded.

"That's only natural and not a miraculous event," Noesis observed casually. "As a consequence, the period of childhood is considerably shortened. And that means a gain in years during the process of formal instruction. But let me go back to your objection to the effect that I seem to put children and adults on the same level."

"Oh, yes," Knox agreed. "We haven't finished that yet."

"I was thinking in terms of the psychological needs and pertinent motivations, such as the will to freedom, the quest for pleasure, both of them being subsumed under the all important feeling of self-love. In this respect, I still maintain that there's no fundamental difference between the motivations of the child and of the adult. Only the means available to both vary, due to their different social position. Daddy drives a Buick and Junior a second-hand car. Daddy's toys are bigger and more expensive and the games he plays are—at times—more dangerous in their consequences. That's all. And if you're still not convinced, I invite you to review one by one the list of the psycho-social needs, and you'll be surprised with the result."

"I think I can see what you mean clearer now," Knox consented. "But we must go back to the unfinished issue of conditioning, remember?"

"I do. I've already said in this respect that conditioning isn't the proper method of educating, because of the basic and essential difference between man and animal."

"Do you realize," Knox observed, "that you're getting very close to the old Platonic and Christian conception of man? Next you'll be saying something on man's immortal soul, his spirituality, and so on. . . ."

"I hope you're just teasing me," Noesis remarked with a smile. "The cause for man's uniqueness—his power to conceptualize, to think and to create—are not supernatural in origin, just plainly

260

the result of the higher stage man has reached in the evolutionary process."

"I see," Knox said. "But with respect to conditioning, again, wouldn't you agree that at least for the very early stages of childhood such as infancy and the few years that follow, it's the only method of education possible? You can't reason with a baby, even if he's a born genius!"

"I would prefer to use the term 'learning' than conditioninig, and even there I would insist that the main task of the educator should consist in creating such an environment that would provide the best opportunities for the child to learn by doing, by experience, to develop those attitudes and habits which will be useful to him, without the harmful effects of negative conditioning."

"Your principles sound good," Knox interposed, "but I wonder how one's supposed to apply them to concrete situations?"

"First let me elaborate on the concept of negative conditioning. Then I'll go into the specifics. My main objection is based on the effects of such a technique, that is, the stifling of the child's individuality. There're many ways to accomplish that. The most effective and most harmful, of course, is what psychology labels as reinforcing the desired reactions by punishment, capitalizing on the child's natural fear and aversion for pain, both psychic and physical. I'm sure you must know that the immediate effect of fear is to inhibit the person's powers and resourcefulness. It reduces him to the level of a scared animal. And the number of the created inhibitions are equated with education. The more inhibited, the better, because better 'adjusted' or 'adapted' to the desires, wishes and objectives of the adults, who praise obedience, modesty, humility as the highest and most desirable virtues. An obedient child gives no trouble. A humble child is ready to submit and to serve. A modest, meek, shy, timid and withdrawn child can be easily dominated, directed and owned. A slave is preferred to an independent, free, self-willed and self-sufficient individual. Should they get such a stubborn rebel, they'll do everything to turn him into an emasculated and impotent neurotic. Occasionally they might also praise and reward

261

a child for his so-called virtues, but they want to make sure that the child never forgets the rod, the 'board of education,' physical punishment meted out to him with a sense of indignant justice and self-righteousness. When they succeeded to kill every trace of the child's unique individuality and transformed him into a well-adjusted, well-rounded, well-adapted, obedient conformist, they're proud of their achievement. They've created a 'good' child."

"If somebody heard you," Knox commented, "he would immediately accuse you of destroying the value of authority and the respect due to it. They would charge you with the dissemination of subversive ideas to suit your purpose of fomenting destruction and rebellion. They'd point to you as a dangerous element, a radical, an extremist, a godless and malicious individual, ripe to be locked up, in order to save the others from your pernicious influence. . . ." Knox stopped for a minute, examining Noesis' face for the effect of his words on him, then he asked: "Are you totally and radically opposed to conformity, obedience and respect?"

Noesis smiled and answered: "Let's submit an important distinction in order to clear up the confusion. I'd say that, by all means, always and without exception, man should conform to the facts of reality. Discover the laws of nature—his own included —accept them and obey them respectfully. For one can control nature only to the extent one knows its laws and learns how to make them work for one's own benefit, and not against it. I should also add, on the side, that all of man's troubles are caused by his irrational wishes to ignore, disregard and bypass the absolute facts and laws of nature. He harms himself every time he chooses to go against reality and nature. If man places himself outside reality, he ends up as a non-entity, a non-being, and death will follow as a natural consequence, as the just punishment. Perhaps you know that at the root of all mental and emotional disturbances you find the same cause—men's irrational wish to go against the laws of nature, offending the principles of identity, non-contradiction and sufficient reason. A neurotic is the maladjusted person who refuses to conform to the absolute facts, the categorical imperative of reality and reason."

"If these are your convictions," Knox broke in with surprise, "why did you speak against conformity a while ago, condemning it so vehemently?"

"Because then I was referring to social conformity, and its fateful effects on the individual."

"You mean that no one should submit to the existing social, political and moral order? That everybody should rebel against all kinds of authority, starting with that of the parents in the family? But would mean total anarchy! I'm sure you couldn't have meant that!"

"I'm glad you grant me this much," Noesis remarked with amusement. "Let me explain myself. I insisted on man's absolute need to accept and respect the laws of nature. Similarly, I urge everybody to accept and respect the laws of his reason, by which he discovers the facts of reality and truth. In other words, I'm saying that man should rebel only against those social, political and moral laws which cannot be justified by reason, because they were instituted only to guarantee the privileged position of those in power. He should do that, knowing that his rights, due to him as an individual, rational, autonomous and self-sufficient being, are violated by the arbitrary restrictions of those who perform the ignoble act of enslaving, commanding, subjecting and exploiting. But I certainly oppose any irrational and irresponsible use of freedom, any rebellion supported by the subversive intentions of the nihilists and anarchists. I hope I made myself clear now."

"More than that," Knox replied. "You see, the reason I asked you that question was my experience with the disastrous effects of parental permissiveness and exaggerated liberalism."

"I couldn't say anything to the contrary," Noesis retorted. "That's the other extreme and you may recall that we've discussed that already, in connection with the parent-child relationship. But I'd like to comment on the 'student rebellion.'"

"I wonder what you're going to say . . ." excited anticipation lit Knox's eyes.

"There you have the best example for the immature and

irresponsible misuse of freedom. It clearly demonstrates what happens when freedom and license are taken as being identical. But I'm not ready to put the blame exclusively on the students, or other marchers and activists for that matter."

"What do you mean?" Knox interrupted in surprise. "Whom are you going to blame then?"

"The so-called educators and your educational methods," Noesis replied with firmness. "In most of your institutions of learning, there's instruction and training for professional purposes, but the formation of the students' character has been abandoned, in the name of, or under the disguise of, some scientific rationalization. I mean to say that, in the name of positivism and factualness, values have been ousted as non-scientific. And with that you've given up the student as a person. You restrict your efforts to factual information only, doing nothing for the formation of the persons' characters."

"But some educators claim that that's not their business. They concern themselves with judgments of facts only, and dismiss all value judgments as relative, subjective and unscientific. I remember that one of my instructors in college, in a course of political economy, stated repeatedly and emphatically that the questions of values have nothing to do with his field. Then I asked him whether the products and money had any value at all for him, whether they stood for something useful rather than useless and harmful. But he dismissed my question with an intimidating and sarcastic remark on my naive ignorance!"

"Well, you see, that's it exactly," Noesis observed with satisfaction. "I regard it not only as the most anti-psychological and anti-educational, but also as destructive and harmful."

"Please explain what you mean."

"You're well aware that neither knowledge nor behavior are innate. Only the potentiality and the ability to learn are innate. Which means, in other words, that both knowledge and behavior are acquired by learning and experience. But this implies also that a child doesn't come into existence equipped with the standards of value he absolutely needs for his own guidance and use. Therefore, he naturally looks for such standards and measures in his environment, in the home, at school and in society at large. He wants to build up for himself a definite set or hierarchy of values, ideas, principles and convictions he needs for the purpose of developing himself into a certain type of a person, to establish a sense or identity of his own, through the form and style he gives to his own character. And now imagine the liberally broadminded and permissive parent or teacher, who tells him with an evasive air of false sophistication that there're no objective standards and values, because these things are a matter of taste only, depending on one's feelings and on how one looks at them; they're subjective and relative. . . . Well then, Edward, think of what this attitude accomplishes in the mind of that student."

"It requires no hard thinking on my part," Knox remarked scornfully, "because I know it all from my own experience. I grew up in such an atmosphere. I was exposed to this kind of liberalism. I was left with nothing to stand on, with nothing to believe in, with nothing to take seriously and respectfully. I was floating in mid-air and I became one of the angry young men, a rebel without a cause. . . ."

"Then, since you see it so clearly for yourself," Noesis concluded, "I don't have to spend more time on it."

"Sure. . . . But where will all this lead? What'll be the outcome of it all? Who's going to stop it?" Knox sounded alarmed. "And suppose it doesn't stop! Then, what about the future of man? You can't call that evolution! It's decadence, decay and final extinction!"

"I understand perfectly what you mean," Noesis replied calmly, "but perhaps I should tell you that your concept of evolution must be improved somewhat. When speaking of evolution on the cultural level, I didn't mean to say that whatever comes later in time is necessarily higher and better. There is, in fact, what you called degeneration or the death of a culture. As you know, there've been many cultures that have disappeared. But, on the other hand, there's no reason for alarm, if you think dialectically."

"I don't quite understand," Knox admitted.

"From the beginning of recorded history, man has tried to give a reasonable account for the problem of evil. Of course, his first attempts were primitive. I mean, mythical and religious. They invented the duality of good and evil. You'll find its traces in all of man's religions. They thought of a 'good' God who was man's friend and of another one, an 'evil' god, who was man's mortal enemy. They also invented, through their frightened imagination and impotent condition, some 'good spirits'—also known as guardian angels—and some 'evil spirits,' the legion of devils of the underworld. And the meaning of human life and history were interpreted as the perpetual clash of these opposite powers, with alternating success and defeat. Of course, man tried to secure the good will of the 'good spirits and gods' by all sorts of superstitious beliefs and rituals, magic included. By that he also meant to exorcise the world from the evil spirits. But to make a long story short, it was only through the rise of the scientific and philosophic frame of mind that this problem received a more acceptable explanation. It was Hegel, as you know, who made most of the dialectical method, while constructing his philosophic system. His system failed, of course, but his method survived. He found a meaning and a justification for evil, which he called the 'tremendous power of the negative,' an antithetical force, an opposition, a No that contradicts every Yes. But this No wasn't meant to be a destructive force. It was understood rather as a challenge, leading to a 'Nevertheless,' to a synthesis on a higher level, to the reconciliation of the opposites in a new force, reaching a temporary and dynamic balance of the opposites, eventually splitting anew and leading to a new strife, demanding a still higher synthesis, and so on."

"But that doesn't explain the extinction of the many cultures," Knox objected.

"If you look at it more closely, you'll see that it does. Take a clue from biology—life presupposes death in the sense that the living survive at the cost or the death of another life. *Mors tua, vita mea*—Your death is the condition for my life and survival. Now apply this to the death of cultures. The death of a culture shouldn't be regarded as final and absolute, because although the specific economic, social and cultural structure—the institutions—

may crumble as a consequence of natural causes or wars; nevertheless, its ideas will survive and become the fertilizing and incubating forces for the preparation and birth of another culture. Thus the principle of continuity is dialectically preserved. The best example would be the culture of the Greeks. Their institutions have long since disappeared and only a few ruins speak of the splendor of their cities. But their ideas, their philosophy, their knowledge survived and became the foundation of your whole Western civilization and culture."

"I understand your explanation," Knox said, "however, since you take the principle of the organic unity and continuity as a cosmic law—dialectically integrated—I'd like to know how does that apply to your more advanced civilization? Is there such a thing as decline, degeneration and corruption in your world?"

"The cosmic law of dialectical continuity and evolution should be applied to our case in the light of the principle of existential limitation. I don't mean anything abstract or metaphysical by this. Remember, we already talked about the problem of evil, then we went on to the power of the negative. Now it should be easy to make the connections."

"I'm sorry," Knox confessed, "but I don't see your point."

"Why don't you try to analyze the meaning of the idea of 'existential limitation?' You would find clues there. Limitation means—both quantitatively and qualitatively—only so much, so far and not more. . . . So much being, so much knowledge, so much freedom, so much progress and not more. Limitation, therefore, is a negation, and every negation is a limitation. It's this limitation which is at the root of all imperfections. To be limited and imperfect means the same thing."

"And how does this idea tie in with dialectics and evolution?" Knox questioned further.

"You can look at limitation—imperfection—as a negative force. Psychologically, you may even call it 'evil,' but I don't use that term, because of its old moral and mythical connotations. In Hegel's language, limitation, as a negative force, would be the antithesis, the opposition, the No-saying spirit. And now, instead of inventing malignant deities and spirits, we take limitation as a challenge, a wonderful enemy to be defeated. And every victory gives us the courage to overcome the next barrier, the next limitation, the imperfections that are still with us. Evolution is a dynamic process, constant strife and war. Instead of waging wars against our fellow human beings, we prefer to fight for more power through knowledge. For knowledge is power, and this is *our* quest for more being. . . ."

"Your ideas sound very interesting!" Knox commented with conviction. "But would you comment on the situation existing here on our planet?"

"You're asking for a lot," Noesis answered. "I'll try to limit myself to the most essential things. As far as your own country goes, I invite you to remember the distinction we drew between civilization and culture. In that sense, I could answer your question very simply—you're civilized and illiterate. In other words, you're well conditioned Pavlovian creatures. Your ideals in life can be subsumed under the slogan of success, measured by the size of your paycheck and the car you drive. You have no philosophy of life and to that extent, you're not really existing. You spend your whole lifetime in accumulating material goods, which you have promoted from simple means to ends in themselves. Finally, I find it a very strange paradox that you are, at the same time, the most technologically advanced people and the least happy. The rising index of mental illness should tell you a lot about it. As there're no values taught in your schools, there're no cultural values present in your lives either. Of course, you Edward are one of the few exceptions."

"Thank you for your compliment," Knox remarked rather drily. "But I'd like to know the outcome of it for the future. I'm a young man and I'd like to know what to expect from life."

"What you can expect from life depends entirely upon what you make of it," Noesis said in earnest. "As to the future . . . well, I haven't much hope, if I think of the immediate future, four or five generations ahead. I think we agreed that the population of this planet is living through the ideological epidemics of rising collectivism. It's the new experiment man's trying out on himself. But we also said before that the eventual triumph of collectivism won't be a final one, only temporary. Man's will to freedom and his quest for more being will fight and defeat the collective dragon."

"Do you have any further remarks or criticism of our system of education?" Knox inquired.

"Why do you ask me this question?" Noesis reacted with surprise. "I think I said what I considered as the most essential."

"Then we could move on to the positive part of our dialogue. I mean, you should talk about the way you, on your planet, have solved those problems."

"Yes, I remember that we had that in mind," Noesis agreed. "So let me start from the very beginning. I mean, the procreation of children."

"I'm glad you start there, because I have to admit that the whole thing is up in the air, as far as I'm concerned. Of course, I haven't forgotten what you've said so far about genetics, the absence of marriage and family, therefore of parents. But I still don't know how it works in the concrete. Who are those who procreate, when and why?"

"Let's take one question at a time," Noesis suggested. "First, I'd say that every man and woman is genetically fit to procreate, which doesn't mean that everybody does so!"

"Then who's the person in authority who makes the choices and gives out the assignment? More important, who makes the selection of the mates? And who keeps a check on the number of children to be born? You know what I mean?" Knox talked rapidly and in confusion.

"Edward, you're asking all your questions at once," Noesis remarked. "Since everybody is qualified genetically, there's no need to select, to accept or to reject, to allow or to forbid. It's done on a voluntary basis and that goes also for the selection of the mate. As to the limitation of the number of births, we need no bureaucrats invested with unlimited powers. Computers do a much better job."

"Before you go on," Knox interrupted, "what'd happen if a case of misgenetion should occur? After all, I don't think that you can prevent that."

"Whenever such cases should occur, though they very rarely do, that individual is sterilized at an age when we can get his voluntary consent. But we talked about this before. As to the motivation why some men and women volunteer for the role of procreation, I can give you a simple answer. It's the desire to share and perpetuate the values and pleasures of a meaningful life for its own sake."

"I can well accept this explanation with regard to the male. But concerning the mother who submits herself to the discomforts of pregnancy and childbirth, knowing all the while that the child she's bearing and will give birth to will actually not be hers. Perhaps she won't even see the child. . . . Well, that'd be more difficult to accept."

"Of course it is, and it'll remain so, as long as one still thinks and feels within the framework of the traditional ideas and values. In the name of maternal instinct—a rather inappropriate, vague expression—every mother thinks of the child as flesh of her flesh, blood of her blood, life of her life, and naturally considers the child as her own. Nevertheless, I'd say that this instinctive attachment to the child decreases with the increase of one's enlightenment. Besides, you know that there're parents in your world who give up their children for adoption. Then you have the cases of unwanted pregnancies, when the unwed mother is only too happy to walk out of the hospital alone, leaving behind the baby she has never even seen, to the care of certain institutions. Some of them even accept money in exchange for their children. Moreover, it wasn't so long ago that parents sold their children, while others are charged, even today, with criminal neglect or abuse, not mentioning those who kill them. . . . Of course, you'll say that these cases are rather rare, that they represent only the exception, and that society brands them as morally corrupt. While there are some immoral aspects present, especially in some of the cases mentioned, I wouldn't make it general. The important point is to learn that so-called 'maternal instinct' isn't an absolute and unconditional imperative, unless you want to equate woman with an animal!"

"I raised that objection mainly because of the almost universal prevalence of our social and moral prejudices. Personally, I have reasons to agree with you. Take my case, for instance. I was only four years old when my mother took off with another man, without a second thought of what would happen to me. . . ."

"And yours isn't a unique case," observed Noesis. "If you remember what we found out about the children's true feelings toward their parents, and of the parents toward the former, then you'll have added reasons not to brand our way of doing things as 'inhuman.' "

"But I've heard it said so often, that 'a child absolutely needs the love and care of the mother, because there can be no substitute for her true love.' "

"I hope that you consider those remarks no more valid then the manifestation of romantic sentimentalism, with a dose of hypocrisy thrown in for good measure."

"That's how I feel about it," Knox confirmed. "My next question is about what happens to the children after delivery."

"Before I go into that, let me mention something I overlooked before, that is, that the period of gestation is reduced to six months only, and that the delivery itself is practically painless."

"I see," Knox acknowledged this new information. "By the way, what is the age you consider ideal for pregnancy and childbirth?"

"I'd say between twenty and thirty, and then no woman goes through more than three pregnancies, spaced at a minimum of three years apart. Thus, the optimum is secured for both mother and child. Now as to the children, they're raised and educated in the best environment our society can provide."

"Is it some kind of a collective nursery?" Knox inquired with suspicion.

"I notice a certain critical tone in your question," Noesis said. "Let me correct the wrong ideas you usually associate with the term 'collective nursery.' First of all, the word 'collective' here is misplaced. Remember that we have no formally established state or government, much less any collective phalansterianism. That idea fits only the totalitarian dictatorships of your present and past. Second, the term 'nursery' is an understatement. You should rather think of an institution, a school equipped with all the

271

facilities needed for the best development of the children, staffed by the most competent professionals. The care of children isn't left to unqualified persons, who substitute love for the necessary knowledge."

"How many children do you have in one of those institutions?"

"Never more than twelve, but usually less. And that's an absolute must, in order to attend to the needs of every child, considered as a unique individual."

"I can well imagine that you provide the best as far as the satisfaction of the child's organic or physical needs go. . . . I'd say the same in regard to formal instruction and learning, the development of the intellect. But what about the child's psychological needs for security, acceptance, belonging, attention and love?"

"I don't understand what you mean!" Noesis said with surprise. "Unless you want to fall back again upon the slogan of motherly love and care!"

"I wasn't going to put it quite that way, but something to that effect," Knox tried to clarify. "After all, those children are, so to say, strangers, they don't belong to the scientists who run those institutions, and. . . ."

". . . You assume that they cannot feel the same things the mother would, is that it?"

"I see that I've made a mistake. . . . Let me think it through. . . ." Knox admitted his blunder. Then he continued after a pause: "Of course it's nonsense. . . . I mean, what I said about the lack of love. . . . Perhaps I could use the example of your gardener. No doubt, he must have loved the flowers he grew and cared for, even though he didn't father them. It must be the love of life and of the living as such, but on much broader terms, that is, not confined to the narrow limits of the family and kin. The love of life and the living!"

"I'm glad you corrected yourself," Noesis replied. "But let me add one more idea with regard to the needs of the child. What a child actually needs is only an environment, physical and social, which can satisfy in the best possible manner and at the proper time all his needs, physical and psychic. If these needs are

272

satisfied, the children naturally react with joy and love. Besides, does a small child—three, four or five years old—really understand the terms 'father' and 'mother'? Who and what those persons are in his life? And why does the child love them or hate them, as each case demands?"

"Obviously a child has no means of knowing the meaning of those terms and his ignorance on that subject remains with him for many years, especially when parents are reluctant to satisfy the child's natural desire to know the truth about procreation and sex. The parents prefer to feed his imagination with absurd tales and stories. . . ."

"And in spite of all that, the child loves his parents," Noesis continued, "but for what reasons?"

"Simply because the parents are the persons who satisfy the child's physical and psychological needs. And I have to conclude that the child would respond in the same way to any other person who'd be in charge of that service. Furthermore, if the child's frustrated in his need-satisfactions in the home, he very frequently turns to those persons outside the home—a teacher or a friend, for example—who does satisfy those needs. Of course, the parents resent these forms of outside attachment and make the child feel guilty about it," Knox concluded with satisfaction.

"You should've also mentioned the advantages our system has over yours with regard to the child's development," Noesis went on. "Remember that we've pointed out before the harms that can be done to children, very early in their lives, when they're helplessly and defenselessly exposed, by the mere accident of birth, to the deleterious influences of unqualified parents. But these are only the preventive measures. Much more important is the positive care and work done for the healthy and normal development of each child."

"Are you referring to the formal education of the mind, teaching or schooling?" Knox inquired.

"Not yet, although that's the other important part of the whole process. Right now I was referring to the period of pre-school age, which in my world ends at the age of four. It's the period during which the child slowly discovers the world around him and develops his abilities to manipulate the objects of his experience. Play is the usual form taken by this need to learn by experience. But in your world this is, to a great extent, left to chance. Even the toys are designed by adults from their point of view, with little concern for the needs of the child living on a different level of consciousness. The toy manufacturers are more concerned with their profits than with the laws governing the development of a child's interests, needs and intelligence. The child is burdened to adjust to a world made by the adults and for the adults. When it comes to the patterns of behavior, they've no qualms about demanding children to live up to the adult standards of behavior. They treat a child's lying, for instance, with the same severity as the premeditated lies of the adults, not realizing that in the mind of a child the real and the imaginary, the rational and the emotional, aren't yet fully differentiated. And all these wrong attitudes create many unwholesome problems for the child."

"What do you have to say on the formal teaching or instruction?" Knox inquired further.

"There isn't enough time to say everything," Noesis observed. "Certainly I intend to evaluate your practices in this respect also. My objections are many. First, even in your rich country, the profession of teaching is held in a rather low esteem, judging by the meager salaries paid to those engaged in this profession, while everybody loudly clamors its all important and noble character, labelling it a vocation. But that's only the posturing of cheap hypocrites. Consequently, your best minds go into the more lucrative professions, leaving the business of teaching to the average or below average individuals, many of whom are women who regard their jobs only as a means of additional income for their families, often only on a part time basis, or by those who are yet single and will quit their positions as soon as they get married. In other words, there're very few teachers really dedicated to their professions."

"I fully agree with you," Knox replied. "And as far as the salaries go, many a truck driver or a plumber is better off than most of our high school and college teachers."

"Take then the method of teaching," Noesis continued. "Most of it is presented ready-made to the student, all problems seem to be solved and settled in advance. The only thing the student's required to do is to accept the information, very often without understanding the issues, and to fill up his memory with an indefinite number of items, just loosely connected or downright disconnected. No wonder his intellect, his ability to think, judge, reason, infer, to induce and to deduce become atrophied, or, at best, only partially developed. Besides, the teacher is hard put to answer all their questions due to the great number of students entrusted to his care."

"What would be the ideal number of students in a class?" Knox asked with curiosity.

"Maximum twelve, but six or eight would be even better."

"That's impossible in our system! There's a critical shortage of schools, and a lack of facilities and funds, which is worst of all."

"While you're spending millions of dollars for military purposes!" Noesis observed with regret.

"That's another ugly truth, and a stain on the conscience of our leaders," Knox remarked with indignation.

"Speaking in positive terms, I'm going to point out only two essential conditions for proper education. First, there's the need to guide the student from insight to insight, leading him through the processes of problem solving and the discovery of the first principles, with as little assistance or tutoring as possible."

"But that presupposes a superior intelligence!"

"It most certainly does," agreed Noesis. "I find your democratic ideal, in urging and practically forcing education for all, very strange. You seem to forget, or rather evade, the obvious evidence that there're different degrees and limits of educability, set by the individually different and innate abilities of the children. As a consequence, your curricula are designed with a view of the lowest common denominator, thus stifling and hurting the bright ones, the few who are capable of creating something new. There are, of course, a few exceptions."

"But that's how our politicians want it," Knox remarked with resignation.

275

"And for the simple reason that it's easier to command, to dominate and to rule a mass of illiterates," Noesis completed Knox's sentence.

"I believe you don't have such problems, assuming that every child is of a superior intelligence," Knox went on. "It must be a pleasure to teach those children."

"Only if you can answer all of their questions," Noesis added. "In fact, however, our children are given all the opportunities to learn by themselves and the role of the teacher is a minimum one. If we want to take it literally, we have no such profession as teaching. Every adult is well qualified to guide a child. Then there's one more point. I believe we touched upon it at the very beginning of our conversations. It's the question of integrating knowledge in a structured system, into a unified whole, in order to do justice to the unity of nature itself."

"Oh, yes!" exclaimed Knox. "You did say something on the disadvantages of specialization. I remember!"

"That's right," Noesis agreed, "and now we aren't going into that again. But perhaps one brief remark is due. I would say that a truly learned and educated or cultured person must be well versed, at least in principles, in all areas of knowledge, and capable to see and to establish the integrated hierarchy of knowledge."

"Do you have institutions specialized in giving professional training?" Knox asked.

"It's very difficult to settle this question with a simple yes or no," Noesis hesitated. "If I told you that all of us are capable and competent in most fields of knowledge, you wouldn't believe it. On the other hand, however, there're individual inclinations and preferences. In addition to the possession of a universal knowledge, most of us select one major field of research, without, however, getting lost in it. As I told you before, we're against narrow specialization. Besides, no one spends his lifetime doing research in one field only. Whenever one project is completed in one field, we turn to another area."

"Do you have research centers, similar to our universities?"

"The theoretical part of the work is done individually as it

276

ought to be. The first condition for any creative effort is privacy and loneliness. There's no such thing as thinking together. But the experimental part and its final translation into some visible product is carried out in our laboratories and production centers."

"Nevertheless, there must be some coordination of your individual efforts," Knox insisted. "And coordination or organization requires communication, consultation, cooperation. Besides, you're not going to deny that the present presupposes the past, which means that we learn from those who went before us and also from those who are with us. Finally, in order to avoid wasteful duplication of efforts, there must be some kind of directives."

"A computer takes care in part of the problems you brought up," answered Noesis. "Then there're libraries, books, periodicals and many other means of securing the information one needs for his work. This doesn't mean, however, that we don't exchange our ideas with our fellow men. Quite to the contrary! I only wanted to make sure that you won't entertain wrong ideas in terms of a collectivist, socialized and centrally regimented teamwork. Your 'organization man' is unknown to us, because no such type can exist in our world. Similarly, we don't have unions, professional organizations or learned societies, with their bureaucratic structure and artificial functioning. Everyone's free and able to contact everybody else, whenever there's a desire to do so."

"Since it's getting late again," Knox said with an eye on his watch, "there's one more question I'd like to ask you before we close our session for tonight."

"What is it?"

"I think it's part of the general topic of education," Knox went on, "it's the question of recreation or the facilities you have for amusements, if any?"

"I'm glad you remembered this problem," Noesis agreed. "In fact, it's necessary to recognize the all-important place pleasure holds in man's life. Pleasure is the natural consequence and reward of any activity performed according to its intrinsic laws. Since life is a spontaneous activity from within, pleasure becomes its natural component. For sure, most people associate happiness

277

with pleasure and joy, and look upon frustration, pain and suffering as its contradiction. Pleasure is a must for every living organism."

"And that's the justification for recreation and amusement," Knox observed.

"You can say that, of course . . ." Noesis remarked.. "However, I have a few critical remarks concerning your conception and attitude toward pleasure and recreation. Before you misunderstand me, I hasten to say that whatever is wrong in this respect is due rather to man's present socio-economic condition and he is given no other choice."

"What are your objections, Noesis?" Knox urged him on.

"From what I've been able to observe so far, I find a rather strange and unwholesome division or split between your work and the time set aside for pleasure of 'fun.' Very few people look upon their work as the main and permanent source of their satisfactions. And I include not only your laborers, your skilled workers in the factories, but also your professionals. Work is being looked upon as the curse of Adam, as an unwanted but necesary burden and evil, as an indispensable means to earn a livelihood. I repeat again that I fully agree that there is not much meaning and pleasure which man can derive from his daily work, especially those who are condemned, so to say, to perform a repetitive and mechanical sequence of motions, while attending to a machine. There is no opportunity provided for the free play of the mind, for individual initiative and creativity. Boredom and frustration are the outcome of this routine. As a necessary consequence, compensations are wanted. They start living only when their working hours, their slavery is over. Pleasure becomes a necessary antidote, apart and divorced from one's daily activity. People have to 'take time out'—a few hours every day or during their weekends and vacations. Since they are utterly bored and frustrated, they are not very discriminating with regard to the sources of their pleasures. . . . They want to forget, to escape into anything, away from reality and its frustrations. Naturally they prefer those 'outlets' which give them the fastest and most radical change,—drugs, alcohol, sex, and so forth. Even the hours spent and lost before their television sets, in the movies and theaters, must be of such nature as to provide some new excitement for their tired senses and imagination. Violence, brutality, crime, sex and abnormalities of all sorts provide the best thrillers and horror shows. You may have noticed that in their livingrooms the bookcase and the piano were replaced by the TV set and the built-in-bar. Very few people read anything worth that effort. The majority never go beyond newspapers, magazine and the products of the yellow press. Then, if we come to their socials, well, just listen to what they talk about. The trivia of the daily rut. They keep themselves carefully aloof of any serious issue belonging to philosophy, science, art and politics. And they justify the utter sterility and shallowness of their conversation by the false pretext of respecting everybody's opinion. They are nice and they don't want to hurt anybody's feelings by disagreeing. At the same time, they insist on the need and the importance of communication, not realizing that they have practically nothing worthwhile or interesting to communicate. They talk and keep on talking, saying nothing at all. . . . Their real fun begins with the pleasures derived from the stimulation of their overwrought and tired senses. As a result, they remain psychologically just as frustrated as before, and keep on compensating themselves by the resourcefulness typical for unfastidious hedonists. Many of them become mentally alienated, insane. . . ."

"What is the solution you would propose?" Knox asked in a challenging manner.

"I'm sure that man on this planet cannot derive his meaningful joys and pleasures from his work, as long as the present methods of production prevail. There is a long way to go until automation will liberate man from the drudgery of physical work. As I said before, in another context, leisure is the necessary condition for the rise of a cultured existence, and the pleasures derived from it."

"I have the impression that in your world most of the pleasures are derived from your philosophic, scientific, and artistic values."

"Your impression is well founded," Noesis agreed. "I'm aware, of course, of the difficulty most people—especially the ignorant

279

and the uneducated—would have to understand and to accept that man can derive permanent joy from the play of his creative mind. If you take someone who never studied or undestood philosophy, science and art—when exposed to these subjects in school—certainly you cannot expect such a person to understand or to share the passionate love and pleasure a cultured intellectual gains from his work. How could he if he never had such an experience and, what's more important, he is not mentally qualified and able to have it? A philosopher, a scientist or an artist are depicted as 'queer,' 'square,' as an 'egghead,' and also abnormal to that extent."

"How true!" Knox exclaimed. "I would say that there is a direct relationship between one's degree of intelligence and what he calls pleasure. The artistic need of a child, for instance, is satisfied with 'Mary had a little lamb.' The average man will be satisfied with the popular and vulgar tunes or folk-songs. And for morons, only moronic things are acceptable."

"You could quote Aristotle's saying," Noesis concluded "that whatever is received, is received according to the dispositions of the receiver."

"It just occured to me," Knox said suddenly, "that we have completely forgotten to discuss the questions pertinent to the formation of the child's character. We spent our time talking on other things, and I remember that you had included this in your plan."

"I realize that," Noesis consented. "It's too late now, so let's leave it for our next session, when we will discuss the problems of ethics and religion. It fits in there perfectly."

"You said also 'religion,'" Knox remarked with surprise.

"I fully understand your astonishment," Noesis smiled, "because of the rather strong condemnation on my part of man's moral and religious practices. This is why my suggestion must have struck you unexpectedly."

"Indeed it did," Knox replied. "I took you for an atheist."

"Remember that Socrates was condemned and executed on grounds of being taken for an atheist," Noesis said. "But he wasn't. . . ."

"Are you trying to suggest that you're not one either?" Knox asked rather excited.

"Not in the sense this term is commonly used and misused," Noesis answered. "But let's leave this question at this point, and we shall discuss it in detail the next time."

"Yes, next time. . . ." Knox muttered thoughtfully. Then he added with uneasiness: "Is this next time also our last one?" He sounded sad, depressed, almost grieved. Noesis immediately understood the full meaning and implications of Knox's anxious question.

"Yes, Edward, it will be our last discussion." And with this he fell silent.

"But I will not be able to finish the whole manuscript within two or three weeks!" Knox said with alarm. "I'm alone now, you see, I have to do the editing and the typing too."

His last remark was meant more as a justification or an excuse. It contained an allusion to his separation from Marisa, but Noesis did not seem willing to pick up that invitation to enter into personal matters. He only said with emphasis:

"I remember that Aristotle, speaking of the great-souled man, stated that such a man is not very fond of companionship, because he happens to be his own best friend. Thus he is never alone." Noesis paused for a while, and then he continued: "As to the manuscript, you don't have a deadline to meet. You need several months to have it all finished and ready for publication. I'm sure that you realize that you have to go over the whole book once more after you finished your first draft. . . . And you'll find certain passages that you'll want to change and rewrite."

Knox was anxious to find out whether Noesis would keep up their relationship after the next session, but his friend's reserved attitude seemed to discourage further inquiries. He pulled himself together, forced a faint smile on his lips and took leave of Noesis. Never before had he experienced the weight of loneliness so intensely. He realized how far he still was from the goal set by Aristotle for the great-souled man.

Chapter Eleven

THE ULTIMATE MEANING OF ETHICS AND RELIGION

No major event disturbed the even flow and succession of Knox's days, spent exclusively in writing. Any outsider or superficial observer would have described his way of life as an utterly uniform and monotonous one, extremely boring and frustrating. Perhaps a social psychologist would have labelled it as a case of extreme maladjustment, bordering on abnormality. Very few people indeed could have understood why and how a young man could live in total seclusion from the world of people and events. Taking a closer look at Knox, he would have seemed the perfect example of introversion, a very dangerous trait in the judgment of most other-directed extroverts. Such an observer would've drawn the picture of a strange individual who spent most of his time in his apartment, almost a prisoner, behind locked doors. Not even eavesdropping would've revealed more than an undisturbed silence broken only occasionally by the mechanical sound of a typewriter. No one ever came to his door, even the salesmen avoided it carefully. No delivery men of any kind stopped in front of his apartment. They all passed by, as if it were non-existent. Many of them must have thought of it as empty. In the afternoons, however, the persistent observers could have seen that young man stepping out of his place, locking his door and walking straight out into the street, without taking notice of the presence of the people who happened to be around. He gave the impression of someone avoiding contact with anyone on purpose, which was the truth. He appeared to be mentally absorbed in some thought of his own, perhaps even obsessed by it, judging from his eyes staring ahead of himself but noticing nothing in particular. His face didn't seem friendly, rather too serious; one could almost say angry. There was an air of impassivity and aloofness about him, a forbidding reserve and distance, that froze the mechanical and socially prescribed smile on the face of the better adjusted and more normal, more human, 'nice people.' Two hours or so later, the same solitary figure reappeared in the hallway, occasionally carrying one or two paper bags, probably containing provisions. He then walked straight to the door of his apartment, looking neither to the right nor to the left, unlocked the door, as if in a hurry to escape being seen, and disappeared as soon as possible behind the door, which he locked again from within. Then, nothing again for another twenty four hours, just silence and the clicking sound of the typewriter.

But Knox didn't look upon himself in this way. He didn't consider himself either seriously maladjusted, mentally obsessed or deluded. He was keenly aware of his situation and considered it as a period of very significant training and learning. He understood it as an endurance test. He wanted to find out how much loneliness he could take without becoming unhappy and miserable about it. He kept before his eyes the image of Aristotle's independent, autonomous, self-sufficient and great-souled man. He knew that Noesis was one of them, but he wasn't equally convinced whether he had at least the basic qualities required to develop himself into that ideal state of being. On the other hand, he would have hated to look upon himself as a gregarious mediocrity, almost a herd animal or a primitive being, who can live and subsist only as a member of his tribe.

As his writing progressed, Knox thought of making the first preliminary contacts with some potential publishers. He was prompted, on that course of action, by his desire to find out what lay in store for him, concerning the future of his book. He disliked immensely any condition of doubt, indecision and ignorance. He wanted to face and solve that crucial problem by a direct frontal attack. At least he would learn what he could expect in this regard. For that purpose he wrote a two page summary, describing the central idea and purpose of his book. He also included a brief sketch about the 'story' of the 'plot' as

284

a unifying background for the succession of the dialogues. Then he composed a brief, formal letter, to accompany the description of the manuscript. He avoided any attempt to indulge in propaganda and self-appraisal. He knew that the book should be accepted, if at all, only on account of its central idea. If that failed to convince the editors, no amount of 'advertising' would do any good. Next, he searched through his drawers for a copy of the list of the publishers, selecting those whom he considered to be more interested in the type of his manuscript. He would send one or two letters every day, thinking that he should have an almost clear picture through their replies by the time the manuscript would be completed. He tried to brace himself beforehand to file away the rejection slips with stoic resignation. . . .

He was positively nonplused and shocked by the unexpected invitation of one of the publishers to visit the editor-in-chief, a certain Evelyn Ross, in order to present the already finished part of his book. Without wasting any time for the all-important interview, Knox made an appointment for the following day in the morning. He was full of torturing anxiety, mixed with hope.

His surprise was even greater when he was showed in by a secretary into the office of the editor-in-chief. He had expected to meet a man, for Evelyn was sometimes a man's name. He had anticipated him to be middle aged, very impressive and austere looking, through the importance of his position. Instead, the person occupying the place accross the desk from him was a young woman. For a moment he thought that there had been a mistake, that he had been brought to the wrong office. But no! There was no mistake! This was actually the editor-in-chief!

As he tried to assess the impact of his personal encounter during the days that followed the interview, he had to admit that his positive reaction to her wasn't due to her physical appearance only. As a matter or fact, Evelyn was in no way the type of an infernal 'femme fatale.' Although she looked attractive in her well-tailored suit, it was rather the total effect of her personality, which found its best expression in her intelligent face, especially her dark and vivacious eyes, holding no trace of nervous tension. The whole interview lasted no longer than fifteen minutes. After the preliminary questions concerning his personal background, Evelyn requested his consent to leave the finished part of the manuscript with her, promising that he would hear from her again in less than three weeks, the time needed for its appraisal. Knox had wanted to go into some discussion about his work, but there was no invitation on her part to do so. She called her secretary to show him out of her office and to allow the next person to take his place.

It was Noesis who announced himself first, after only two weeks. He invited Knox to come to his apartment in the afternoon. He was pleasantly surprised when Gynea opened the door for him, greeting him with the familiarity of an old friend. She informed him that Noesis was to join them as soon as he had finished some unspecified business. Knox was unable to conceal altogether his helpless embarrassment due to this unexpected circumstance. He didn't know what to say or do until Noesis would arrive. There was no sense in starting the dialogue without him.

Gynea must have guessed his confusion and came to his rescue. She started talking about her travels to the different parts of the globe. She described colorfully the strange reactions of people when sighting their space craft in the skies. Knowing of the amount of fear present in all the persons when faced with that unknown phenomenon, she told Knox that they always chose uninhabited areas for landing. To Knox's question as to how they managed to find transportation to the cities, Gynea told him about the arrangements they make in advance with their fellow space men who happen to be nearby at that time, and who drive to the spot with an earthly automobile to transport them further. Knox also learned that they have at least a few people of their kind in almost every great city throughout the entire planet. They're helpful as guides and interpreters. He noticed, however, that she never once mentioned the names of the places she had been to. He expected her to ask about Marisa, but apparently Noesis had informed her about his new situation. During the whole conversation, it was Gynea who did most of the talking. She inquired about the progress of his work, and he was glad to report to her the news about one publisher willing to evaluate it. But he didn't mention Evelyn.

Noesis' arrival was welcome especially by Knox, who had a sense of being relieved from the inexplicable tensions he had felt during the time he had been alone with Gynea. He knew that his performance had been rather awkward. Since it was dinner time, they decided to get that out of their way before starting their conversation. For dessert, they had some kind of tropical fruit unknown to Knox, which Gynea must have brought with her. Noesis listened with interest to Knox's report on his work and his hopes with regard to the publisher's initial interest in his book.

After dinner, Noesis took a magazine out of his briefcase, opened it at the section on crimes, and handed it over to Knox, inviting him to read it. It was a report on a couple who had killed their seven children. They had been arrested on charges of criminal neglect and first degree murder on seven counts. There was in that same section another article, much shorter, on a teenage boy who had shot his father, because the latter had dared to express his dissatisfaction with his son's report card. And yet another, which dealt with the case of a man who shot his wife, their three children, committing suicide afterwards. Knox did not seem to be unduly shaken by these gruesome acts. There was nothing new or unusual about them to him. It only reinforced his contempt and disgust with human beings, whom people like to identify as the highest species of the living, created after the likeness and image of God. . . . He felt also ashamed of belonging to the same glorious kind of anthropoids. He handed the magazine back to Noesis, and observed drily:

"I know the reason why you wanted me to read these articles. You consider them as a proof and an evidence that justifies your devastating criticism of our way of life. And, unfortunately, I can do nothing else, but accept the facts as they stand."

"I had another purpose too," Noesis remarked. "It serves as a good introduction to our discussion of today on the topics of ethics and religion. It dramatically illustrates the basic issue of good and evil."

287

"That question has not been settled yet," Knox affirmed pensively. "Any student of cultural history and anthropology is bound to end up as a skeptic, an agnostic, a relativist and a subjectivist. . . . Certain patterns of behavior are regarded as evil in one place, and only a few hundred miles away you'll find them praised as virtues. Because of this circumstance I have to admit that I myself do not find my way clearly through this confusion."

"Could it be," interrupted Gynea, "that the questions about good and evil, right and wrong, virtue and vice, were placed and viewed in the wrong perspective?"

"That might be the case," Knox admitted rather passively. Apparently he did not have much hope as to the outcome of their discussion.

"Well, then, let me elaborate on my suggestion," Gynea continued. "I'm going to use the fitting distinction made by Nietzsche between slave morality and noble or master morality."

"That distinction could be well taken," Knox observed, "but I'm afraid that my readers will not like it. Perhaps you don't know of the many accusations hurled at him by the extremists of the right and of the left alike. The popular image of this lonely thinker is that of a godless monster, a proto-Nazi, an advocate of the will to power over men, a ruthless paranoic, deluded by his vision of the superman, fashioned after the image of the nordic blond beast."

"But this caricature of Nietzsche doesn't hold with those who have taken the time and trouble to learn from his writing what he actually thought and advocated," Noesis stated with conviction. "To my mind, Nietzsche was the first one to assail the fallacies of a morality based on supernatural authority, because of its harmful consequences for man's life on earth. He was just as vehement in denouncing the secularized version of the moral world order," Noesis continued. "I mean, the ethics of altruism, sympathy, and pity."

"If we want to start from the very beginning," Gynea remarked, "we should mention the first premise underlying the many versions of slave morality, namely the doctrine about man's original sin."

"You mean the mythical legend about Adam, Eve, the serpent and the apple, in the idyllic surroundings of the garden of Eden?" Knox interposed sarcastically.

"I'm much more concerned with the implications of that story and what it accomplishes in every human being who believes in it," Gynea continued. "It means nothing less than the invitation to consider man as a 'fallen' creature, a corrupt and degenerate being, whose 'intellect darkened' and whose 'will was bent toward evil.' I think you realize what destructive effects this doctrine has on man's whole attitude toward himself. He is forced to look upon himself as a moral criminal as long as he lives, as a despicable and hateful misfit, worthy of contempt and punishment. It destroys man's most precious psychological and moral qualification, such as his natural love for himself, his will to live, to create, to be proud of his achievements and values, his self-esteem, self-respect and dignity. As a born evildoer, he will live in fear and guilt, taking his suffering as his natural state of being. He will learn to look upon life and the world as an unwanted burden, as a place of exile, a penal colony, a 'vale of tears,' and a place of horrible crimes. Then there are also the cynical ones, who will take advantage of this situation, committing the most evil and lecherous crimes as long as they can get away with them, shrugging their shoulders in disdain, saying 'we are born criminals, anyway.' " . . .

"But the picture you've just drawn," Knox commented in a little more lively manner, "fits the profile of a mentally and emotionally imbalanced person, a perfect neurotic and maybe even worse."

"That is absolutely true," Gynea agreed.

"Whoever invented that story," Knox went on, "must have been sick too, the first pessimist and nihilist to boot."

"Much worse, Edward," Noesis suggested. "He was the first sadist, motivated by an unlimited lust to perpetuate suffering, to make life identical with evil itself, to reduce people to the level of emasculated puppets, ready to be enslaved, to suffer, to submit, to take all sorts of misfortunes as their natural condition. And that was the birth of the morality designed for slaves."

"It's just another instance, in fact the first one," Gynea observed, "of the will to power, the lust for power over man, a passion possible only to a deluded mind that finds pleasure in expressing his basic hatred for all of life and the living."

"But the most remarkable thing about all this is that it's been accepted and obeyed, and for God knows how long!" Knox exclaimed with excitement. "I wonder why?"

"The success of this sadist can be explained, at least in part, if you recall that he had some very powerful things on his side to build his case upon."

"What are you thinking of?" Knox asked.

"I mean the undeniable presence of suffering in man's life," Noesis explained. "Then, if you consider also the circumstances and the time when this doctrine was invented, man was helpless and could not find an alternate explanation for his miseries. Living on a very primitive level, without the aid of science and philosophy to rescue him from his pre-logical or pre-conceptual, rather superstitious and mythical mode of thinking, he was a powerless prey for the first man deluded by his paranoic lust for power."

"Your explanation accounts only for the initial success of this strategy," Knox remarked critically. "It does not tell me, however, how this doctrine survived three thousand years or more, and why it's still accepted today?"

"You did not take into account many other factors," Noesis continued. "First, you should have remembered that the doctrine was presented as a 'revelation,' that is, as a superior, higher, and indisputable truth, coming directly from the mouth of God. Second, you must bear in mind that even today and much more so in the past, religion still has a strong hold over most of the population. And, unfortunately, it's bound to survive as long as man behaves as a religious animal. On the other hand, you know of course that this 'dogma' of the original sin has been challenged recently by some progressive theologians too. . . . So there's reason to hope for its death."

"Let's hope so!" Knox agreed. "But I'd like to see you applying this first premise to the issue of morality."

"It's very simple!" Gynea took over. "You have all the necessary ingredients in that doctrine to work out an authoritarian system of ethics designed for slaves. There's the concept of sin, guilt, suffering, punishment and even the psychological dispositions required to make it work. Its domineering and paternalistic character is contained in the brief formula of 'thou shalt not,' by which they introduced the restrictions, prohibitions, proscriptions, taboos, all the negative imperatives, designed so as to accomplish one thing only—the creation of all kinds of inhibitions in man, thus forcing him to give up his natural desire for pleasure, happiness and life. Of course, you have to add to it also the doctrine on immortality, which means another powerful weapon to enforce and reinforce man's will to submit and obey. There's heaven for the few, for the 'good and the just,' the chosen minority, and hell, eternal punishment—described in the most gruesome words and imagery—for all those who dare to rebel, to disobey, to think, to say Yes to life and to live it."

"Moreover, you have to remember that the so-called commandments were formulated in such a way as to condemn man's strongest desires and needs," Noesis interposed. "The will to freedom, the quest for independence, the natural desire for pleasure—sex could serve as the best example, and man's natural curiosity, his pursuit of more knowledge. All these basic tendencies were branded as evil, imposed by the devil himself, who, incidentally is another useful invention of the sadists. He is, in one person, God's secret agent who performs a useful service for him. He acts both as an *agent provocateur*, a tempter, a spy, and an executioner, providing an eternal thriller or horror show for the delight of the 'redeemed.' "

"If the facts of past and present cultural history didn't stand in one's way," Knox commented with disgust, "I would say that it's almost unbelievable that such morbid ideas could have determined the course of human history. But there's no way to deny it, and much less reason to embellish or justify it. It's a crime committed against mankind, in the name of morality itself. That shows also its perversity. Are we ever going to free ourselves from this revolting nonsense?"

"Remember, Edward," Noesis answered, "that we already agreed that science and philosophy—which stand for the forbidden fruit of knowledge—is man's only hope for success. The more man thinks and knows, the less inclined he becomes to accept the idiosyncrasies of faith."

"On the other hand, I have one difficulty," Knox continued. "You also mentioned that, in the process of evolution, every stage is a necessary one."

"Yes, I recall having said that," Noesis agreed. "But what's your point? Are you trying to build up a justification for the ethics of obedience and conformity?"

"Not as far as the doctrine goes," Knox reflected. "But you have to agree with me that—considering man's primitive condition at the beginning of his civilization—that was the only form of morality that could accomplish the necessary goal of keeping the unruly herd animals from running amuck."

"I agree with you, as long as you mean only the primitive past," Noesis answered. "But I can't find any justification for its survival in the modern age of science and philosophy."

"That's true," Knox consented. "One ought to expect that any educated man, who has developed a scientific, analytic and critical frame of mind, would submit his moral and religious beliefs to the same scrutiny."

"But he doesn't," Noesis retorted. "In fact, he appears to us as a strange paradox. In the field of science, he behaves according to the strict code of scientific method and carefully obeys the laws of his reason and reality. The next moment, or perhaps on the weekends only, the same man seems to have forgotten the dictates of his intellectual honesty and integrity, because you find him as a sorrowful penitent. . . ."

"Wouldn't you say that there's a great deal of hypocrisy in that dignified spectacle?" Knox asked.

"Which only makes it worse and even more shameful," Noesis concluded.

"All right! I agree with you that there's no excuse for the educated people," Knox commented. "But you can't expect those who belong to the rabble, the populace, the mob—the large majority of the population—to sit down and philosophize on the merits and demerits of their moral and religious beliefs. . . ."

"I don't expect them to do any such thing," Noesis remarked. "Therefore, I'd say that, for the time being, the ethics of conformity is a necessary evil. But I hope that this isn't going to last forever. In fact, I know that it can't. It all depends on how soon and how fast ignorance is overcome. Until that day, the maintenance of the social order requires the virtues of obedience and submission."

"You haven't said anything so far on the ethics of altruism," Knox observed.

"I believe we already said enough on self-love and its opposite, self-sacrifice, so I don't feel that we should waste time on that."

"Then let's move on to the ethics of the superior man," Knox proposed.

"You used the term 'superior men,'" Noesis said. "I wonder what you mean by that idea? What mental associations take place in your mind when you think of it?"

"By 'superior men' I mean the rational and free persons," Knox answered. "Similarly, I take the irrational and all sorts of bondage as the marks of inferiority."

"What do you mean by the quality of rationality?" Noesis went on.

"Reason is man's highest perfection, through which he is set apart and above the animals, who're bound to and guided by their instincts only."

"What does reason accomplish for man?"

"Reason is the source of man's intellectual knowledge," replied Knox. "It interprets, integrates and identifies the materials collected by his sense organs. Through reason, man surpasses the mere perceptual or sensorial level of consciousness—and thus he becomes aware of himself, he lives as a self-conscious subject, a person."

"Go on," insisted Noesis. "You haven't said all there is to say."

"Well, let me see . . ." Knox reflected. "I guess I have to elaborate in more detail on the process of intellectual knowledge, that is, on man's power to form concepts or ideas, integrate them

293

through the acts of judgments, formulate the first principles of reason and reality, and reason his way toward particular conclusions. In a word, to think."

"What are these first principles you alluded to?" Noesis asked again.

"The principle of identity, of non-contradiction, and that of sufficient reason or causality," Knox answered. Then he added: "But why do you ask me all these questions? What's their significance in relation to ethics?"

"But can't you see it?" Noesis asked with surprise. "Remember that we've rejected the supernatural origin and foundation of morality! Consequently, we have to provide a natural basis for the new ethics. Can't you see my point?"

"I'm not quite sure . . ." Knox hesitated. "Probably you want to say that the conditions of morality are reason, reality and free choice. But that's the whole of man's life!"

"That's correct," agreed Noesis. "And that's the way it should be, unless you want to reestablish a 'moral world order,' apart from life and in opposition to it."

"No, I don't want to do that," Knox remarked. "But then I have to conclude that man's life and morality are strictly coextensive, they overlap. Man's a moral being by virtue of his rational and free nature."

"Very well taken," Noesis observed. "However, this also means that there's nothing non-moral about man. He's either morally good or morally bad. Sometimes even evil."

"If what you said is true, then I must conclude that the rational is the good, while the irrational is the evil," Knox declared.

"You couldn't have stated it better or more precisely," Noesis said. "But, tell me, exactly what do you mean by the rational and irrational?"

"The rational makes sense, there's meaning to it," Knox answered as if undergoing an oral examination. "And the irrational is senseless, it's stupid, absurd, contradictory, it makes no sense, it's meaningless."

"You said contradictory, right?"

"Right. That's what I said."

"Contradictory to what?" Noesis persisted.

"To the facts of reality, of course," Knox stated.

"And what do you mean by reality?"

"You don't give up, do you?" Knox remarked with a smile. "I believe you must be driving at some important conclusion. Well, since there's no way to define reality, I'd describe it as that which is or can be—physical reality, the world, the universe, its elements, the phenomena or events that take place in it, people, and so forth. . . ."

"Your description is almost complete," Noesis agreed. "However, I want to emphasize one part of it, the one you called 'people.' That term is vague, it's an abstraction only. I'd prefer to speak of the concrete, singular and unique individuals as the only carriers of life. Then I invite you to connect reason and reality. . . . What do you get?"

"I already mentioned that it's the function of reason to interpret, integrate and identify the nature of whatever falls within the scope of its knowledge."

"On what assumption?" Noesis insisted.

"On the assumption that 'a thing is what it is, and not something else.'" Knox quoted Aristotle. Then he said: "To be, to exist, to be real and actual, means to be something specific, I mean, whatever is, is because it possesses a definite nature, essence or substance, that is, a permanent set of properties, characteristics and attributes that make up its identity."

"That's fine," Noesis commented. "Now answer this question—what would you call the result or the success of reason in identifying the objects of reality?"

"That's simple. It's called truth, understood as the statement or the expression of that which is or exists, independently of the knower."

"Did you attend a course in philosophy in college?" Noesis inquired with satisfaction.

"Yes, I did, and it was an introduction to Aristotle's theory of knowledge."

"I'd have given you an A," Noesis said in sincere appreciation. "But I have a few more questions. . . ."

"You're really giving Edward a hard time!" observed Gynea teasingly.

"I don't mind it," Knox replied, "as long as I can defend my own. . . ."

"Well, then, now connect the ideas of reason, reality and truth with that of the good."

"I did that already, when I said that the good is the rational," Knox said. "I'll now add that the good is the true, and evil is the false. Does that satisfy you?"

"Sure," Noesis consented. "But there's one more connection to be established. Would you associate the idea of virtue and vice with truth and falsity, respectively?"

"No doubt about that! It's only logical, I mean, expressing the facts of reality."

"Before we say anything else on virtue, I'd like to discuss man's nature and identity," suggested Noesis.

"That's not to be done so easily!" Knox frowned, "I became rather confused with Sartre's statement that—regarding man—existence comes before essence. If I understand him correctly, he wanted to say that the human person comes into existence without being anything more than an openness, a possibility, a potentiality. Then, each man, in the course of his life, gives himself some form through an endless change in acting out certain roles, by playing some part on the stage of life, thus trying to give himself some kind of identity or essence. He also remarked that most people just live in any random way, leading an inauthentic existence in almost total alienation from themselves and their fellow human beings. Then he concludes, of course, that most of life makes no sense, it's meaningless and absurd, it progresses toward the absolute nothing, death, which puts an end to this farce and comedy. He seems to make a great deal of freedom, speaks of anguish, despair and dread, but doesn't seem to lead anywhere. The whole thing ends up in the well known celebration of nihilistic moods, nausea being the predominant tone. And I haven't found out what the authentic mode of existence could be, if one starts with the premise that nothing makes any sense at all."

296

"You seem to have digested it all right," Noesis observed. "As to my own reaction to all that, I'd subscribe only to the first half of what he said."

"What do you mean?" Knox raised his voice in surprise.

"I mean that I agree with Sartre's ideas—in fact only a modern version of Aristotle's idea—that man comes into existence as a potentiality only, possessing no more identity than the sum of his innate dispositions and tendencies. His mind is just a *tabula rasa*, a blank tablet. Man has the ability to think, but the contents of his mind—his ideas, principles and values—must be acquired through the free exercise of his intellect. In this sense, I also agree that there's no a priori, ready made identity or essence, no definite or final meaning or purpose given to any man with his birth certificate. And since only very few people really think, and even those who do so may make mistakes along the way, I have to agree that the mode of existence, the existential situation or condition of most men is inauthentic, insignificant, of no consequence, even absurdly irrational, at times comical, then tragical, perhaps both. . . . As to the second half of your statement, concerning the tragic finale of life crowned by death, I disagree with Sartre. If he had been consistent with his views, he would've acted upon it by killing himself. . . . But he didn't. Apparently, he derives some masochistic pleasure in contemplating the ugly debacle of existence. Or else, there could be a good dose of hypocritical posturing to it."

"You may be correct in your way of looking at it," conceded Knox. "But I'd rather listen to what you have to propose as a remedy."

"Granted that there is no immediate or ultimate meaning given with the fact of existence, it still doesn't follow that man cannot give a meaning, a purpose, an identity or essence to himself."

"How is he going to do that?" Knox asked skeptically.

"Simply by living according to what his reason tells him about his own potentialities or abilities, and the facts of reality. And with this, we're back again in the field of ethics."

"It's your turn now to elaborate on your ideas," Knox remarked with expectation.

"And I'll be glad to do it. Think back a few minutes and focus your mind on the ideas we've analyzed so far: reason, reality, truth and virtue. Do those things tell you something in terms of the purpose, value and meaning of life?"

"I'd rather hear you say it," Knox replied.

"Fine. All I want to say is that there's another kind of ethics, the morality of the higher men, and we called it the noble morality, in contradistinction to the morality of obedience and penance."

"How does it work?"

"I shall elaborate on two ideas mainly, freedom and virtue. Freedom can be defined as man's power of self-determination in the light of the knowledge available to him through the exercise of his reason. Concentrate on the concept of self-determination. You'll see that it means man's ability to determine by himself and for himself the contents, the direction, the purpose and the meaning of his own existence. Thus he develops into a self-made, self-created being. His own choice, the intelligent use of his own freedom, is the only justification and sanction for his whole being and existence. As we said before, he belongs to himself only. His life is his, and only his. He exists for his own sake. He's free to accept his existence or to reject it by the act of suicide. If he accepts it, it's up to him alone to do what he will with it. He's free to misuse his freedom, to corrupt his mind, to exploit himself, thus becoming his worst enemy and executioner. But, similarly, he's free to discover his own potentialities, abilites and needs, and to actualize and develop them to their highest limit. And that's a work of a whole lifetime. It follows, therefore, that freedom implies the moral concept of responsibility. Man and only man is responsible for his own life, within the limitations of his own being. Thus, ethics becomes identical with the whole process of life. But it's a self-chosen and self-imposed code of values."

"What do you mean by values?" Knox questioned.

"First let me explain the concept of virtue," Noesis replied. "Then it'll be easier to identify the meaning of value. You may recall that the Greeks had a very concrete and precise conception of virtue. They associated it with ability, skill, power, and perfection. Each craftsman was supposed to possess a virtue, that is, the ability to perform his skills in the best way possible for him. And the man of no virtue was equated with the man of no ability and power. Then they thought of the perfection which is proper to man, independently of his skills, and they concluded that man's highest virtue—ability and perfection—resided in the power of his reason, his mind and thought. The quest for knowledge and the contemplation of truth was regarded as man's noblest activity, the purpose and the meaning of his life. And now apply this to the question of values."

"It follows from what you said that, by value one should mean almost the same thing as ability, power and virtue. . . ."

"Or, in one more comprehensive term, goodness," Noesis added. "Because the Greeks always spoke of the 'good life,' whenever they discussed those questions."

"But, as you know, there are individual differences. Abilities vary, and, besides, there are those who refuse to think, to know and to act in the light of their knowledge," Knox observed.

"That shouldn't disturb you in the least," Noesis said, "because I'd look upon it—no matter how large their number—as man's failure to live according to his own nature, his refusal to live according to reason and reality, giving preference to the misuse of his own powers and freedom."

"You said that no outside justification or sanction is needed for the ethics of the noble men . . ." Knox remarked inquisitively.

"I said that for a very simple reason. There's the principle of causality, which—when applied to ethics—means that the nature of the action determines the nature of its results and consequences. And it works as an immanent principle of justice, built into the very nature of the acts themselves. Thus man shall learn that it is for his own benefit and interest to live according to reason, reality, truth, virtue and goodness, because those actions, through their own nature, will reward man with pleasure and happiness. Similarly, man will soon find out that vice, the irrational, the false or the evil, will demand of him a just payment in the form of his own confusion, misery and suffering. You can

299

see, therefore, that there's no need at all for any outside sanctions or justification. Heaven and hell were invented as useful devices for conditioning man to act out of fear. . . . But an action performed under the pressure of fear is not a free act, and to that extent it's not morally good either."

"If I'm to put all these things together and apply them to our own condition," Knox said, "I'll have to conclude that the moral being as you understand him is practically non-existent."

"You conclusion is true, even if it hurts," Noesis stated. "You ought to remember, though, that Aristotle made a distinction between man as he actually is and man as he ought to be, because he could be. He spoke of the ordinary, vulgar and ignorant man in opposition to the noble and proud men of wisdom and virtue."

"So far, you said practically nothing on the social aspects of ethics," Knox observed.

"There is not much to say on that account," Noesis answered matter of factly. "What is society, mankind, humanity, the people and the public you seem to make so much out of? What's mankind apart from the individual persons? Can't you see that those concepts stand only for abstractions? I'm not willing to accept any of the socialistic or collectivistic doctrines that invest society with a being, a reality, an existence of its own, apart and above the individual, in order to justify their demand for the individual's subordination and enslavement to the collective. Actually, the individuals become enslaved by the gang of ruthless individuals who have seized power and control the machinery of politics. Of course, they can't accept this truth. They have to dress up their immoral and sometimes even brutal actions by some collectivist creed—altruism, for instance—telling man that he is his brothers' keeper, that he belongs to everybody but to himself and the meaning of his life should consist in sacrificing it for the benefit of others."

"Nevertheless, man has certain social obligations," Knox insisted.

"Which are or should be no different from the obligations man owes to himself, namely, to live according to reason, reality and

300

truth. Can you imagine what marvelous changes could occur, even in your own society, if every single individual assumed the responsibility for his own life? If he lived according to reason and reality, if he respected the law of identity, non-contradiction and sufficient reason? For one thing, there would be no need for welfare organizations and all the social workers would be out of business. I've observed that only those persons oppose individualism who are wont to accept the responsibility that goes with an independent life. Edward, it's much easier to live as a parasite and to rationalize the immorality of it in the name of his needs, the love we owe to everybody and all sorts of social responsibilities."

"Would you say that it is due to these false ideas that there is so much crime and immorality in our world?" Knox asked.

"That's partially true," Noesis said. "I would add, for instance, that many of the crimes or sins committed by your fellow men are due mainly to the following causes: the prevalent moral and religious beliefs, which forbid life, pleasure and happiness to man; then you have the amount of ignorance as another source of ill-doings; finally, there is the economic factor, I mean your specific system of production, distribution and consumption, that creates inequality, injustice, thus breeding the feelings of frustration along with the desire for revenge, to get even."

"I'd like if you gave me some examples," Knox asked.

"Let me do it," Gynea stepped in after a long silence. "I would approach this problem somewhat differently. Let's start from the principle of need satisfaction. I submit that no person would assume all the risks involved in doing any wrong thing, if all his needs—physical, psychic, social and cultural—were satisfied. To give you a few examples, why do people steal? Is it because they have all they need, or perhaps the opposite is true? Can you imagine somebody stealing a piece of bread after a delicious dinner, knowing also that he can eat as much as he wants to, whenever he feels like doing it? Why is there aggression, brutality and violence? Simply because some of man's psychic and social needs have been frustrated, such as his need for freedom, respect, justice, importance, status, and so forth. Then take the sex-crimes,

301

rape, for instance. It's only the sexually hungry and frustrated individual who cannot find the normal and peaceful means to satisfy his needs who is driven to such action. . . . Why do people lie, cheat and betray? Think of need frustration and need satisfaction again, and you'll have the answer. Why is there prostitution? Because your moral, religious and social codes, due to their antinatural attitude toward sex, forbid the normal satisfaction of that need, forcing the individual to put up with a whore. Finally, I'd invite you to go over your so-called commandments, one by one, and ask always this question: what new restriction and frustration does it create? Forbid a man to sit down, declare it to be a sin, and very soon you'll find a few who will insist on sitting down, if for no other reason than the desire to assert their freedom. Now, if you think of my last example as silly, I'll remind you of the meat or no meat on Fridays and a host of other equally nonsensical prohibitions. . . ."

"Then I have to assume that there is no crime committed in your world, since everybody has everything and all provisions were taken to satisfy all of the person's needs. . . ." Knox observed.

"That's the only correct assumption you can have, since it expresses the reality of facts," Gynea agreed.

"On the other hand, this also means that crime shall be with us as long as our moral, religious, social, political and economic institutions?" Knox questioned.

"Certainly! And I want to emphasize that, speaking of need satisfaction, you have to include all of man's needs. I say this because there have ben some who believed that once the material needs of man had been satisfied, by raising everybody's standard of living to an optimum, man would become morally perfect. But such is not the case. . . . You have the steady increase in the white-collar crimes because of the psycho-social frustrations of the individuals concerned."

"You seem to make little of the crimes committed by the mentally disturbed," Knox remarked critically.

"That's not so," Gynea answered. "I was going to mention it with the remark that even in this specific instance—representing the minority of all cases concerned—one should ask the question, to what extent your present institutions are responsible for abnormal behavior? I have the impression that many of your present moral and religious beliefs breed neurosis and other, more serious forms of mental alienation. On the other hand, I don't want to say that there are no organic causes also responsible for the disorders of this type."

"Am I again correct in assuming that mental disease is unknown to you?" Knox inquired.

"It's only the logical conclusion following from our premises," Gynea replied.

"I'd like to go back to the question of virtues," Knox suggested, turning toward Noesis. "So far we've only talked about it in principle, but we haven't considered any virtue in particular."

"I'm glad you said that," Noesis assented. "However, I'd much prefer to use the term 'personal qualities' instead of virtues, because the latter has an abstract connotation. For instance, you'll find in many books an impressive list of virtues, such as justice, fortitude, prudence, temperance, courage, etc., and they are treated as if they were some self-subsisting ideal essences, apart from the living individuals, similar to Plato's essences or ideas."

"That's true," Knox agreed. "Then people start a collection of virtues, arranging them in a neat hierarchy and the whole thing is reduced to the level of a hobby like collecting antiques."

"Well, then," Noesis went on, "speaking of the moral qualities of a person, I'll mention only the most essential ones, I mean, those which are absolutely necessary for living a healthy and meaningful existence. In the first place, there is self-love, which should not be confused with ordinary selfishness of the inferior man. But self-love is possible only to the person who knows of himself as the possessor of values he appropriated by his own efforts and abilities. And I don't mean only the visible achievements or success. There are certain qualities of the person, such as the development of his mind, of his freedom from things and people, his detachment from the trivial concerns of the ordinary man. It's the awareness of this personal power, achieved through the arduous task of self-overcoming."

"Isn't there a danger in going too far in this respect," Knox interposed, "reaching the stoic ideal of indifference?"

"I know what you mean," Noesis answered. "Certainly, I'm against such exaggeration, because it involves the danger of uprooting man's passionate self, the fount of his vitality and creative energy. On the other hand, though, I prefer a certain amount of tranquility, serenity, imperturbability or peace of mind, to the state of chronic worry and anxiety. There is no dignity in it. Therefore, I'd suggest the combination of a passionate involvement and detachment at the same time. And I don't see any contradiction in it. It means only that the person's freedom is always maintained. There is no danger of losing oneself in whatever one is doing."

"What other qualities do you want to mention?" Knox urged him on.

"There are certain qualities that are the immediate consequence of self-love, such as self-esteem, self-respect, self-confidence and self-sufficiency."

"I have certain doubts about self-sufficiency," Knox admitted. "I don't think that anybody can reach the height and the perfection of absolute independence. After all," Knox went on, "I interpret life as a continued process of need satisfaction. Man is a dependent and needy being, physically, psychologically, socially and culturally."

"Perhaps you misunderstand the meaning of self-sufficiency," Noesis observed. "I meant no more than the ability of the person to provide for himself and by himself, using his own resources and abilities, without becoming a dependent on others for his needs."

"However, this new interpretation doesn't rule out the fact that even in your society there is some degree of mutual dependence and cooperation," Knox insisted.

"No doubt there is," Noesis agreed, "but I call it the free exchange of ideas and values. The principle of truth and justice requires that you do not accept anything without returning an equal value for it. Similarly, you can't claim anything without offering an equal value in exchange."

"Is this your definition of justice?" Knox asked.

"Take it rather as a description only," Noesis remarked. "If you want to work out a definition for yourself, you'll have to include a reference to reason, reality, truth, and ability."

"I assume that in your world there are no such things as commandments," Knox ventured. "You must know, of course, that we are blessed with quite a collection of them."

"And most of you live in direct opposition to them" Noesis stated critically. "Perhaps you could say that men's actions match the picture of the Ten Commandments perfectly, but taken in reverse. However, to come back to your idea, I would say that there is only one commandment, and we called it—as you remember—the commandment of truth, I mean, man's respect for reality, reason, the principles of identity, non-contradiction and causality."

"Do you realize, Noesis," Knox said, "that we omitted an important topic in our previous discussions? If I'm not mistaken, it was the relationship between education and the formation of the moral character."

"You're correct," Noesis agreed. "And you can take our observations on virtue as part of that question. However, there are a few more things to add, such as the relationship between values, the integration of the person's varied tendencies into a whole and their significance for the meaning of his life."

"Since I don't feel prepared to tackle these complex problems, I expect you to do most of the talking, unless Gynea wants to take a turn," Knox stated unceremoniously. Gynea accepted the invitation and said:

"First we have to clarify the question of values. And the only way to say something worthwhile on it, is to consider values always in relation to man's life. In this sense, I would say that by values I mean all those objective perfections or qualities that are fit to satisfy man's needs as a man."

"However, this means that you're subordinating all values to man, thus making all of them relative and useful only," Knox objected.

"Did you expect me to discourse on absolute, eternal and

ideal things or essences that transcend man's existence in every respect and belong to the heaven of Plato? Suppose that there were such ideal and metaphysical entities. How would that affect man? And what's the use of them anyway?"

"I know what you mean," Knox replied. "It would only create a frustrating and irreparable chasm between the ideal and the real. Instead of promoting man's quest or desire for more perfections, it would only serve as a reminder of his tragic limitations and imperfections. He would think of values as something beyond his reach and, sooner or later, he would resign himself to his imperfect condition, thus creating an obstacle for the progress of evolution. On the other hand, you see, to put all values on the same level, considering them as mere utilities or means only, doesn't seem to do justice to the obvious differences among them."

"Could you clarify the meaning of your last remark?" Gynea said attentively.

"Suppose I enumerate first, the main value categories or the large dimensions of man's value experiences," Knox elaborated. "As you know, there are the religious, moral, philosophic, scientific, artistic, social, political and economic values. Now, do you consider them all on the same level, regarding them as mere utilities or commodities?"

"Do you realize that there are two different things fused together in your loaded question?" Gynea said. "So let's take them apart. First, as to the charge of considering all values as use-values only. I'm not going to take it back and retreat into qualifying excuses. Of course, you may label me as a pragmatist. But I don't see how you could associate value or worth with total uselessness, in order to satisfy your position. If something is of no use whatsoever for man, then it's of no value for him."

"I'm sorry, but apparently you misunderstood me," Knox observed. "Therefore, I'm going to give a few examples. I'm sure you're not going to consider religion, ethics, philosophy, science and art as mere utilitarian concerns like food, clothing and shelter. At least we, on this planet, like to say, with Aristotle, that knowledge is wanted for the sake of knowledge only.

Similarly, that art is cultivated for the sake of art itself—*l'art pour l'art*. . . . The same considerations are due also to the moral and religious values."

"Sorry to disappoint you and to go against Aristotle's revered authority, but I can't agree with you, Edward. Are you ready to conclude that art is useless, that knowledge is impractical, that philosophy is no more than disinterested contemplation? And as to religion, I prefer to say nothing."

"But I remember quite well," Knox persisted, "that Noesis called us, from the very beginning on, mechanized and motorized barbarians. Then, to justify his remarks, he went on to make an all-important distinction between civilization and culture, drawing a very clear line of demarcation between certain value categories, implying also the polarities, antinomies or conflicts existing among them. . . ."

"I guess I'll have to defend my position," Noesis broke in readily. "In fact, I did say all the things you mentioned. However, I didn't say, neither did I imply, that I consider the values of culture as useless, on the contrary. . . ."

"Then you side with Gynea?" Knox asked with genuine surprise.

"If I do so, it's only because I consider her words as the expression of truth," Noesis said firmly. "And let me give you my reasons. Perhaps you should take the term 'useful' analogously, and not univocally. With this distinction in mind, I'd say that both the economic and the artistic values are useful, but in different ways. The economic values are useful insofar as they satisfy man's organic needs. . . . The artistic values are useful to the extent that they satisfy man's need for beauty and symbolism, and so forth."

"Then, again, you are putting all values on the same level." Knox said in confusion.

"Quite frankly, I don't follow your mode of thinking," Noesis observed. "I kept on insisting on the different nature and quality of the needs satisfied by different values, and you're still insisting on the term 'same level.' "

"Then I have to conclude that you consider the cultural values as above, higher and superior to those of civilization," Knox inquired.

"If I said yes, you would immediately accuse me of reintroducing a dualism or dichotomy in man's nature just as Plato did with all the negative consequences to it. Therefore, I invite you to remember our conversation on man's psychosomatic unity, wholeness and integrity. On certain occasions I said that *Bios* and *Logos* are only two inseparable aspects of the same reality, man."

"However, you also stated that *Bios* comes before *Logos*." Knox persisted. "Then, on other occasions, you reverted your position, saying that *Logos* comes before *Bios*."

"Indeed, I did say all those things," Noesis continued calmly. "But I don't see any contradiction in it. So, let me explain myself. Try to look upon man from this point of view—regard him as a unity, a totality, a wholeness, made out of the well integrated complexity and variety of his many natural dispositions, tendencies and needs. Try to understand the full meaning of these expressions: unity in variety, and integrity in complexity. Thus the differences among values should be regarded qualitatively and not gradatively as higher and lower. They are of different quality, because fulfilling different needs in man's complex nature."

"Nevertheless, I believe that you'd put more emphasis on the cultural value than on those belonging to civilization only."

"If I agree with you, I'll have to qualify it again," Noesis answered. "I'd never consent to separate that which should be kept together by its very nature. In other words, I'm neither for civilization apart from culture, nor for culture divorced from civilization. In fact, my whole criticism of your present condition was aimed at this point only. I said that you're civilized barbarians, insisting all the time that your next stage in the evolutionary process should be geared to the creation of cultural values in order to reach the balanced integrity of your lives, individually and collectively considered. For man as man, is neither a brute nor a ghost, he must be the synthesis of his animality and rationality."

"I'm glad you cleared up this confusion in my mind," Knox

acknowledged gratefully. "You're neither a materialist nor an idealist. . . ."

"But a realist, if you like to pigeon-hole me," Noesis completed his sentence. "But this discussion was a useful introduction to finish the problem of the development of man's moral character. Since you have all the elements in your hands now, I invite you to do it for me."

"I'll try," Knox consented. "And I hope it'll be to your satisfaction. Since you agreed to be called a realist, I take that to stand for the unity of the physical and psychic. And I surmise that this should also be the principle or the premise directing the development of man's character from childhood on. The problem, therefore, is to design such a program of education, or, even better, to create the type of environment, which will provide for the satisfaction of all of man's needs in proper sequence and order, keeping in mind the qualitative differences among values and also the individuality of the child. The ultimate goal of this program, of course, should be the attainment of an integrated character and personality. All the values should be assimilated or appropriated without creating either a narrow limitation or an one-sided development, resulting in a caricature."

"So far it's very good," Noesis commented. "However, in order to make it less academic and abstract, could you think of an example or perhaps an analogy?"

"Since you seem to have one, or perhaps even more, why don't you take over?" Knox suggested.

"All right. I had in mind an example taken from the field of aesthetics, more specifically, the values of beauty and symbolism. Have you ever tried to identify the elements, the necessary ingredients or qualities belonging to beauty? What makes you call something beautiful?"

"My first answer would be in line with the traditional doctrine which claims that beauty is that which is pleasing to the eye. But I realize—knowing you by now—that you would immediately ask me: why does it please the eye? What is there in the object, which you call a work of art, that causes such a subjective reaction in the viewer? And I'll answer that it's integrity, wholeness, totality, unity, order, form, harmony, balance, proportion, and style, as the necessary qualities of the beautiful. Conversely, the absence of these qualities accounts for disorder, disharmony, imbalance, disproportion, which makes us call a thing ugly."

"All this is fine," Noesis commented. "In fact, I couldn't have stated it any better. Therefore, what you have to do now is to apply these ideas to man, conceived as a work of art."

"But that's easy!" Knox remarked gladly. "Every individual has to develop himself into wholeness, integrity and unity, not only physically but psychically too. Consequently, he has to assimilate all values in proper order and measure. Through that the individual will develop all of his innate potentialities, inclinations and abilities. Then, he has to give a special form or style to his whole being, in conformity with the uniqueness of his individuality. This, however, could prove to be rather difficult, if one thinks of the dangers of narrow specialization resulting in onesidedness. Considering, however, the superior intelligence of your children and the advanced state of your civilization and culture, such dangers could be averted much easier, than in our world. The next point would be, I think, the development of all those personal traits or qualities—virtues—that we described before. And this is all I can say on this point."

"Do you have any question that you'd like to ask?" Noesis said.

"Yes, I do have one or two," Knox answered. "First, could you give me a hierarchy or a structured articulation of values which you'd consider the best? I don't say ideal, because you don't like that expression."

Noesis smiled in approval and said: "I propose the following order: morality or ethics, standing for character or the condition of the good life; philosophy, as the foundation of science, which comes next; then art, as the expression of beauty and symbolism; the social, political and economic values would complete the list."

"Of course, you realize that you left out the religious value altogether," was Knox' critical remark.

"Yes, I did so for the following reason. While you usually posit the religious value as the first and the highest one, I prefer to

310

leave it for the last. The reason for this choice of mine will be discussed later tonight."

"My second question concerns the problem of individuality," Knox continued. "On several occasions you rejected the ideas of uniformity, conformity, equality, and all kinds of collectivist slogans. But this gives rise to the following dilemma: either everybody follows the pattern you described as the best one for the appropriation of all values, and to that extent you'll have uniformity—or nobody does. But then you'll have certain imbalances to the extent that they deviate from the pattern."

"Or else, there is a third possibility, that is, all the values are present in everyone, but in a due individualized form. Perhaps you had the impression that everybody is everything in one person. You even called it a universal genius. Then you must have imagined that everybody concerns himself with the same ideas, thinks of the same problems and performs the same work. But this would be totally wrong. I'll give you some examples. Take, for instance, your musicians, and take the same theme worked out by many composers, such as a requiem mass. I'm sure that you're not ready to put Mozart and Verdi in the same category, simply because both of them composed a piece of music on the same theme. Or take your scientists. You know, of course, that there is more than one theory concerning the nature of light, for example. And each scientist can defend his own position even through experimental evidence. Or, finally, think of the variety of the solutions proposed by your philosophers with regard to the nature of knowledge and its value. . . . These examples should tell you that your dilemma is not a true one."

"I'm not ready to give up yet," Knox protested. "Your examples are fit to illustrate the conditions existing on our planet, due to the amount of ignorance we have to labor under. But it doesn't apply to your advanced situation."

"I hope you don't consider us as omniscient creatures!" Noesis smiled. "In spite of our advanced knowledge, we do not call it absolute and final, immortal, eternal and immutable dogmas. We don't have any person who would claim infallibility either. We are after one thing only, that is, the accumulation of more

311

evidence and more knowledge. Considering our boundless universe, there is no danger that we shall sit around idly, because we reached the limits of knowledge."

"Do you have any cases of one individual being better, in the same field, than another? Or, even worse, that one individual is deprived of abilities in one or another field? And should this be the case, doesn't that create conflicts?" Knox went on.

"I don't see the reason why it should," Noesis remarked. "An intelligent person should realize that no individual can possess all the abilities and values of life. Some limitation is given with the nature of individuality as such. But, on the other hand, every individual is the personification of a set of perfections from which he can derive the necessary qualities of self-love, self-respect and pride. So there should be no reason for developing inferiority complexes. Moreover, an intelligent person also understands both the uselessness and the destructive consequences of resentment, envy and jealousy. Respect and admiration for another person's qualities are, therefore, the proper attitude, and one that creates the basis for meaningful and constructive relationships among men."

"Unfortunately, this is not our case," Knox said regretfully. Then he went on: "There is one more set of problems we still have to consider tonight, and it's the all important question about the global or ultimate meaning of existence. It's an issue usually debated by philosophers and theologians. You recall, of course, that we've touched upon this question several times and decided to discuss it at the end. You've even rejected the label of an atheist when we had talked about it. I wonder, therefore, what you have to say on these questions."

"Let's talk about the meaning of life first," proposed Noesis, "and let's consider this problem from its negative aspect, I mean, the most frequent forms or ways men on your planet try to work out some justification for their existence. In the first place, I want to mention the religious or transcendental answer given to this question. It starts with the anthropomorphistic image of a personal god, thought of as the creator of the universe and the father of mankind. Since there is no evidence to substantiate such

312

claims, faith became an absolute necessity along with the acceptance of 'revealed' truths. I should mention in parenthesis, that faith is opposed to reason. Faith requires the sacrifice of man's intellect and will. It demands submission and obedience. Next come the doctrines on original sin, divine providence, redemption and eternal life, either in heaven or in hell. Everybody is believed to have an immortal soul and is being told that the meaning of life is beyond life; you start living and enjoying yourself after you're dead. Resurrection was invented to remove some of the blatant contradictions. Those who accept these ideas on blind faith—perhaps they just believe in their belief—are ready to stop looking for any immediate meaning and value in life while still living. All values become devalued, insignificant and of no consequence in the perspective of the promise of an eternal bliss. For 'one thing only is needful,' that is, to prepare yourself for heaven by the acts of self-denial, mortification and sacrificial sufferings of all sorts. This world is openly condemned and denounced as a 'vale of tears,' a penal colony, where you're serving time for your original and non-original sins. Every value becomes only something limited, imperfect, and temporal. In the name of their supernatural expectations, the believers become holy nihilists and pessimists, enemies of knowledge, progress and all kinds of pleasure. I don't think it's necessary to go into the details of what this doctrine destroys in man, because everybody can draw the obvious conclusions. Perhaps I should mention one curious aspect of this strange situation. Practically nobody takes the belief in the afterworld seriously, because it's psychologically impossible. Therefore, most people work out some odd form of compromise according to the formula of rendering to Caesar the things that are Caesar's and to God the things that are God's. Naturally, there you find a great deal of false pretense and hypocrisy."

"Do you realize that if it were not for man's fear of eternal punishment, everybody would run wild. . . ." Knox remarked seriously.

"I know that," Noesis admitted. "And it's another evidence that your people act out of fear only. If they do the good, it's not because it's the good and it's also to their own rational advantage and benefit—as it should be—but because they expect an outside sanction and justification, that is, eternal reward or punishment."

"I believe, though, that this situation will continue until man's mind develops to such a degree that there will be no more room left for any superstitious beliefs," Knox submitted.

"That's the natural trend of cultural evolution," Noesis agreed. "But let's move now on to the other means by which man is trying to find some meaning in life. I have in mind the unruly and exaggerated cultivation or pursuit of material values. Please, do not interpret my words in the sense of any mystical or supernatural hatred and contempt for material well being. I meant only the reversal in man's valuations. Material goods and values perform a rather limited, but very important function in life. As you already know, civilization—understood as a liberating factor—is a necessary condition, a stepping stone toward the coming of culture. The fallacy within the worship of wealth consists in overextending its legitimate value and significance. Being only a part of life, it should not be made into the whole of life, because it doesn't work, and it turns out to be just a compensation for psychic frustrations, or else a base means to attain power over other human beings."

"Which is another self-defeating goal in life," Knox remarked.

"Give me the reasons why you said this," invited Noesis.

"Because power over others brutalizes and corrupts man, leading only to another form of slavery. Every tyrant is also a slave of his passionate lust for power and of those he enslaved. . . . It's a dead end, because such a man undertook something immoral, and the nature of his actions will destroy him before it does anybody else. It may also develop into a paranoic obsession. And I consider all this as the exact opposite of meaning and value."

"Since we got this delusion out of our way along with the undue worship of wealth," Noesis went on, "let's turn now to the other forms of creating the illusion of meaning and happiness in life. I am thinking now of the social idols, such as success, fame, glory, status, prestige and what not. I object to these false values, because of the psychological fallacy involved in them. I

314

mean the same thing I've already mentioned: the impossibility of finding the meaning of one's life in the life of another. Besides, it creates the atmosphere of competition, conflicts, tensions, envy, jealousy, resentment and social unrest."

"Don't you have any famous man or woman in your world, whom you consider a hero, perhaps on a cosmic scale?"

"We respect and admire everybody's values and abilities," was Noesis' answer. "But we don't like the theatrical dramatizing of it. There is an element of comedy and immaturity in it. Besides, you have to remember that each one of us considers his own life as the highest value."

"What do you think of those who consider the quest for more knowledge, such as philosophy, science and art, as the source and the cause of their happiness?" Knox questioned.

"I knew that this would be your next question," remarked Noesis, "and I am in full agreement with this goal, because I consider it as the best means to fulfill man's desire for lasting happiness. However, I want to dwell on this topic in more detail. Therefore, I'll go back to the nature of life itself and I'll emphasize one of its essential traits or laws: it's the phenomenon of growth. I selected this characteristic because it ties in perfectly with the meaning of evolution in our ever expanding and growing universe. Then I'm going to associate the idea of growth with the quest for more being, that is, the universal law of constantly surpassing and transcending the stages that had already been reached, in view of the next and the next stage of being, a state that integrates all the perfections contained in the previous stages, with the new qualities proper to the next."

"May I interrupt you for a second?" Knox said. "I notice that the premise you started out with bears no relation to a transcendent, absolute and infinite being, usually called God. You seem to stay within the cosmos only. . . ."

"Your observation is very fitting and accurate," Noesis observed. "To our minds it makes no sense at all to look for a being of any kind that would be outside, apart and above reality itself. For reality is the existing universe. To imagine such a being apart from that which is, is to deal with contradictions, and it

315

turns out to be the opposite of what it was meant to be in the first place, namely, non-being."

"Then your position is that of cosmic immanence, I mean, you defend pantheism."

"I don't like that term at all because of its theistic-religious connotation. I prefer 'panontism,' but this term does not exist in your vocabulary."

"It also follows that you reject the idea of a personal god, a creator, a provident father, a redeemer, and so forth." Knox remarked.

"Yes, I do," Noesis affirmed with conviction. "The only absolute I accept is the existence, the reality of the cosmos which is identical and coextensive with matter or energy. You know from science that matter can neither be created nor destroyed, and that the amount of energy in the universe is constant, though variously distributed in space and time. A creation out of nothing is another contradiction in terms, as you should know."

"Ruling out all forms of transcendence," Knox went on, "the only place where you can find meaning to your existence is in, and within, existence itself."

"This is only natural and logical," Noesis answered. "I'm sure that you didn't expect me to speak on resurrection, heaven and hell. . . . But let me go back now to the ideas of the quest for more knowledge and more being. It's through knowledge that we assimilate and appropriate the mode of being and the perfections proper to the existents other than ourselves. In this sense we grow, we evolve, we become more and more perfect, we transcend the limitations and the imperfections of our present condition. Herein lies the essence, the meaning and the purpose of one's existence."

"However, you had stated before that some limitation and imperfection—which you associated with the ideas of evil or the power of the negative—will always be part of your lives."

"I did so, indeed," Noesis agreed, "but what do you want to say about that?"

"I only meant to say that this implies that you'll be always on the way, always going, always progressing, developing, evolving, without ever reaching a final destination. Unless you want to say that the progression toward death is the goal of your journey. . . ."

"Since that would be absurd to say, do you expect me to invent a heaven and a hell for you, both as a consolation and a deterrent?" Noesis pressed his question.

"No, I know that you can't do that," Knox said. "But you could regard death as absolute and final and settle down with it."

"Exactly in the manner proposed by the existentialists?" Noesis questioned his friend. "I know that they project the long shadow of death over the whole of their lives, they live under its depressing power, and end up as practical nihilists and pessimists. They sentenced themselves to death while still alive, thus living out an absurd existence."

"Well, that's what they're doing," mused Knox. "And if one thinks of it, their point seems to be well taken, because death without a resurrection reduces everything to nothing at all."

"And yet they still keep on living, most of them as practical hedonists, snatching up all the pleasures they can, until their devil takes them to nowhere!" Noesis concluded with contempt.

"But is there anything else left for man?" Knox insisted. "What's your alternate proposition?"

"I've already suggested it tonight, but let me state it in more specific terms. The only meaning, value and purpose of life, its only justification and sanction, is life itself. But this should be understood in the light of what I said before on the essence of life as activity, growth, self-transcendence, and the satisfaction or pleasure that accompany this process. The fact that death ends this process doesn't mean that it nullifies the value of life, emptying it of all meaning. I look upon your contemporary atheists as children who, having lost their parents and home, keep on crying and bewailing their tragedy. They celebrate the death of God with tears in their eyes, because they lost their illusions, their belief, their comforting hopes, and now feel estranged, alienated, lost in an absurd world. They're both comical and tragical clowns, or, perhaps even better, neurotics."

"But while emphasizing the absurdity of life and existence," Knox declared defensively, "they refuse to accept it as their guilt."

"And whom are they accusing then? Because they've lost their heavenly father and the promise of a beatific vision, they blame it all on someone who—by their own premise—doesn't even exist. They're thrashing straw and making a lot of wind with their odd and pitiful posturing," Noesis remarked with contempt.

"You seem to make little of death," Knox observed.

"And you seem to make too much fuss about a very natural fact," retorted Noesis. "But let me try to get my point across to you, if I can. I repeat once more that the meaning of life is to live it the way I described it. I think that the trouble with all those who cultivate the philosophy of dread, anguish, despair and nausea is psychological. I submit the suggestion that they've never become anything, they've never accomplished anything remarkable and of lasting value, and those who're talented among them wasted their abilities in writing new editions on the lamentations of Jeremiah, their forerunner and prototype. For it's much easier to blame, accuse, rationalize, find excuses for one's impotence, than to get down to some form of creative activity that would reward them with pleasures and satisfactions. Thus I come to my final question. Please try to take it in all and consider it seriously. If I spent all the days of my life in the service of creative work, in the pursuit of more knowledge and being, and if I come now to the end of that journey, tell me, is there any meaning to ask and to expect anything else? Such a life is its own justification, meaning and reward. There's nothing more to ask for. A creative life contains its own meaning and value, and there's nothing more to ask for. A creative life contains its own meaning and value, and there's no way to go beyond that into the region of hallucinations and delusions. Finally, I'd like to remind you, for the last time, of the gardener."

"Yes, of course, your gardener and his flowers," Knox replied pensively.

"Since you mentioned flowers," Noesis continued, "I want to ask you, why don't you also demand immortality for them, and for every blade of grass, every bird and animal in the forest? Perhaps you should include also all sorts of insects to do justice to whatever lives and dies. . . ."

318

"If you expect me to say that it's only man who has an immortal soul," Knox replied, "you're not going to hear it, because I don't believe in it. Nevertheless, I'd say that man shouldn't be put on the same level as birds and animals and plants. After all, he's a self conscious, free and creative being."

"These perfections aren't enough to warrant immortality," Noesis said. "From the very beginning, I made it clear that we look upon man as a natural phenomenon, as the product of evolution, and the difference between man and the other forms of life is only one of degree and not of kind."

"I have to confess to you," Knox observed, "that perhaps because of my being conditioned the way I am, it's rather difficult for me to go along wholeheartedly with your idea, although I have to acknowledge its logic and rationality."

"Why don't you quote Pascal then, who said that 'the heart has certain reasons unknown to reason itself'?" Noesis suggested.

"Because I'm not ready to embrace his mystical sentimentality," Knox replied with uneasiness. "But to change the subject, I don't think you can ignore that there's a certain order in the cosmos, that there're universally valid laws, principles, and also evident purpose in the whole process. And if you don't dismiss them, I wonder how you interpret them in the light of the principle of sufficient reason?"

"You expect me to repeat the arguments of Aristotle and Aquinas in favor of God's existence?" Noesis challenged.

"You said you're not an atheist," Knox retorted.

"Neither did I claim to believe in an absolute being! On the contrary! But as to your remark on order, law, purpose, design and causality, I'll say this—suppose I consider all that as the natural outcome of the code, of the blueprint, present in matter itself, as part of its own nature and being, the formal aspect of its being what it is? And this position requires no outside cause to put that code or the formal principle of its structural organization and functioning in it. It's part of matter itself. In fact, it would be absurd to think of any existent, from the hydrogen atom on to the most complex structure, as existing without possessing a definite nature and form of its own. Total amorphy is absurd. . . . It's non-being."

"But then you're an atheist after all!" Knox insisted.

"If you take that term in its ordinary meaning," Noesis replied, "then you're right. I am an atheist. But if you can think of the whole of the universe as the totality of being, existence, unity, truth, and goodness, then I'm not."

"Is this what you meant by your term 'panontism'?"

"You can consider it as that," Noesis consented.

"What about the origin of the universe?" Knox inquired further.

"Are you looking for a father, a mother, or both?" Noesis asked.

"I'm asking you a question about a first cause!" replied Knox, somewhat irritated.

"The idea of a first cause that would precede being and existence makes no sense at all. Causality apart from reality is meaningless. Reality and causality are coexistent and coextensive. As I told you before, matter can be neither created nor destroyed."

"This being so, I have to conclude that the first and the last principle of your philosophy consists in the idea of the eternal recurrence. . . ."

". . . Of the same, under different forms," completed Noesis, with an air of finality. And that was sufficient to indicate that he considered the discussion closed and ended.

There followed a sudden silence. Noesis sat motionless in his armchair, his unflinching gaze resting on Knox's face. He seemed to be much more serious, collected and reserved than ever before. His detachment and aloofness appeared to increase with the passing of each moment, becoming almost severe and forbidding. Its immediate effect on any stranger would have been that of tension, uneasiness and fear.

Knox, though familiar by now with his friend's strange character, became rather disturbed and nervous. He felt helpless, not knowing what to do. He felt for a cigarette in his pocket, and lit it mechanically, just to do something, to break the unbearable pressure and tension for which he could find no explanation. His mind refused to function, resisting the command of his will to coordinate the unruly associations of dismembered ideas and feelings. Gynea sat a little further away, near the window. She must have sensed what was going on in Knox's mind, because she kept on looking back and forth at Knox and Noesis, as if expecting one of them to break the silence.

After a while, Noesis got up, walked to the table on which his briefcase was lying. With slow and measured precision, he took out an envelope, somewhat larger than usual, walked up to Knox and handed it to him, without ever uttering a word.

Knox, not knowing what to expect in the envelope, tore it open with nervous impatience. A deep feeling of frustration overcame him as soon as he became aware of its contents, twelve or fifteen one hundred dollar bills, and nothing else. He put them back in the envelope, which he placed on the little table in front of him, and raised his eyes at Noesis, waiting for an explanation. But Noesis' attitude was just as unyielding as before. Knox realized that by now it was up to him to say something.

"It's very generous of you to give me this money," he said with an unsteady voice. "Should I look upon it as an invitation to terminate our relationship? It's both very impersonal and businesslike. I shouldn't accept it, since it's beyond the terms of our agreement, and I haven't earned it yet."

"But you will," answered Noesis tersely.

"In other words, this is the end," Knox went on with frustration and bitterness. "I accepted your proposal, then we went through our discussions, I wrote them down, at least partially, and now, since there's nothing else to discuss, it's time to say good-bye."

"That's only natural," Noesis commented objectively. Then he added: "You seem to have become somewhat sentimental."

Knox took this remark as offensive and almost crude. He immediately pulled himself together, and forced an impersonal attitude upon himself. Then he said curtly:

"I won't discuss that. What I had in mind was actually some unfinished *business*." He put an undue emphasis upon the last word. "I thought you'd have wanted to see the finished manuscript before it goes to print."

321

"I don't see the reason why I should," Noesis replied. "What I've seen so far is sufficient indication that the rest will be just as good. Besides, it's in your own interest, first of all, to make it as appealing as possible to the reader."

"You don't seem to attach much significance to it, though," Knox observed critically.

"What reasons make you say that?" Noesis took up the challenge. "Do you measure one's interest by the amount of feelings one displays?"

"That's one way to assess it."

"But not the best, let me tell you," Noesis said firmly. "According to what we've said on the relation between one's reason and feelings, you should know better by now."

"But of course! You allow yourself only the emotions which you previously filtered through and controlled by your reason. And you must proceed accordingly in all situations and experiences, such as friendship, separation and death. . . ." Knox observed with bitterness.

"I realize that our attitude may seem rather unnatural from your point of view, just as your emotional involvement appears strange to us. We live according to reason and reality, not according to wishes, whims and beautiful sentiments. Knowing the everchanging, therefore, very unstable nature of emotions, we think it's better to assess the value and the meaning of everything in the light of reason and reality," Noesis answered.

"However, I'll have to return to you the memory cells after I finish using them," Knox said without knowing why he had made that remark.

"You may keep them, if you want to," Noesis said.

"Are you going back to your own world very soon?" Knox went on.

"Why do you ask this question?" Noesis inquired with reserve.

"Well, . . . forget it!" Knox muttered in confusion. "It was a silly idea anyway."

"What were you thinking of?" Gynea asked with curiosity.

"I meant to ask you whether you ever took anybody from our planet to your world," Knox said uneasily.

"No, we haven't," Gynea answered with understanding. "It wouldn't do any good to any person."

"You mean that the physical environment is unfit for our organism?"

"No, that's a minor problem only. I mean that the social and cultural environment would be such that no man from this planet could survive."

"But why not?" Knox insisted. "After all, if all of your people are like you and Noesis, I don't see why an intelligent person couldn't live with you to his greatest satisfaction."

"Well, I'll give you an example. Perhaps that will help you understand," Noesis broke in. "Have you observed that children prefer the company of other children to that of adults? Similarly, you must have heard about the complaint of many mothers who are forced to spend many long hours in the company of their children. Or, even better, the rather strange and almost queer behavior of your men of genius, some of them going insane, because they were condemned to live in a society of people who couldn't understand their ideas? The gap between the genius and the average person is even greater than that between a moron and an average person?"

"In other words," Knox said with sadness, "anyone of us, maybe even the best of us, would be that child or perhaps even just a moron in your society, and it is for this reason that he could never adjust himself. . . ."

"I'm glad you understand," Noesis answered.

"But couldn't he learn, in order to match the level of your culture?" Knox insisted.

"There are two things you should recall," Noesis explained. "First, there are no jumps in nature and its evolution. Every stage is a necessary one. No child can turn into an adult overnight, no matter how bright he is. Second, there are limits to learning and educability and that's a matter of genetics and eugenics."

Noesis' words sounded implacable and final. Knox realized that the final moment had come. Slowly he got up from his seat, picked up the memory cell and the envelope. His friends could see how much effort and self-control he needed not to betray

323

his emotions. First, he walked up to Gynea, who held out her hand as a gesture of friendship and farewell. Then he turned to Noesis. He stood before him motionless, much longer than needed. He was being held again by Noesis' eyes, by the same power he had first experienced during that memorable evening on the hill. They revealed to him once more the qualities of a superior type of being, who existed in power and freedom. . . .

CHAPTER TWELVE

EPILOGUE

It must have been close to daybreak when Knox left Noesis'
apartment. He was completely crushed by the shock of their final
separation. At first, he tried to recollect himself, to check and
control his intense and profound sense of loss. He tried to follow
Noesis' advice to be reasonable, to use the power of his mind,
to look at his present situation objectively. But every attempt
on his part failed to produce the desired change. It only added
the feelings of anger and shame to his totally abject condition.
He felt like sinking down on the sidewalk, covering his face with
his hands and letting the torrent of his tears gush forth from
his eyes.

Then anger took hold of him again and he felt like hitting or
hurting himself, to punish himself for his lack of courage and
dignity. But he did neither. He just kept on walking, slowly,
staggering to the right and to the left, as if he were drunk. He
felt tired, exhausted. His body ached all over, ready to collapse.
His mind was numb and paralyzed. Instead of the normal stream
of consciousness, there were moments of total forgetfulness, an
almost abnormal standstill, followed by the sudden emergence
of some isolated image or thought. He kept on walking, his head
sunk to his chest, his unsteady legs carried the loose and droop-
ing gait of his body. Once in a while he stopped, for no reason
at all.

As he reeled along the street, his lips moved silently, as if in
a soundless dialogue with himself. Occasionally he dismissed
some unwanted thought with an impatient wave of his hand
and resumed his heedless wandering. He saw a deserted bench

in front of a darkened store and hastened his steps in that direction. He welcomed the chance to sit down and allow himself some rest. He closed his eyes, as though trying to erase the oppressing weight of the reality around him. Instead of succeeding in blanking it out, there it was, on the screen of his imagination, the clear and vivid image of Noesis' penetrating eyes, that kept on growing out of proportion. He jumped to his feet and began walking rapidly, as if running from something frightful, towards some important destination. Had there been an open tavern nearby, he would have walked in and drunk himself into total oblivion.

Very soon the city seemed to come alive. More and more cars, trucks and buses began zooming up and down the streets in all directions, creating an infernal noise. People appeared on the sidewalks, hurrying past to some place. Knox looked up and realized that it was past dawn. The street lights had been turned off without his noticing it. He found himself in an unfamiliar section of the city. It must have been the section where foreigners lived, for he heard some words he could not understand. He was too exhausted to continue his wandering. He longed to be back in his apartment, to close his door behind him, to shut out the world. . . . He managed to get into a cab and gave his address to the driver.

As soon as he found himself in his apartment, he threw himself on his couch, not bothering to get undressed. He hoped to find in sleep a refuge from his painful feeling and overwrought imagination. As he lay there motionless, stretched out on his sofa, his eyes closed, his body seemed to take advantage of the opportunity to rest. The tension in his muscles gradually gave way to a sensation of total relaxation and abandonment. His mind, however, was unable to slacken. His imagination kept on working, knitting together its plays and games, free from the watchful eyes of his reason. . . .

He was looking intently at the figure of a man who seemed somewhat familiar to him, except for his unusual height—he was more than seven feet tall. He stood alone on some strange structure, and Knox couldn't see whether it touched the ground or not. It appeared to him, more as if it were suspended in mid-air, alternating between complete standstill and sudden bursts of motion. The man standing on it was waving to him and motioning him to approach. Knox was both eager and afraid to move, but he felt himself being drawn toward that man who was now climbing up and down on the bars of that unfamiliar object. Knox managed to take hold of the lowest bar of that moving contraption, which as soon as he grasped the bar, thrust itself upward with constantly increasing speed. Knox began to scream in terror. . . . The stranger looked down at him with severe reprehension, as if telling him to behave and to hold on. His eyes resembled two luminous spots of light, flashing and glaring incessantly, emitting waves of heat on Knox's face. He felt that his strength was lapsing, his grip weakened with every moment as he hung on the speeding craft. Soon one of his hands had slipped and now he hung, one arm flying free. He closed his eyes, to avoid the terrifying look of the man above him. Then, he was falling, falling freely, faster and faster, toward the ground below, which ran toward him at fantastic rate. He heard the sound of a hideous laughter accompanying him in his dive to sure death.

Knox was now sitting comfortably at a table at the same sidewalk café he had so often frequented, in a not too distant past. As he looked around himself, he saw that everything had changed. He didn't recognize the waiter, who was rather reluctant and slow in serving him. Something unusual and strange must have happened to his person, he thought, there must have been something odd in his appearance, because the waiter kept looking at him with suspicion and disapproval. Walking up to some guests, seated at another table, he began talking to them excitedly, while pointing his finger at Knox. The other customers listened attentively to the waiter's words, nodding in sign of approval of whatever he was saying. He tried hard but unsuccessfully to find out what they were so eagerly discussing. One or another word reached him only, and they sounded like accusations . . . "subversive!" . . . "godless!" . . . "dangerous radical! . . . "pernicious rebel!" . . . "hater of humanity!" . . . "destroyer of family and love" . . . "communist!" . . . were the expressions hurled at him by those people, under the instigations of the waiter. Knox tried to identify the faces of those hostile individuals. They were young, college age, girls and boys. Their voices sounded familiar to him and he was quite sure he had seen them before and often. But their faces were unlike the well known expression of their eyes.

The men were clean shaven, very neatly dressed, matching to the last detail the image of the well-adjusted, middle-class bourgeois. The girls stood close to their dates, repeating ever more loudly the insults of their companions. Some of them shouted "mother!" . . . "child!" . . .

The agitation and the noise was gathering momentum step by step. . . . Suddenly, the waiter turned around and started toward Knox. His black uniform was now more like a cassock. There could be no doubt as to his intentions. He was approaching with the determination of an aggressor, his eyes glowing with hatred, his hand raised above his head, holding an empty bottle. The crowd followed behind, shouting in a frenzy: "Give it to him!" . . . "Finish him off!" . . . "Kill the bastard!" . . . Knox jumped to his feet and ran as fast as his feet could carry him. The shouts of his pursuers were dying in the distance, yet Knox kept on running in despair. . . .

Then Knox wasn't in the park any longer. He was in a nightclub. . . . The place was crowded with people. Some of them sat close to the stage to have a better view of the show, but the majority of them were more interested in the contents of their glasses. Knox felt drowsy, dizzy after his first drink.

Everybody was unusually excited, noisy, shouting and laughing hysterically, unable to control themselves. He got up from his place at the bar and moved over, right in front of the stage. Somebody had just shouted into the loudspeaker that a new attraction was about to begin.

The music flared up with deafening violence, and the wild rhythm drowned completely all traces of a melody. . . . A young woman walked onto the stage, her motions attuned to the beat of the music. She was dressed in an evening gown, glistening silver in color. Her face was hidden behind a red veil. She proceeded to strip her attire, beginning with her gloves, followed by the cape, then the dress, while moving around in circles to the sound of the orchestra. When she was already topless, almost totally naked, except for her high heeled slippers and a few inches of cloth covering her loins, she fell into a fit of frenzy, trying to keep up with the speed of the music. She looked like a demented creature, suffering from some horrid disease. Her convulsions came to an abrupt halt with the finale of the music. She tore the veil off her face, walked to the edge of the stage and stared straight at Knox, without paying any attention to the roar of applauses of the public. Knox was held transfixed with horror at the expression of those eyes! There was in them the anomalous glow of an almost deluded mind, the abhorrent and disgusting gloating of depravity, the foul and cadaverous air surrounding the degenerate and dying. . . . He wanted to take his eyes off that repellent face, but he couldn't. He was terrified and dreadfully shocked to recognize Marisa's eyes in the pale setting of her tired face, that seemed to have aged too much and too fast.

Then, the anguished weeping of a child was heard, coming from behind the stage. . . . Marisa shuddered with fright, turned toward the direction of the wailing, as if waiting. A small child, around a year old, came staggering with uncertain steps onto the stage, babbling: "Mommy, Mommy, Mommy!" in despair. Marisa picked the child up, grabbed a glass from a nearby table and poured its contents into the child's open mouth. Then she turned toward Knox again, piercing him with a fierce glance, lifted the child up above her head. Her body was shaking with an uncontrolled fit of repulsive laughter, as she thrust the child violently on Knox's table. The music drowned the horrified cry of the people, and Marisa was back on the stage, performing her convulsive contortions. . . .

Knox began to run filled with horror. . . . He was on a meadow, approaching a hill at some distance. He saw a blinking light on top of that hill. In spite of his extreme exhaustion, he kept on running, faster and faster, fearful that the light might disappear at any moment. He didn't look back once, though he had the vivid sensation that he was being followed. Once or twice he heard a faint cry, the sound of someone calling his name. Finally, he made it up the hill. . . . His heart was throbbing, he felt his blood hammering in his brains and couldn't control the panting of his breathless chest. Not more than fifty yards from him, he saw a space craft, saucer shaped, its lights running around its rim with regularity. An intense light was coming from an opening on the side of the craft. Two human shapes could be clearly distinguished. They were standing next to the craft, ready to go aboard. Only their faces could be seen with some clarity, their bodies being covered with long capes that swept the ground.

Knox was startled and overwhelmed with joy at the wonderful sight of his friends. Noesis and Gynea looked at him steadily. . . . Their faces glared with beauty in the white light from the craft. Noesis waved to him with a friendly gesture, followed by Gynea. Knox began running toward them, but at that moment, Noesis and Gynea had already disappeared inside the craft which took off immediately. In no time even its blinking lights were not to be seen any more. . . .

He remained motionless for a long while, looking up into the limitless depth of the skies. . . . Then he again heard the sound of his name coming from the foot of the hill. He turned around slowly, and looking down, began scanning the ground below him. He saw a shapeless shadow, somewhat darker than the ground itself, trying to move upward. But with every effort, the unidentified figure seemed to slide downward instead.

As he walked closer to it, he saw a woman on her hands and knees, desperately trying to crawl uphill toward him, but sliding back again. After each failure, he heard the muffled sounds of subdued sobbing and the weak sound of his name, "Ed. . . . Help me! . . . It's me. . . . Ed, are you still there?" He rushed down toward her, for it was Marisa! She was lying motionless on her side, her face touching the ground. Her fingers were still clutching the scant grass with lifeless rigidity. There was an empty stare in her motionless eyes. . . .

A sudden clap of thunder filled the void of oppressing stillness.

Lightnings ripped apart the heavy mass of clouds that covered the earth as an immense black bowl turned upside down. Heavy drops of rain began hitting Knox from all sides. He knelt down to lift Marisa's lifeless body, but he could see nothing on the spot where she had fallen. A fierce wind blew the torrents of rain right into his face.

Knox started toward the city with staggering steps. He was soaked to his bones and a nervous shudder ran through his whole body. Then he began trembling and shivering all over. The whistling of the wind and the barbaric sound of the orchestra split his brain with persistent blows. Most painful was the shrill and shricking sound coming from some instrument unknown to him. It was a high-pitched sound that lasted only for a few seconds, followed by a short period of silence, but then it started off again, on and off, on and off, intermittently. . . . Each time he felt the same sensation of acute pain drilling its way into his brain. The mechanical regularity of the recurrent sound filled even the brief moments of silence with indescribable anxiety. Every new attack was more intense and violent than the previous one. He couldn't take it any longer. He put his fingers into his ears and emitted a fearful cry of anguish, that shook his whole body with a violent jerk. . . .

Knox jumped up from the sofa, his eyes wide open in bewilderment, staring in front of himself with a blank expression. It was the ringing of his phone that awoke him from his agonizing nightmare, throwing him back into reality. He hurried to the phone and lifted the receiver with a nervous reaction. The normal sound of a calm human voice produced a soothing effect on his overworked and overstrained mind.

It was the secretary from Evelyn's office, asking him to come and see her at ten in the morning of the next day.